ON THE FREUD WATCH:
Public Memoirs

ALSO BY PAUL ROAZEN
Freud: Political and Social Thought (1968, 1986, 1999)
Brother Animal: The Story of Freud and Tausk (1969, 1990)
Freud and His Followers (1975)
Erik H. Erikson: The Power and Limits of a Vision (1976)
Helene Deutsch: A Psychoanalyst's Life (1985, 1992)
Encountering Freud: The Politics and Histories of Psychoanalysis (1990)
Meeting Freud's Family (1993)
How Freud Worked: First-Hand Accounts of Patients (1995)
Heresy: Sandor Rado and the Psychoanalytic Movement
(with Bluma Swerdloff) (1995)
Canada's King: An Essay in Political Psychology (1998)
Oedipus in Britain: Edward Glover and the Struggle Over Klein (2000)
Political Theory and the Psychology of the Unconscious (2000)
The Historiography of Psychoanalysis (2001)
The Trauma of Freud: Controversies in Psychoanalysis (2002)
Cultural Foundations of Political Psychology (2003)
Oedipus in Italy: Edoardo Weiss and the Founding of Psychoanalysis

EDITED BY PAUL ROAZEN
Sigmund Freud (1973)
Louis Hartz, *The Necessity of Choice: Nineteenth Century
Political Theory* (1990)
Helene Deutsch, *The Psychoanalysis of the Sexual Functions
of Women* (1991)
Victor Tausk, *Sexuality, War, and Schizophrenia: Collected
Psychoanalytic Papers* (1991)
Helene Deutsch, *The Therapeutic Process, the Self, and Female
Psychology: Collected Psychoanalytic Papers* (1991)

ON THE FREUD WATCH:
Public Memoirs

Paul Roazen

Free Association Books
FA^B

First published 2003
by Free Association Books
57 Warren Street W1T 5NR

© 2003 Paul Roazen

All rights reserved. No part of this publication
may be reproduced, stored in a retrieval system,
or transmitted, in any form or by any means,
without the prior permission in writing
of the publisher.

This book is sold subject to the condition
that it shall not, by way of trade or otherwise,
be lent, resold, hired out or otherwise circulated
without the publisher's prior consent in any form
other than that supplied by the publisher.

British Library Cataloguing in Publication Data
A catalogue record for this book is available from the British Library

Produced by Bookchase (UK) Ltd
Printed and bound in England

ISBN 1 853435 68 6

For Samuel H. Beer

CONTENTS

Introduction: Memories of the Boston "Psycho"		8
1	The Importance of the Past	13
2	Charles Rycroft and Ablation	27
3	Freud's Analysis of Anna	41
4	The Problem of Silence: Training Analyses	51
5	The Eissler Problem	58
6	Dickens's *David Copperfield*	81
7	Eugene O'Neill's *Long Day's Journey Into Night*	94
8	A Life in Controversy: Letters	101
9	Freud's Correspondences with Ferenczi & Abraham	125
10	Freud and His Followers	140
11	Canada: Political Psychology	158
12	Using Oral History: A Case in Freud's "Secret Essay"	174
13	Winners and Losers in Historiography	190
14	The Vitality of Neurosis	206
A Personal Epilogue: Secret Spaces		217
Index		221

INTRODUCTION
MEMORIES OF THE BOSTON "PSYCHO"

The time I spent going to clinical psychiatric conferences in 1964-65 was a memorable part of my becoming knowledgeable about the strengths and limitations of psychoanalytic psychology, and I think it worth reflecting back on. Since I spent most of my adult life in universities, it is therefore inevitable for me to think about how theoretical and clinical concepts can best be taught. Although, at least within the social sciences, I do not remember having read an account of what can be learned from witnessing such case presentations, that year stands out in my mind as a landmark in my education.

Massachusetts Mental Health Center was then affectionately known within psychiatric circles as "Psycho." The place had an honorable heritage as the Boston Psychopathic Hospital, which was venerable in terms of the history of modern American psychiatry; it also then boasted a considerable roster of senior psychoanalytic training figures. I had, by the fall of 1964, completed my Ph.D. dissertation on "Freud and Political Theory" in the Government Department at Harvard. I had a fairly heavy teaching schedule, as the last year of my Teaching Fellowships, and was anxiously concerned about whether I would succeed in being promoted to a full-time teaching position at Harvard.

My interest in psychoanalysis, indeed in any form of psychology or psychiatry, was professionally viewed as something of an aberration, even though it had started while I was still an undergraduate studying political philosophy. Political scientists like to think of themselves as hard-headedly concerned with the successful pursuit of power; the History Department, and the people who then made up the Department of Social Relations, would have been more sympathetic to my preoccupations. I assumed from the outset that all the social sciences formed a unity, academic distinctions

INTRODUCTION

as they existed between departments being the result of accidental university forces, and that a theory of human nature was essential to all the human disciplines. When I told one senior member of my Department about what I proposed to do at "Psycho," the reaction I got was so grimly unfavorable that there was no reason for me to repeat the unwelcome news to anyone else. I was determined to forward my education; I knew enough to realize how ignorant I was of practical clinical issues. I had extra time on my hands, since my thesis was completed, and was passionately curious about what I might learn.

No one of course was paying me to do what I did. I cannot now recall the specific steps by which I went about getting the information and permission necessary to attend the conferences. It seems to me that what remains important is that there were absolutely no bureaucratic barriers that obstructed me. I recall briefly seeing some high hospital officials; everything was wonderfully informal. And soon I was traveling several times a week from Cambridge to the other side of the Charles River.

I am afraid I did not have the patience to sit in on enough ward meetings, although ideally that would have been desirable. My own background had meant learning primarily from lectures and seminars, along with solitary sessions in Harvard and Oxford "tutorials." So it was natural for me to head for the formal sessions at "Psycho" where psychiatric patients would be presented by residents to senior consultants and the staff. At first I went to a broad range of such presentations; in time, however, I selected those sessions to which the senior people I wanted to hear would be at work.

The most memorable single figure was Dr. Elvin Semrad. He was already legendary as someone who could hear the grass grow. I had been told how successful he could be in getting patients to open up in a large group of people. But nothing prepared for how interesting, in a low-key way, his clinical performances were. I remember one winter meeting especially; we had had a bad snowstorm, and almost no one else came. The patient under discussion was a recovered paranoiac, and the highly intellectual resident had complicated theories to explain his success. So few people were present that Semrad went around the room asking each of us what we thought; I think it was the only time I ever spoke up. It seemed to me, when asked, that the source of the recovery was that the resident had somehow managed to stay with his patient during her time of great troubles. It did not suit the resident to hear his elaborate constructions reduced to the role of being emotionally supportive, but I think Semrad appeared to approve what I had said.

Semrad may have had an outstanding reputation for understanding the severely ill, but he had written next to nothing, and that little only in conjunction with others. He almost masked sophistication by means of a midwestern naiveté; in those days "Psycho" had plenty of residents all too full of theoretical commitments, and Semrad's approach seemed to be all to the good. A couple of years later I invited him to give a lecture in my first undergraduate course at Harvard, "Psychology and Politics," and his down-to-earthness proved a great success with my students. Yet when I once heard him elsewhere lecturing on the history of concepts of psychosis, I was as horrified to find out those obvious thinkers he had left out, such as Carl G. Jung, as those unlikely candidates he had chosen to include, such as Anna Freud; traditionalist pieties afflicted his thinking more than I would have supposed.

Other senior teachers had different temperaments, and some could be downright doctrinaire; I remember one woman consultant predicting that in the end psychiatry would be "on its knees" to psychoanalysis; she was that certain of the ultimate triumph of her own point of view. (There were some friendly smiles exchanged in the audience about the intransigent spirit implicit in her metaphor.)

In the end, though, it is the patients who stand out in my mind. For instance one young man had been found sitting on top of a table in his university cafeteria; he wore a silent smirk throughout the clinical presentation, never said a single word, and seemed to me straight out of Melville's "Bartelby the Scrivener". Another case comes to mind: a depressed, impotent truck-driver, being interviewed by a well-educated psychiatrist struggling, unsuccessfully I thought, to overcome the immense class barriers between them. One young girl, about whom I later wrote something, was at first diagnosed as schizophrenic, until the senior analyst objected that the lack of psychotic symptoms meant she was more probably a "hippie" or a "pseudo-hippie"; he gave a memorable denunciation of the implications of a facile diagnosis of psychosis, and the resident who was treating her did admit that he had disapproved of her general behavior, as well as her hairstyle. Also, I can recall one outpatient, who had staged a manipulative suicide attempt, being interviewed, but I think I saw almost entirely in-patients.

In those days "Psycho" felt threatened as a teaching institution, since a new requirement had been enacted that the hospital service the local "catchment" area as defined by a recent community mental health act. The young psychiatrists I met were unhappy about cases they now were obliged to see which did not suit the needs of their research or strictly psychological interest.

On the whole I think my year at "Psycho" made me more skeptical of the written material that until then had been the mainstay of what I thought I knew. A couple of residents gave reports of their work as psychiatrists in the Peace Corps, an alternative then to their being drafted into the military, and I was horrified at what they deemed deviance, and how easily they conformed to the purposes of a bureaucratic organization; I had thought that psychoanalytic psychology was devoted to the autonomy of the individual self, and yet here were people who were intent on using the terms that I had thought sacred in the history of Western liberalism, but invoking them for the sake of sustaining group pressures. One young man was alleged to have had "shaky ego boundaries" while in love with a native girl, and according to Peace Corps policy he was being transported back to the States before any marriage could be possible; it struck me that uncertain ego boundaries was an appropriate response to any such proposed union.

I should say, and I hope it does not sound ungrateful of me for the opportunity that I had been given, that I did not think that the medical background of the residents was anything like ideal for their future professions. I recall a young resident who provoked laughter in a room when he proposed what he called a "definitive" treatment program for a patient, as if life could not be counted upon to bring with it uncontrollable and interesting surprises. It did seem to me peculiarly unfortunate that, unlike in my own special field, there was no secure way of telling him that he did not know what he was talking about.

Nonetheless I did have confirmed for me that year, in an absolutely unforgettable way, how great psychotic upheavals, however they might have started, involve a patient's whole being, physical as well as emotional. In those days relatively little attention was paid to drugs; they must have been prescribed, and perhaps I would have heard more about them at ward meetings, but not much emphasis seemed to be placed on them. Of course my own interests were social and psychological, yet I do not think that my bias can have blocked out a reality which, given my own medical ignorance, would have been bound to have mystified me and interfered with my following what was going on. I do recall Semrad once weighing in against the use of electric shock therapy, but no one there seemed at all in favor of its use. And I will never forget – although I could not then begin to reconstruct his thought processes – a spine-tinglingly clairvoyant way a young resident made human sense out of a bizarre schizophrenic delusion.

One meeting held about a schizophrenic patient still stands out in my mind: she had committed suicide by ingesting a hundred aspirin tablets. She first had, however, woken up in the middle of the night, told a nurse on duty what had happened, and then been transported to a general hospital; in the emergency room she was given an injection meant for another patient, which covered up her symptoms sufficiently for her to be returned the next day to "Psycho." She started hemorrhaging and died. It was a horrifying tale of a medical mix-up, and after the conference was over people asked each other whether the other hospital even knew what had ultimately happened. But the senior psychoanalytic consultant had spent the whole public session exploring the psychological roots of schizophrenia, and that meeting still represents for me, as it did then, the irrelevance of such conjecturing in the face of clinical reality.

It is hard to know how students learn, and no doubt the unofficial contacts, in the lunchroom as well as the corridors, had much to teach on their own. I can even reconstruct certain memorable conversations with certain people. On the whole, however, the formal presentations meant the most to me, or at least they were the distinctive part of my experiences at "Psycho."

After approximately eight or nine months of these meetings, I had research projects that seemed to be pressuring me for time, and I ended my involvement at "Psycho." Healthy Harvard undergraduates helped lure me away from clinical material that had to strike me then as unsettling. I have been back there since, once for a talk on Freud in 1970, and then again in 1985 for another lecture. Times have so changed, and ideological fashions altered, that I think it worthwhile to bring to public attention what circumstances once were like at "Psycho." If social scientists had regular bases for being in touch with clinical work, by means I worked out or some other possible mechanisms, then I think interdisciplinary cooperation would be enhanced. For we in university life not only have something to learn from such experiences, but also hopefully can add an important dimension to the way clinical thinking evolves.

I would like to mention that appallingly little attention gets paid to how psychoanalytic psychology should get taught. Lawrence Kubie tried to hypothesize what an ideal institute might be like, but his example has scarcely ever been followed up. But I would like to emphasize, in behalf of what those of us from within academic life can bring to the pursuit of knowledge, how our sense of time is wholly unlike that of most practicing clinicians. Although we have classroom commitments, and writing deadlines, the amount of our leisure is immense; and that means we are free at will to read, books as well as articles, in a way that is usually impossible for therapists. The idea that psychoanalytic literature – or anything else for that matter – can be taught on evenings when everyone is more or less exhausted is not my idea of a proper educational setting. And yet I know that many psychoanalytic institutes continue to perpetuate such an undesirable state of affairs.

The quest for understanding that underlay my own involvement at "Psycho" was fully matched by those I met. From a contemporary perspective what went on then must seem strangely antiquarian by now. Nevertheless, despite having spent so many more years by now in universities, I cannot single out any other time when I participated in a more sustained or devoted search for meaning.

Subsequently to my time at "Psycho," while reading a book on psychosurgery I was surprised to learn that in the late 1950s lobotomies had still been performed there. And although almost every case I saw was diagnosed as schizophrenic, and not one as manic depressive, nowadays the development of new medication means that the pendulum has swung radically toward new nosological categories. My experience leads me to suspect all forms of dogmatism, and I think that the current wave of positivism, associated with DSM thinking, represents another form of technological reasoning, as potentially misleading as the old reliance on the private practice use of the couch for neurotics. As Americans we tend to discount the enduring importance of power, and how it can get wielded surreptitiously. History, even of a personal nature, can give us some precious distance towards life today, which leads directly to the next essay in this collection.

1

THE IMPORTANCE OF THE PAST

One might think the importance of the past would be an embarrassingly unnecessary topic in any civilized context. Freud made so much of the significance of history for each individual, as well as the repeated emphasis he put on the story of the early development of psychoanalysis itself, that one could suppose that there would be no need to pursue the point. But Freud did take a somewhat special approach to life histories, singling out for example the critical importance of early traumas, with the idea that once they were reconstructed neuroses could be overcome; and he, as well as his supporters, polemicized so early about the origins of his "movement" that it has taken considerable subsequent effort to come up with alternative narratives. Further, he tended in principle to isolate clinical material from social realities in a way that can now be considered ahistorical. Nobody has followed up on his commitment to the inheritance of acquired characteristics, nor his fascination with Egyptian archeology; these were historically significant aspects to his work (including his interest in telepathy) that are apt to be skipped-by today.

The main problem we have to confront now seems to be that story-telling itself appears to some to be the central enterprise with which psychoanalysts are concerned, as if old-fashioned truth could afford to take a back-seat clinically. For no matter how impossible it may be to approach God-like omniscience, without some such ideal goal of the truth history is in danger of becoming merely a weapon in partisan warfare. Propagandizing, as well as the possibilities of suggestion, are so common an occurrence that we need to think of trying to construct many kinds of barriers against them.

An immense amount of the world's great literature has had to do with the past and how we conceive it. Poets and novelists have come up with a host of imaginative reflections on the subject. Objectivity has itself come under a cloud, and not much deserves to survive of Freud's frequent use of the image comparing his therapy with surgery. (The current fashionable reliance on classification and diagnoses like those in DSM III & IV can show how little modesty we have learned since turn of the twentieth century psychiatry.) Psychoanalysts have been on stronger ground for being among those to be centrally concerned with memory, including the perils of avoidance as well as the vagaries of recapturing lost time. Historians themselves, whose professional subject-matter so many different kinds of amateurs have trespassed upon, only relatively rarely seem willing to pause in reflecting on the broadest generalizations connected with their field; consequently even the word "historiography" seems off-putting to most, about as attractive-sounding as "bibliography."

My own approach to the importance of the past starts by hinging on the question of power, which has generally been considered the key concept in political science, the subject in which I was professionally educated. Machiavelli and Hobbes both put power so at the center of their respective approaches that it was subsequently hard for political thinkers to dodge it. Yet the study of politics remains one of the human sciences – like psychoanalysis. The difference consists in that political life is concerned with the outside world, where success is considered the great objective; while psychoanalysis, also simultaneously an art as well as a science, is centrally preoccupied with the inner world in which failure deserves to be respected. For me psychology and politics have been complementary disciplines that can add to each other; the external world should belong at least within the broadest scope of a psychologist's concern, just as fallibilities and weaknesses ought not to be scornfully brushed aside by political observers.

Power as a subject has never attained much legitimacy within psychoanalysis. It is true that in "Analysis Terminable and Interminable" Freud did rely on the writer Anatole France's liberal maxim that "when a man is endowed with power it is hard for him not to misuse it."[1] Freud also could acknowledge the legitimacy of the question of whether psychoanalysis could cause harm: "if a knife does not cut, it can not be used for healing either."[2] But on the whole it would be others, unsympathetic to the revolution in ideas Freud initiated, who would point out the power elements within psychoanalytic practice. Wielding authority ought not to be automatically suspect, although authoritarianism is another matter. Rousseau, a great leader in the history of education, once famously proposed the paradox of "forcing" people to be "free," an idea that foreshadowed many of the ethical dilemmas implicit in later psychological thinking.

If I were starting out as a young man today, it might no longer be as necessary to point out the abusive possibilities within so-called classical psychoanalysis, now evidently a rare enough procedure; but the main object of contemporary legitimate concern could be the ease with which striking power can unknowingly be wielded by naive enthusiasts for so-called biological psychiatry. (A variety of different schools of thought, including existential analysis and an interpersonal approach, should not be compressed into the arbitrary dichotomy between psychoanalysis and biological psychiatry.[3]) Drugs whose side-effects are only partially known, or addictive, are too often being prescribed — even to young children — without enough adequate knowledge of the complex human beings being treated. A potentially lethal drug like lithium can be recommended, to ambulatory patients, on the basis of a telephone conversation.[4] Technical diagnoses are being bandied about, and heredity made central, as if we were living a hundred years ago and no one had ever criticized the drawbacks to such a highly formalistic approach.[5]

The past should be a central concern; for without our understanding history we are left surrendering to the present. Imagine what it would be like to think politically without any memory of World War I and II, or the Vietnam War, for example. Or how would we like to be without knowledge of the ways in which civil liberties can be threatened in time of war? And yet some such strictly contemporaneous approach is all-too common in clinical fields. One central temptation that needs combating is the assumption that whatever is must be right. I am suggesting that the main way of avoiding the implicit premise that we are living in the best of all possible worlds is an awareness of the past. Although analysts at least pay lip service to historical sequences, in virtually every psychoanalytic training center I know about Freud's writings are extracted from their intellectual context so that they are read in isolation from whatever opponents he might have been trying to contest. In psychiatry too practitioners are encouraged to think in terms of technique rather than the values and beliefs of the past.

But the history of dentistry, for example, does not bear the same relation to the work of today's dentists as the history of psychotherapy should be vital for contemporary practitioners of that different craft. Every field has its hidden as well as open sectarianism. Even dentists, however, would acknowledge that we in the United States go in for orthodontics in a way that is unique in the modern world. In general we must try to get people to see that suffering and pain are to a large degree defined culturally, mediated by social expectations. It is not necessary to join in any simplistic antipsychiatry movement in order to acknowledge that different societies look on human problems in their culturally characteristic ways.

In America, for example, we need to be especially aware that we are likely to be misled by our traditional faith in progress. If one were knowledgeable enough in comparative cultures it would be possible to write about the manner in which different countries construct their past in distinctive ways. Although it can be perilous to engage in conjectures concerned with the subject that used to be known as "national character", the speculative dangers that might be involved are worth risking given what can be expected to be learned.

A famous literary example would be Henry James's study of Nathaniel Hawthorne in which James sympathized with how the young artist was confronted with "the coldness, the thinness, the blankness" of early nineteenth century American life. James was writing in 1879, after having taken up permanent residence in England three years earlier. James was convinced that "later in life" Hawthorne had felt after he had "made the acquaintance of the denser, richer, warmer European spectacle" that "it takes such an accumulation of history and custom, such a complexity of manners and types, to form a fund of suggestion for a novelist." James's words enumerating "the items of high civilization, as it exists in other countries, which are absent from the texture of American life" have become famous:

> No State, in the European sense of the word, and indeed barely a specific national name. No sovereign, no court, no personal loyalty, no aristocracy, no church, no clergy, no army, no diplomatic service, no country gentlemen, no palaces, no castles, nor manors, nor old country-houses, nor parsonages, nor thatched cottages, nor ivied ruins; no cathedrals, nor abbeys, nor little Norman churches; no great Universities nor public schools – no Oxford, nor Eton, nor Harrow; no literature, no novels, no museums, no pictures, no political society, no sporting class – no Epsom nor Ascot!

James did not seem to realize how narrow his own snobbism was going to make him subsequently look like; instead, he felt that "the natural remark, in the almost lurid light of such an indictment, would be that if these things are left out, everything is left out."[6]

James thought he had found in Hawthorne a writer after his own heart, and was able to quote him along his own preferred lines. Hawthorne had once written: "No author, without a trial, can conceive of the difficulty of writing a romance about a country where there is no shadow, no antiquity, no mystery, no picturesque and gloomy wrong, nor anything but a commonplace prosperity, in broad and simple daylight, as is happily the case with my dear native land."[7] Although at the time James may have been helping to introduce Hawthorne as a writer, by means of James's long "critical essay," from our own point of view it is a bit hard to believe that James could ever have so misunderstood Hawthorne's achievements. For Hawthorne had inherited the distinctively American version of Puritanism, as obsessed with the sins of the past as one could imagine. Hawthorne was hardly the ideal spokesperson to pick for "a commonplace prosperity," and I suspect that Hawthorne could have been ironic when he wrote about the "broad and simple daylight" supposedly characteristic of his "dear native land." *The Scarlet Letter* (1850) was not only in gloomy contrast to such a simple-minded outlook, but deeply rooted in the Salem past. *The House of the Seven Gables* (1851) also demonstrated Hawthorne's convictions about how history powerfully influences the present. Hawthorne's earliest short stories, or "tales," from the 1830s demonstrated his belief in human rootedness; he filled his writings with almost a doom-filled atmospherics associated not just with the heritage of the American Revolution but of the New England version of Puritanism. Somehow Henry James as late as 1879 could still think that "history, as yet, has left in the United States but so thin and impalpable a deposit that we very soon touch the hard substratum of nature...."[8] I think that in general Hawthorne should have been a writer among those least likely to support James's point of view.

Even if James was demonstrably wrong in what he had to say about Hawthorne, James may have nonetheless been onto a sound comparative point about America. When one thinks of the whole revolutionary period itself, the Founding Fathers proceeded to reason in a peculiarly anti-historical manner. Madison, Hamilton, and Jay, for example in *The Federalist* papers, tried to appeal to universal principles about human motives. In their defense of the new Constitution they were proposing to proceed with full confidence in the power of reason and reflection. Although they took for granted dissatisfaction with life under the Articles of Confederation, it is striking that they did not appeal back to the long historical experience they had shared as colonies of Great Britain.

We have been so peculiarly fortunate as a country that we almost do not notice the way others have found it necessary to ablate their pasts, a subject we will return to in Chapter 2. In Japan, for example, the post-World War II offices of General MacArthur have been allowed to vanish. Italians too have been apt to have a blind spot when it comes to the Mussolini period. In Germany the break occasioned by the Hitler period has left in its wake both guilt and cynicism about the past. (At the same time Germans publish facsimile editions of books on a scale that we would never dream of producing.) The collapse of the Soviet Union has left a series of countries having to come to terms with the problem of who in their pasts might have collaborated with dictatorial regimes. In Budapest recently I was impressed by how they had preserved, in a theme-park outside the city run by a commercial free-lancer, huge relics of their Stalinist past; within the city itself a slab of the Berlin wall had been donated by a Germany grateful for Hungary's opening its gates to refugees at a critical moment. Hungary may be an exception that defies many of the historiographical rules I have tried to explicate. But the experience of the rest of the world when it comes to history has been so much more textured with tragedy than what has been the case with Americans that it is hard not in spite of everything to think that Henry James was onto something when he developed the theme of American innocence.

I do not want to dwell on the momentous events of Sep. 11th. Still it seems to me that we have before then felt uniquely protected in an unrealistic way; thirty billion dollars a year on intelligence spending still left us vulnerable and exposed. It was not just a massive failure in intelligence, but I want to point to the characteristic American avoidance of even the dirty-sounding word "spying," in preference to the neutral sounding and idealistic concept of "intelligence."

Abroad, in older cultures, art restorers are more likely to be aware that fixing up deteriorating frescoes, for example, inevitably means changing the painting to something different from what it now is or for that matter once was; but a decision to leave it alone simply invites a different sort of change. Federico Fellini did a film about Rome in which an archeologist watching over digging for construction witnessed an ancient chamber being penetrated; the walls turned out to contain twentieth-century drawings, but the entrance of fresh air meant that they immediately began to disintegrate. Fellini had a fine European sense of irony about history.

In the midst of nineteenth century England's romance with evolution Lord Acton once declared that "Progress [is] the religion of those who have none."[9] Now technology itself does in fact progress, but we in America have hardly been moving upward and onward ever since the Pilgrims landed on Plymouth Rock, or the Founding Fathers organized our Constitution. It is true that our national cultural myths do encourage such a naively progressive orientation; and the Supreme Court, for instance, tries to maintain a kind of seamless connection between us and the past, so that we can appear to be living under an eighteenth century document which has been adapted for current times without discontinuities.

And it is characteristic of us to think in terms of what the historian David Brion Davis has recently called generational chauvinism – that we are somehow inherently superior to previous times. Some degree of present-mindedness is inevitable, and today's concerns do inevitably have to shape what interests us. But it ought to be clear that any progressive approach to history means that we ourselves are certain to be soon left-behind in the rubbish-heap that such an outlook entails. A few short years from now any fool will be able to look back on us as prejudiced and dumb. (A cyclical view of history can of course be equally misleading.) We ought to have the foresight to see that relying on any chauvinistic hindsight based on a strictly developmental perspective is bound to be deadly even to our own best efforts.

Just as we must never allow ourselves the complacent assumption that everything now is the best of all possible worlds, so we must acknowledge that it is in the nature of ideals to be permanently at odds with reality. Norms have to be in contrast to facts, and we should not take for granted that some incoming tide will automatically lift us onto higher ground. The way to improve things is always to be chasing after ideals that are in principle unattainable although they remain inherently desirable. It is the tension between what ought to be and that which is that helps motivate us to action. So neither conservatism nor utopianism suits the full reality of the human condition.[10]

A field like dentistry has undeniably progressed, but how securely can we say exactly the same for psychotherapy? Every clinical encounter is, I believe, simultaneously an ethical one[11]; and in the world of moral values we encounter choices all of whose merits cannot ever be proven one way or other. I am not suggesting that in philosophizing everything is relativistic or equally up-for-grabs. But at the same time science cannot hope to settle things in a way that in principle could make everyone equally satisfied. Morality gets us inevitably into a murky area that is, at least for some, unsatisfactory in its ambiguity and cloudiness; but I think we are better off acknowledging the reality of ethical dilemmas, and how values can be inherently at odds with each other. This is a point that my supervisor and tutor in political theory at Oxford, Sir Isaiah Berlin, liked to expand on.[12]

Taking certain medication can be at the expense of creativity, and antidepressants are known to be hard on the sexual drive; but how can we calibrate the pros and cons of what can be gained as opposed to what is likely to get lost? Practitioners of rival psychotherapeutic schools have had contrasting moral outlooks, and it is characteristic of American optimism not to want to weigh the disadvantages of so-called progress. The better educated one is the more likely that choices get made in an informed context. One of the reasons why the history of controversies in psychoanalysis has held my attention is the extent to which such quarrels were about rival conceptions of the good life.[13]

How we ought to live, and the best ways of organizing society in order to promote objectives that we might have in mind, are bound to be questions that civilized people are able to disagree about. Much of world philosophy has been concerned with competing outlooks on the good life. Alfred Adler, to mention only one example, was a socialist, and it can be no accident that psychologists whose testimony was relied on by the Supreme Court in its 1954 Brown decision on desegregation traced their intellectual ancestry back to Adler; nor can the Menningers be proud of how their family refused to cooperate in undertaking that historic lawsuit against a Topeka school board. In general, by becoming acquainted with the past we should be better able to come up with sophisticated judgments; there is little in human affairs that is really new under the sun. The history of ideas is a rich subject precisely because it offers concrete examples of how people under different social and political conditions have chosen options that might enlighten us about our own situations.

The past is gone, and only at best partially recoverable. The future, though, is almost completely unknown, and a matter largely for prophecy. To reiterate: as we try to live in the present the main resource we have for challenging that which exists has to come from our knowledge of the past. It is history that provides us with the enlightenment with which we can deal with what we encounter. It is not only concepts from history that can help us, but the examples of how people have lived. So that the explicit teachings that Freud or his early disciples may have promoted can be supplemented by the complex examples of their lives. How people do behave is at least as instructive as what they preach. Psychoanalysis became a profession almost uniquely open to women, and Freud was defying a younger generation in Vienna when he ignored the views of those opposed to allowing female practitioners to be full members of his psychoanalytic group.[14]

Within psychoanalysis itself there has naturally been a tremendous amount of attention given to Freud himself. But biographical accounts of Freud have often been unusual and unspoken vehicles of partisanship. Vested interests have added to this acrimoniousness, and rival groups of interested parties have used observations about Freud's life for the sake of promoting their own points of view. Students of Freud need to be alert not just to the spin he could put on his own career, but to the variety of biases that inevitably enter into accounts of Freud's life. However critical of him that one might be inclined to be, nobody could contest that he was a highly educated intellectual full of ideas, and that he succeeded in attracting to him a fascinating group of people whose lives, whatever one might now think of the merits of what they proposed, have to be considered, I believe, as models of interesting originality. In talking about the early days of psychoanalysis, or the struggles of Freud's tortured genius, one is not dealing with the uninteresting sort of bureaucracy that, let us say, we confront with today's International Psychoanalytic Association (IPA).

Any organization with approximately 10,000 members has to be a completely different matter than a narrative connected with the tiny group of people involved, for example, with the early strife between Freud, Jung and Adler. I mention these names because they are so intimately associated with the central founding myths of the discipline. My own approach has been that of an outsider willing to reconsider all past professional difficulties. As an intellectual historian I have found this a rich field precisely because there were, when I started out some forty years ago, so many examples of central figures who were neglected, ignored, or misunderstood. Filling in some of the silences seemed an intellectual adventure in keeping with Freud's own stated aim of correcting amnesias. Challenging collective family romances, and re-arranging various lineages, was in keeping with what intellectual historians are supposed to be doing.

At the outset of my work the early editions of Freud's letters were being regularly bowdlerized. It was only with the publication of my *Brother Animal: The Story of Freud and Tausk* that when I cited a particular shocking example of a suppression in a Freud letter to Lou Andreas-Salomé I put an end to such tendentious tampering.[15] (That is the reason why correspondences in this field are now called "complete". There is a downside here, since although a book of letters between Helene Deutsch and her husband Felix might be a good idea, the German publisher I have consulted on the matter hesitates to bring out anything less than all the letters, fearing accusation of partisanship.) The English page proofs of the correspondence between Freud and Lou Andreas-Salomé had to be withdrawn from circulation, and the book finally came out with those critical key words of Freud's reinstated. I felt I was then launching a scholarly torpedo, but that was my youth; even so I am afraid I have fairly regularly continued to drop little scholarly bombshells, not fully aware of how provocative that I think it is the job of a political philosopher to be. The Jung family still has to face up to all sorts of private papers not yet released, such as the extensive existing correspondence between Jung and his wife.

Right now I am still continuing at the same old game, although we are in a different phase of scholarship. The editing of the Freud-Ferenczi letters was so unsatisfactory and inadequate that through the publishers of the English edition of the Freud-Binswanger correspondence I inadvertently slowed things down by suggesting pre-publication editorial changes. And I worked hard on the revised edition of the Freud-Abraham letters in order to help ensure that the editing is more up to what I consider scratch. I wish there were many others who could also actively share in this sort of pulling up of our socks, so that in the future students of the history of ideas would have an even better appreciation of what once went on the in past.

Forty years ago Freud himself was within my field of political science not widely considered a legitimate field of inquiry. A career in political theory could have been advanced more readily by an attention to the ideas of Locke, Hobbes, Rousseau, even Thomas Aquinas or Augustine. In the years since I started out American political science has been moving even closer to economics, and away from political theory or the outlook of a professional pioneer like Harold Lasswell, who was once closely connected with people like Karen Horney and Harry Stack Sullivan. And yet I like to think that the central points in past political theorists were concerned with ideas about human nature which have been newly contested within psychoanalysis.[16]

Sectarianism has partially thrived within psychoanalysis precisely because of these fundamental clashes between alternative visions of the good life. The more uncertain the field, the more fanatically held convictions can be. And the fragility of the acceptance of the field can mean that it seem unpatriotic, if not treasonous, to march independently. But ideally history is not supposed to be written solely for celebratory purposes. Historical cheer-leading is not anything that interests me.

History-writing at its best is inherently subversive and upsetting. No authoritarian political regime has ever been able to put up with genuine historical research. To burrow in the past means at least potentially to attack the established present. When Peter Gay subtitled his biography of

Freud "A Life For Out Time," he was being presentistic; a journalistic tag-phrase that no doubt helped sell copies of books gave away the lack of proper detachment. To write in order to make analysts feel good about themselves would be to betray the obligation of the historian to disturb the present by means of the past for the sake of the future. So Gay could leave the name of Wilhelm Reich entirely out of his text, since the story associated with Reich would have complicated the narrative purposes of prettifying the history of psychoanalysis for today. (Oddly enough a recent excellent biography of Freud, the critical best we have had, has also succeeded in avoiding the apparently dread name Reich.[17]) Trade-unionists are entitled to want histories that promote their cause, just as corporations or famous families can appoint (and pay) scholars to present them in the best possible light. The supports that come from having joined the crowd are apt to be greater than the rewards for being willing to go against the grain.

As I look back on my own work, it was traumatic for me to be assailed in two full-length books by Kurt R. Eissler, the founder of the Freud Archives, and to find out that Anna Freud too viewed me as a "menace." (Three decades ago that particular party had a lot of allies with clout.) Yet I like to think that I am capable of being even-handed when I recently felt shocked to find how Anna Freud's position in England seems to have been swamped by those analysts who now ignore what she tried to accomplish. Anna Freud was so singularly lacking in political talent (or perhaps committed to altruistic surrender) that she put her mind to a "defense" of her father more than to securing her own position. Kleinianism is as curiously triumphant in Britain as Lacan has been successful in having an impact in France. These are as much cultural matters as tales of comparative national politics. One of the earliest interests in this subject I had was the story of the national reception of Freud in different national cultures – England and America, for example.

As the years have passed, and I grew more familiar with a broader range of countries and their individual traditions, my original focus has been extended as well as broadened. But there are bound to be losers as well as winners in as rich a tale as the history of psychoanalysis; and for instance to cite the ill-understood example of Wagner-Jauregg, a contemporary of Freud and the first psychiatrist ever to win a Nobel Prize, seems to me a matter of course and not any sign of "anti-psychoanalytic" bias. Someday scholars will also present accounts of the receptions of lithium, lobotomy, shock treatment, family therapy, self-psychology and goodness knows how many other movements within psychotherapy.

To work with the past means, I think, to engage in a kind of anthropological field-work. It is culture that defines what we should be trying to get at; different eras naturally define things in their own special way. The study of great literature – which is how I would characterize Freud's achievement – challenges us to get beyond today's conventional ways of thinking. The history of science itself is self-correcting, but even after all Freud's works may appear to have been beached in an intellectual Smithsonian they should retain their artistic unity. To examine any such texts involves our trying to comprehend the special orientations the past has to offer; this means an opportunity not only to get outside of ourselves, and into the minds of people different from us, but thanks to that intellectual voyage there is a possibility of returning with an enhanced perspective on how we think nowadays. History should not be undertaken either for the sake of enhancing our own sense of superiority or for the purpose of moralistically denouncing past ways of proceeding. The more educated we become the better able we should be to take critical distance toward today's ways of thinking. I am afraid that most psychoanalytic articles in our professional journals, which characteristically proceed by citing bibliographies of past literature, are constructing mythical bridges to the past, a procedure for establishing false continuities that unknowingly legitimates the status quo now.

To be fair to the past means to respect human variety, without insisting that everything valuable in history must necessarily lend support to how we proceed now. How we ought to live should be an open question, requiring tentativeness and a sympathetic imagination on our part. In my own early work I found it a convenient short-cut to interview psychoanalytic pioneers; even after all these years I am still assimilating the significance of what I once learned. The human context for ideas can be an essential road to understanding. Works of psychotherapeutic interest do not arise out of the sky of abstract philosophical reasoning, but rather from the complex struggles people have in dealing with enduring human mysteries. I do not fear that the latest fashions in psychiatric classification will exhaust the complexities of human motives. It is not necessary for any of us to be Luddites about psychopharmacological developments, or the thinking that encourages them. But I do find demeaning the way diagnoses of patients can be used for the sake of pigeon-holing; some things in life are unfixable, and need to be lived through. The human soul has triumphed before over such excessive rationalism as seems today so psychiatrically fashionable. I find it puzzling that Otto Fenichel, whose giant textbook can be seen as a handbook of old mistakes, should be attracting contemporary interest. If one yearns for encyclopaedic knowledge Henri Ellenberger would seem to me far more admirable.[18]

If one were presenting these ideas about the importance of the past in any other national setting, it would be necessary to adapt things radically. I once gave a talk in Paris entitled "What Is Wrong with French Psychoanalysis?"[19] and the place was mobbed. The French are used to serious intellectual exchanges, especially on the level of moral theory, even if one suspects that part of the price for that sort of vitality is a lack of conviction that civilization exists outside Paris. (The Chinese can be even more frustratingly self-confident because their ancient culture predates ours.) The French can unfortunately be crassly anti-American, as in the way they have been apt to dismiss the growth of ego psychology as only a matter of conformism.

In work as in life one makes choices, hopefully doing the best one can. If I have learned anything from my studies it is how essential in all the human sciences can be the injunction to guard against fanaticism. One of the best characterizations of how Freud's mind could work can be found, I think, in Solzhenitsyn's novel *Lenin in Zurich*.[20] Splitting a movement, reducing it down to its hard-core in the faith the future will redeem such purity, does remind me of Freud's way of proceeding before World War I. At least in the short-run he conquered against his opponents. And elsewhere that tenacious Bolshevik-like spirit has brought others remarkable psychoanalytic rewards. In the long run, however, I have a perhaps mistaken faith that the more modest people, those humble enough to allow themselves to be at least for a time forgotten, will also succeed in getting a hearing. So it is in behalf of those who have for one reason or another been neglected or unfairly treated that I have tried to work.

My coming of age in the 1950s meant that intellectual history — the power of ideas — was a live central faith. Max Weber writing on the role of the protestant ethic in promoting capitalism seemed a powerful answer to any dismissal of the central significance of the life of the mind. Marxists then had a way of dismissing the so-called superstructure, just as psychoanalysts could be high-handed about "rationalizations". But Freud too had staked his basic claims on the idealistic foundation that the way we think about things can be an independent variable in how we choose to live. Lord Keynes concluded his path-breaking *The General Theory of Employment, Interest and Money* (1936) with words that got indelibly etched on my mind:

> the ideas of economists and political philosophers, both when they are right and when they are wrong, are more powerful than is commonly understood. Indeed the world is ruled by little else. Practical men, who believe themselves to be quite exempt from any intellectual influences, are usually the slaves of some defunct economist. Madmen in authority, who hear voices in the air, are distilling their frenzy from some academic scribbler of a few years back. I am sure that the power of vested interests is vastly exaggerated compared with the gradual encroachment of ideas.

Keynes right away went on in the same paragraph:

> Not, indeed, immediately, but after a certain interval; for in the field of economic and political philosophy there are not many who are influenced by new theories after they are twenty-five or thirty years of age, so that the ideas which civil servants and politicians

and even agitators apply to current events are not likely to be the newest. But, soon or late, it is ideas, not vested interests, which are dangerous for good or evil.[21]

(I am unable authoritatively to support the hunch, but a guess is that Keynes was in this paragraph, stylistically so at odds with the rest of the book, still competing with his great old friend and rival Lytton Strachey. Strachey had first written the final memorable paragraph to his book on Queen Victoria, and then proceeded to write the rest of the text itself. This point does not appear in the otherwise excellent standard biography of Keynes.[22])

I hope Keynes was right about the long-run weakness of "vested interests." But I should confess that no matter how important intellectual history may be in preparing for the future, it has its own inherent fascination. Still, remember also that Nazism was an idea, and combating it was no easy matter for liberalism. The mind is only superior to the body up to a point. A faith in the autonomy of the human spirit goes back, at least politically, as far as John Milton.

I believe that studying the past is truly an end in itself, a legitimate part of trying to become a cultured person. The ideal of living an examined life is an ancient Greek one. Books that recreate something where before there was nothing succeed in their own terms. The pursuit of knowledge does constitute, as a practical by-product, a challenge to power, yet remains I think intrinsically self-justifying.

NOTES

1 "Analysis Terminable and Interminable," *The Standard Edition of the Complete Psychological Works of Sigmund Freud*, ed. James Strachey (London, The Hogarth Press, 1953-1974), Vol. 23, p. 249. Hereafter this edition of Freud's works will be referred to simply as *Standard Edition*.
2 "Introductory Lectures on Psychoanalysis," *Standard Edition*, Vol. 16, p. 463.
3 For example, compare and contrast the splendid approach in Leston L. Havens, *Approaches to the Mind: Movement of the Psychiatric Schools From Sects Toward Science* (Boston, Little Brown, 1973) to Edward Shorter, *A History of Psychiatry: From the Era of the Asylum to the Age of Prozac* (N.Y., Wiley, 1997).
4 Ronald R. Fieve, *Moodswing* (N. Y., Bantam, 1975).
5 Paul Roazen, *Canada's King: An Essay in Political Psychology* (Oakville, Ontario & Buffalo, N.Y., Mosaic Press, 1998), Ch. 2.
6 Henry James, *Hawthorne* (Ithaca, Cornell University Press, 1956), pp. 34-35.
7 *Ibid.*, p. 33. See Nathaniel Hawthorne, *The Marble Faun* (New York, Pocket Library, 1958), p. xi.
8 James, *op. cit.*, p. 10.

9 Quoted in Gertrude Himmelfarb, *Victorian Minds* (New York, Harper, 1970), p. 179. See also Roland Hill, *Lord Acton* (New Haven, Yale University Press, 2000).
10 Louis Hartz, *The Necessity of Choice: Nineteenth-Century Political Thought*, ed. Paul Roazen (New Brunswick, N.J., Transaction Publishers, 1990).
11 See Peter Lomas, *Doing Good? Psychotherapy Out of Its Depth* (N.Y., Oxford University Press, 1999).
12 Isaiah Berlin, *The Proper Study of Mankind: An Anthology of Essays*, ed. Henry Hardy and Roger Hausheer (New York, Farrar, Straus & Giroux, 1998); see also John Gray, *Isaiah Berlin* (Princeton, Princeton University Press, 1996) and Michael Ignatieff, *Isaiah Berlin: A Life* (New York, Metropolitan Books, 1998).
13 Paul Roazen, *The Trauma of Freud: Controversies in Psychoanalysis* (New Brunswick, N.J., Transaction Publishers, 2002).
14 Paul Roazen, *The Cultural Foundations of Political Psychology* (New Brunswick, N.J., Transaction, 2003), Conclusions.
15 Paul Roazen, *Brother Animal: The Story of Freud and Tausk*, 2nd edition with new Introduction (New Brunswick, Transaction Publishers, 1990), pp. 139-40.
16 Paul Roazen, *Political Theory and the Psychology of the Unconscious* (London, Open Gate Press, 2000).
17 Louis Breger, *Freud: Darkness in the Midst of Vision* (New York, Wiley, 2000).
18 See *Beyond The Unconscious: Essays of Henri Ellenberger in the History of Psychiatry*, ed. Mark S. Micale (Princeton, Princeton University Press, 1993), and Henri Ellenberger, *The Discovery of the Unconscious: The History and Evolution of Dynamic Psychiatry* (New York, Basic Books, 1970).
19 Paul Roazen, "What Is Wrong with French Psychoanalysis?", in Jean-Michel Rabaté, ed., *Jacques Lacan and the Cultural Unconscious* (New York, Other Press, 2000), pp. 41-60.
20 Alexander Solzhenitsyn, *Lenin in Zurich*, translated by H. T. Willetts (New York, Farrar, Straus & Giroux, 1976).
21 John Maynard Keynes, *The General Theory of Employment, Interest and Money* (London, Macmillan, 1957), pp. 383-84.
22 Robert Skidelsky, *John Maynard Keynes*, Vol. I: *Hopes Betrayed: 1883-1920* (New York, Penguin Books, 1983), *John Maynard Keynes*, Vol. II: *The Economist as Savior: 1920-1937* (New York, Penguin Books, 1995), *John Maynard Keynes*, Vol. III: *Fighting for Britain: 1937-1946* (New York, Penguin Books, 2002).

2
CHARLES RYCROFT AND ABLATION

It is a pleasure for me to try to pay tribute to Charles Rycroft's originality within psychoanalysis; I knew him from 1965 until his death in 1998, and I would guess that he was shy enough not to have appreciated his success as an independent thinker. We had fallen into a pattern of usually seeing each other at dinner when I happened to come over to London, but I have checked my files and there are also approximately eighty letters from Charles there. On one of our last evenings together, he did remark that he felt his career as an analyst had been "ruined" by the respective power of two women, Melanie Klein and Anna Freud. It is no doubt true that Charles's reputation and standing temporarily suffered from the complex politics of British psychoanalysis then, when ideological contests made it difficult for independent-minded people to win recognition. Although his *A Critical Dictionary of Psychoanalysis*[1] has become influential and widely sold, a book like *The Innocence of Dreams*[2], even though admired by someone like Graham Greene, did not do as well in terms of sales as one might expect.

At the same time I think that it would be understandable if Charles underestimated his own achievement; although books of essays and reviews[3] cannot be expected to prosper commercially, his work was, if only because of the impact of his publishing in *The New York Review of Books*, capable of being widely influential. Charles was like other early psychoanalytic pioneers in being broadly well-educated and cultured. It seems to me that in the face of the transitory fads and bureaucratic lethargy that afflict all fields, Charles did succeed in being a distinctive and original voice. Even though we no longer have the personal pleasure of Charles's intellect and person, I find there is no problem in bringing to mind some of his most characteristic ways of thinking.

Psychoanalysis has had its distinctive manner of proceeding, and British analysts worked out their own special ways of conceptualizing things. Although a little over a hundred years of Freud's school may not seem historically long, it has been enough to establish certain notable traditions of thought. Custom exerts its deleterious ways of inhibiting us, yet Donald Winnicott has been notably quoted on how impossible it would be to become creative apart from any received ways of thinking. In some sense Charles was curiously restricted by past ideas; like for most of us his background did constrict how far he was able to go intellectually. And still I think he managed to break through independently on a variety of fronts.

I have chosen to talk about Charles's paper "On Ablation of the Parental Images, or The Illusion of Having Created Oneself".[4] According to the Oxford English Dictionary, the word "ablation" started in the 16th century to mean "removal"; and ablation has come to signify cessation or remission within surgical, medical and geological contexts. For a good while I did think "ablation" had religious connotations, which a Catholic friend of mine assures me is in fact the case, but I now realize I had mainly mixed up the term with that of "oblation." It seems to me important that Charles implicitly was distinguishing ablation from either repression or denial, both of which he dealt with in his critical dictionary. I have picked this particular essay on ablation, which first came out in 1985, because it seems to me Charles at his best, and at the same time the most relevant to my own special concerns connected with the history of psychoanalysis.

I first met Charles in the summer of 1965, when I was over in England interviewing early analysts about Freud. I also happened to be working on Jones's unsorted papers in the basement of the British Psychoanalytic Society; I came across Charles's own name primarily because of his regularly reviewing then for the Sunday *Observer*, and I saw him once at his office. (He showed me then a scrap-book he had kept of the various newspaper reviews he had published; and I also have a distinct memory of his helpfully tutoring me in which order I should read various chapters of Winnicott's *Collected Papers*[5].) One time I saw Charles that summer I took notes; he had just got back from Italy, the Sunday before a bank holiday, and he rang me up when his car was not ready. Our talk that day lasted according to my records nine-and-a-half hours; but the first subject I marked down – and this was the only occasion with Charles on which I made any such written report – concerned the issue of "self-created fantasies," the obliterating of the parent of the same sex, which could be "destructive" and also "creative". I understood Charles to be proposing an interesting variation on the familiar story of Oedipus.

I noted for myself, probably thinking of Freud, Charles's point that if one is both ego and father, then opposition to oneself becomes *lèse majesté* – the gods themselves have been offended. (That would help account, Charles thought, for one of the sources of Freud's intolerances about other people's ideas.) In my first book (1968) I cited Charles on how Freud's long-standing desire to get to Rome could be interpreted symbolically, as the wish to transcend the religion of obedience to the father by the religion of love.[6] In this connection I had recommended to Charles the early biography of Freud by Helen Walker Puner[7], and he read it; this point of Charles's about Freud and Christianity came up in a letter to me as part of his response to Puner's work. But Charles's more general idea was that if someone is to become his own father, then he has to create himself – which imposes quite a task, which can only be accomplished by a life-work. Genealogy of analysts is important, and what any father did to earn a livelihood matters. But if one has obliterated one's biological parents, a lot remains to atone for – one must make up for it somehow.

It turns out that the original version of the Ablation essay had been written in 1965, but was rejected by both the editors of the *International Journal of Psychoanalysis* as well as by the editors of the International Psychoanalytic Library, which brought out Charles's *Imagination and Reality*. It was, Charles later wrote, thought "impolitic to publish an essay which discussed some of the psychopathological reasons which may lead people to become psychoanalysts."[8] After I had published a book on Erik H. Erikson, Charles wrote (Nov. 10, 1976) to me as follows:

> A propos Erikson's name change: Some years ago I wrote a paper called On Ablation of the Parental Images or The Illusion of Having Created Oneself in which I described a group of patients who attempted to disown their pasts entirely, who denied that their parents had had any effect on them whatsoever, and who, if they were drawn to analysis as they often seemed to be, dated their lives from the moment they started analysis and regarded their true parent (sic) as having been their analyst and their true ancestry his or her analytical lineage. Such people, I said, aspired to be self-made in the most literal sense of the word or, if they couldn't achieve that, to have parents whom they themselves chose. When I read this paper to a group of analysts, I was embarrassed to discover that my thesis applied too well to too many analysts; most of the examples I had chosen were people who had aspired unsuccessfully to become analysts, but my paper gave the impression of being a roman à clef about actual analysts. It sounds as though Erikson exemplifies my thesis up to a point though I certainly didn't have him in mind when I wrote it.

Charles then, evidently in response to what I wrote him, sent me (Nov. 29, 1976) a manuscript of his "On Ablation" paper, which did not appear in print for almost another decade. Incidentally, Charles commented in sending me that typescript: "If you ever think of having another go at my collected papers, read them in reverse order of printing. About half way through I started eliminating technical terms from my style and the later papers are quite readable."

As I once again re-read Charles's Ablation essay for purposes of this presentation, I was struck at the outset by his referring to "the ahistorical tendency characteristic of ablators of parental images...."[9] If I may repeat a point already made: history-writing is inherently a subversive activity; students of history necessarily undermine generally received wisdom. Authoritarian regimes all through time have not been friendly to genuine historical activity. I am putting aside purely celebratory work, what in the States we would call flag-waving, in favor of the objective of history to expand our imaginations. Condescension about the past can be expressed in a variety of ways, such as righteous present-mindedness.

A typical lack of respect for historical sequences has, I think, bedeviled the writing about psychoanalysis to an exceptional extent. In my recent book about Edward Glover[10] (someone whom Charles admired as a clinician – for a time they both practiced as part of the same suite at 18 Wimpole Street) I was essentially trying to introduce a complicating element into the generally received Family Romance among British analysts. Any simple line from Freud to Abraham or Ferenczi to Klein needs, I believe, to be seriously complicated. And Charles in general was also putting his finger on another typical feature of the literature about analysis when he commented on how ablators "seek out 'ideal' intellectual ancestors to replace the actual ones they have dismissed."[11]

The issue for the intellectual historian of establishing continuities as well as discontinuities within psychoanalysis, which I have found to be an essential problem with the literature, would appear to be entirely consistent with Charles's thesis about ablation. When Charles refers to patients who do not attend the funerals of their parents, or "feel relief rather than grief afterwards," he might well have cited the example of Freud's own reaction to the death of his mother.[12] Charles intended to suggest that "the creativeness, the falsity and the dishonesty all derive from the same source," ablation. And he also had in mind that "persons of this kind may be drawn to psychoanalysis and the psychoanalytic movement in a way that may, perhaps, be beneficial to them but is harmful to psychoanalysis."[13] The process of re-creating the self "can be regarded as imaginative and creative," but "it is also false, since it can only be squared with the dreary truth by suppression of some facts, by distortion of others and by subordination of memory to mythopoeisis."[14]

In the erasing of the past and starting afresh, "the original parental values continue to operate unconsciously in an unmodified form."

> This unconscious survival of the consciously ablated parental images is responsible for the paradoxical picture such people often

present to the world; messianic in their advocacy of their own self-created ideas, but shifty and ill at ease in their way of presenting them. If they write scientific papers their acknowledgements are either scanty or obscure, or, contrariwise, so extensive that their real indebtedness is hidden as successfully as a needle in a haystack. They are uniformly anti-historical, or rather ahistorical. . . .[15]

Charles was arguing that their "denial of indebtedness...makes them creative."[16] And he used a passage from Sartre's autobiography *Words* in order show how "despair evoked by the absence of a living paternal image and by alienation from the body can be warded off by self-idealization."[17] Charles also thought that his series of patients who were "ablators" were characteristically "incapable of grief."[18]

Although ablators come to psychoanalysis for "genuine" reasons, "corrupt" ones also intrude: "there are certain aspects of the psychoanalytic situation which appeal to ablators because they seem to them to be designed to enhance the myth of self-creation and to provide opportunities for strengthening, not dissolving, their defensive system."[19]

> Patients and student analysands who do in fact succeed in being analysed by the analyst of their own choice often, it seems to me, become proselytizers of their analyst's theories as much out of personal vanity as out of genuine appreciation and gratitude for his understanding and skill. In such cases, the patient or analysand patronizes his analyst, while basking in the reflected glory of someone whom he has himself elected to idealize and whom he believes he has discovered; thereby reversing the humiliating biological fact that he did not choose his own parents.[20]

Psychoanalysis is still recent enough for ablators "to argue, while remaining this side of madness, that nothing was known about human nature before Freud."[21] Charles was explicitly linking his argument to the state of British psychoanalysis. He pointed to

> the mere existence within the British Psycho-analytic Society of three – or it is more? – different schools of theory and technique, all of which claim to have better therapeutic results than the others. For such a bizarre situation to have arisen and to be still existing, some people must be deceiving themselves, some people must be idealizing their own ideas and work or that of their analysts, and objective criteria for deciding what kinds of patients are suitable for treatment and what sorts of results should be deemed successes must be entirely lacking.[22]

Charles sounded concerned lest it be "unduly cynical" for him to propose that "in such a nebulous, ill-defined field, inauthentic, spurious characters can survive and flourish."[23] Charles was importantly proposing that psychoanalysis "has a special attraction for people whose own relationship to their bodies and their past is ambiguous and whose own inner frames of reference are ill-defined."[24]

Charles pointed out that such ablators could be led "to idealization of the training analysis and of the so-called 'apostolic succession,' and to a tendency to believe that an analyst's competence derives solely from his personal analysis."[25] (The problem of training analyses, and possible drawbacks or even its history, has been I think a curiously neglected subject to be discussed in Chapter 4.) He was also alluding to a factor leading to "the social isolation of psychoanalysts," who could pursue their work "not as a profession but as a calling."[26] And he was calling attention to the possible neglect of the significance of both biology and genetics. He concluded his paper, in his re-written 1973 form, by citing Winnicott's distinction between the "true self" and the "false self": "the 'true self'. . .is the depository of what the individual inherits from his parents, and can elaborate into something which is truly and uniquely himself, whereas it is the false self which harbours the defences, the disguises and the pretensions."[27]

Now why does this paper of Charles's, entirely aside from the merits of its theses, seem so important to me? First of all, his argument has antecedents within my own psychoanalytic upbringing. One of the early people who inspired me, in the course of my interviewing her, was Helene Deutsch; and she had published an early paper on pathological lying, and wrote some famous articles on the absence of grief, imposters, and what she called the "as-if" personality.[28] She was also interested in "parthenogenesis" as an aspect of female psychology.[29] While in no way denying Freud's stature in intellectual history, Helene had been trying to point to other aspects of human psychology that lay beyond the strict Oedipus complex.

Neurosis implies the presence of structured inner conflicts, whereas Helene Deutsch – and Charles also on ablators – was going beyond classical psychoanalytic thought. I remember her teaching me, in her 90s, that "the absence of affect is a feeling too." Here I think that great literature, including even Shakespeare, can easily be misleading; Macbeth, Hamlet, Lear, and Othello are all examples of tragic heroes whose rich emotional responses are apt to seem prototypical. Yet in reality many of us often fall into the category of what Freud more than once dismissed as "riff-raff," people incapable of fulfilling the demanding example of the greatest literary models. In real life people do not live up to the psychological glamour of Tolstoy's Anna Karenina or Flaubert's Emma Bovary. It would be a romantic fallacy to think that Conrad's Lord Jim or any other great literary character were anything other than exceptional; when Conrad treats a self-destruction or suicide as a sign of the presence of character, he was promoting a special idealistic view of human nature.

But little attention is apt to get paid to the issue of the relative absence of character. If I illustrate this with the example of Erik Erikson, I hope it should be taken for granted that I consider him one of the most creative analysts in the whole history of the field. But his name change was part and parcel of the new identity that early psychoanalysis could offer people; I am thinking of Otto Rank's also inventing his own last name. Although genuine ancestry took a distinct backseat in Erikson's efforts at autobiographical self-presentation, at the same time he exaggerated his own direct lineage to Freud. According to Erikson's most thorough biographer, when the Eriksons left Vienna in 1933 "Freud came to the railroad station to see his family off, urging Erik to have a kind and loving heart."[30]

Now the truth is that by 1933 Freud was a sick old man who had had his jaw cancer for ten years; Erikson had only recently been accepted as a member of the Vienna Psychoanalytic Society, and was of no notable standing either among the analysts or to Freud personally. Leaving Vienna was in general hardly favored by Freud, even if Erikson had been jumped from associate membership to being a full member for the sake of being possible "export ware." For me it seems preposterous to believe that Freud actually came to that railroad station, whatever Erikson may have told the one source that his biographer later relied on. To me Erikson was engaged in fabricating a family romance of his own. (Perhaps Erikson was unconsciously competing with his later rival Heinz Kohut, who reportedly had gone to the railroad station in Vienna to see Freud off in 1938.)

Erikson's own tortured relation to his parents got him in public trouble when he appeared to be guilty of autobiographical bad faith in connection with disguising his wholly Jewish ancestry. Yet this heavily ambivalent family background had not only helped stimulate his professional fantasies about his origins within the family of psychoanalysts, but later interfered with his own parenting. Not only was Erikson less than ideal in fulfilling his own standard of "generativity" when it came to helping his own students (Erikson did not notably assist them), but his daughter has been publicly campaigning against Erikson as having been a disappointingly poor father to her. Remember, biological families are full of natural injustices – discrepancies of talent, birth order, emotional preference – from which any intelligent person can need to escape.

With all the psychoanalytic piety that has been associated with the figure of Freud himself, it seems to me that analysts themselves have had a striking lack of natural filial allegiance. A Paris analyst I know had a mother who was a professional painter, and when the Hartmanns were passing through on their way eventually to the States she painted a portrait of Dora Hartmann. When my friend mentioned that she still had the painting, implying that it belonged elsewhere, I suggested that perhaps one of the Hartmann sons would want it. But when I asked them about it, not only was there no special eagerness for it but I got asked: "Was it a good painting?" At the same time it seems to me worth pointing out how young grandchildren of Ernst and Marianne Kris wrote to Anna Freud as if she were a realistic family member.

Charles's concept of ablation helps to highlight something missing in many of the early analysts. To take an instance that has become notable: Anna Freud's analysis by her father, which we will specifically discuss in Chapter 3. It could be asked to what extent the psychoanalytic parentage overtook the familial one. And subsequently Anna Freud proposed, within the context of dealing with legal custody problems for children, the notion of psychological parenthood as opposed to biological parenthood. (She accorded the psychological caretaker special preferential standing.) The analysis of Anna by her father remained for many years a secret, thanks to people like Marianne Kris and others; one has to ask for what purposes of family devotion these people were being defensive.

Charles's notion of the significance of ablation can help us to understand elements of phoniness and creativity. Inauthenticity can involve more subtle problems than one might imagine, and these help to account for the way the scholarship associated with so much in the professional literature strikes someone like me as a Potemkin village of artificial constructs. When in the course of my once interviewing Helene Deutsch I asked her whether she would like me to bring in to her the autobiography of her early mentor Julius Wagner-Jauregg, she really had no interest in the subject. Although Wagner had once been a great figure in her life, after she became an analyst he was in a sense gone, almost as if he had ceased to exist for her. It might go perhaps without saying that Helene Deutsch, like so many of the other early analysts, had successfully escaped from her own Polish origins into the psychoanalytic family. Lest I needlessly leave others out of this ablation story, Melanie Klein's attempt to hold onto Abraham as a the legitimizing source of her work really amounted to a hollow attempt to sustain her own psychoanalytic lineage. One would think it obvious that Freud's own extremely harsh private judgment about her contribution was after his death partly being enacted by Anna Freud and Edward Glover in the course of the struggle in Britain known as the Controversial Discussions.

The establishing of credentials becomes a key to often spurious, recurrent aspects of important thinkers throughout the history of psychoanalysis. Bruno Bettelheim was as inventive about his past as anybody in this regard.[31] And Masud Khan's first biographer had to be surprised to find, despite Khan's earlier claims, that there was no record at Balliol College, Oxford, of his ever having attended there.[32] The examples that one might assemble to illustrate the significance of ablation within psychoanalysis are almost too numerous to mention. How any of us deals with the past is partly a cultural matter, and differs as we have discussed already from country to country; but Charles was pointing to ablation being a psychological question as well.

The students any prominent analyst acquires become part of the legends within the family. Although Charles and I never discussed those he had trained, perhaps now would be the time to mention that among his analysands were such distinguished people as Alan Tyson, R. D. Laing, and Peter Lomas, to list only a few of those talented people who sought Charles out. As much attention has been given in the field to constructing an informal family tree of who was whose analyst, everybody has steered clear of the emotionally charged issue of the real children of analysts and what they might have to report. Melanie Klein's daughter Melitta Schmideberg would be at the extreme end of the spectrum of those who relished hatred of her mother, but alas not alone in her bitterness toward analytic parenting.

It has to be curious how little attention has also been given to the gratifications and frustrations of being a training analyst. For Charles, though, the difficulties between Melanie Klein and Anna Freud made for a family row that he wanted to stand back from. Sylvia Payne was I think right in considering it unfortunate for Charles that so soon after World War II he got pushed into officeholding within the British Psychoanalytic Society. Although his stepping outside traditionalist lines came to be one of his sources of originality, this reward was balanced by how easy it could be for others to ignore his contributions. The peril of ostracism for having betrayed the psychoanalytic family can be harsh; although heresy can be attractive to some, unconscious conformism can be even more inhibiting to many. Charles's security, stemming from his integrity as well as partly from his aristocratic social position, may have made him sensitive to the false pretensions of others. (My own American ignorance of proper British social rules could have helped Charles relax with me.)

In his writing about the significance of ablation within psychoanalysis Charles had succeeded in highlighting a central aspect of my own interest in this field. For me what has counted more than anything was the history of psychoanalysis; and it was precisely because of the anti-historical or ahistorical bias within the field, which Charles had been trying to explain, that intellectual historians like myself could find so much of enduring interest. Even now, with all that has been published, I think there is a relative dearth of real historical scholarship in this whole area. Which theorist came before which other thinker still remains largely unexplored; as much as Winnicott admired Erik Erikson, for example, at least one book about Winnicott makes no mention of Erikson. As I have already mentioned, it has been possible for recent biographies of Freud to proceed without once raising the name of Wilhelm Reich. And Heinz Kohut skipped over the work of Franz Alexander, just as Alexander had dodged Jung. I have long been convinced that the early analysts were a fascinating group of pioneers whose lives and ideas will continue to be of historical interest. As a matter of fact I would want to contend that the people involved in early analysis, and the fascinating stories that surround them, may be much the most important part of what the future needs to be reminded of. These analysts can be models of the problems that creative individuals have to deal with.

At least this is the historiographical side of things that I mainly talked about with Charles; and I regularly sent him examples of what I had most recently written. It is my impression that as the years passed he grew bolder and more emancipated. And I am not alluding here to his allowing his membership in the British Psycho-Analytic Society to lapse. When my *Brother Animal*, exploring Freud's relationship to Victor Tausk, first came out in 1969, Charles must have had difficulties with it; his introverted review, which I do not think we ever discussed and he failed to reprint, was I think hobbled by the constraints of traditionalist thinking.[33] Charles's published view of my book might have lacked anything easily quotable for publicity purposes, but what he wrote was enough for Kurt Eissler to include Charles as part of Eissler's wholesale denunciation of *Brother Animal*; Charles was resentful enough to write Eissler in protest. Anthony Storr, although I had only met him well after I was first in contact with Charles, had come from such a different intellectual tradition that he had no difficulty welcoming the book in an enthusiastic review. Peter Lomas, who I only later found out had been trained by Charles, was also unambivalent about *Brother Animal*. When Charles later reviewed the Freud-Jung letters for *The New York Review of Books*, he was so startled that he wondered whether they should ever have been published. The more time passed, the freer Charles could be in his thinking.

I cannot help wondering now what he would have thought of recent findings of mine in connection with how Freud, Anna Freud, and Jones dealt with the problem posed for the International Psychoanalytic Association by the rise to power of the Nazis.[34] The main culprit of the tale, Ernest Jones, threw a retrospective smokescreen over what happened. (I felt so badly about the unfortunate role Jones played in my Glover book that I put in a particularly sympathetic photograph of Jones in his last days.) Charles had personal familiarity with Jones, who had interviewed him as an analytic candidate, and then later, when Jones was traveling in America for the sake of celebrating Freud's hundredth birthday, temporarily transferred to Charles a long-standing patient of Jones's from one of Britain's most prominent families. Does the concept of ablation help make comprehensible Jones's many idealizations of Freud? I am inclined to be less charitable about Jones than Charles's concept might imply; for when it came to Jones's own behavior in behalf of the IPA, and how he later tried to cover it up in his biography of Freud, it is hard for me not to think that Jones was deliberating lying about what had happened. To compress the story into a nutshell: the IPA reacted to the Nazis organizationally very much the way Jung had, in that a category of direct international membership got created for those Jewish analysts in Germany who would otherwise not have had psychoanalytic legitimacy. But Charles's concept of ablation does help to understand why legitimate psychoanalytic credentials have always mattered so much.

As an intellectual I think Charles would have been intrigued by the story of post-World War II psychoanalysis in Germany. An analyst (Carl Müller-Braunschweig) who, we now know, gave away in code the names of Jewish Italian analysts to the German authorities later became, following the collapse of the Nazi regime, along with a tiny handful of others – including one former Nazi party member – the leader of what became a huge group of IPA German analysts. Collaboration with Adler and Jung was deemed more objectionable to IPA authorities than whatever had happened with Hitler, and "revisionist" German analysts got excluded from the IPA. The German analysts have had to deal with their own questionable past, and ablation has not proven wholly successful. But Charles, I think, had managed to raise a key aspect of their psychological need for legitimate succession.

I suppose that with this small paper of mine I am trying to fit my own work into some sort of historical lineage. If my sort of thinking was O.K. with Charles, then perhaps Anna Freud might have been wrong when she once declared in a letter to Eva Rosenfeld: "All I can say is that Roazen is a menace whatever he writes."[35] (The fact that in England Eva Rosenfeld successfully disguised her own prior analysis with Felix Boehm in Berlin could also be interpreted within Charles's concept of ablation.[36] Charles had in 1965 encouraged me to see Eva as someone likely to be uninhibited, and he seemed pleased later to have proven right.) When I presented some of my ideas about Edward Glover at the Portman Clinic in 2000, I was a bit bewildered to be told by one member of the audience that I ought to be presenting them at the Anna Freud Centre. I like to think that what is valuable about my work on Glover is that I succeeded in showing that the controversy about him fits none of the standard stereotypes. Myth-making about "heretics" like Adler and Jung, who remain even today psychoanalysis's "usual suspects," is part of the mythopoesis Charles wrote about. When I had evidently in reviewing Charles's *Psycho-Analysis and Beyond* for *The New Statesman* twitted him about ignoring one of his own analysts, Sylvia Payne, Charles wrote me (Sept. 20, 1985): "So far from minding about your reservations I am pleased to receive constructive criticism – your implication that I am a bit of an ablator myself must, I think, be right." I was of course pleased when Charles quoted me in 1990 while reviewing a book of Peter Gay's in the *Times Literary Supplement*.[37]

Peter Ackroyd's biography of Dickens contained a passage that reminded me of the general significance of Charles's notion of ablation; Ackroyd was referring to a "kind of filial betrayal" on Dickens's part:

> in a sense he had rejected both of his parents when he recreated himself in language. In that self-engendering which takes place in the act of composition he was in a sense divesting himself of ori-

gins and claiming a kind of imaginative orphanhood. Partly out of ambition, partly out of egoism.[38]

Dickens, who carefully assembled the outlines and corrections for each of his books, ideal children, could be appallingly inadequate with his natural offspring, which we will come back to in Chapter 6. However central an issue in artistic creativity ablation may be, I think it has special relevance for psychoanalysis. Once in Paris an analyst took me aside to show me that he had acquired at auction the ring that Freud had once bestowed on Marie Bonaparte. And I remember how struck I once was by Erik Erikson's having dedicated a book to Anna Freud at a time when she was keeping her distance from his work. Above all, perhaps, ablation as a concept can help understood why it has been so often a case of *lèse majesté* to talk about Freud within the regular categories of intellectual history.

The illusion of having created oneself played a role in Freud's biography even at the time of his death. For in deciding to have himself cremated, at odds with Jewish custom, and the arrangement by which his ashes were placed in an ancient Greek urn given him by Marie Bonaparte, meant that Freud was being self-creative one final time. (His more traditionally Jewish wife, at whose later funeral there was a rabbi, nevertheless asked to have her own ashes added to Freud's. Since there was not enough room, some of her remains were scattered.) The concept of ablation also helps to understand the complexities of Freud's relationship with his intellectual predecessors, as well as how he could be throughout his career so preoccupied with the theme of plagiarism.

I hope that my paying tribute to the memory of Charles reflects the conviction that he succeeded in making himself into a genuinely original thinker within the tradition he matured in. The spiritual daring I found in Charles was in a sense an extension of Freud's own historic independence, even though that common trait had inevitably to lead in different directions. I found Charles's brilliance was fully matched by his broad humanity, and this chapter is partly intended to try to ensure that my gratitude for Charles's life and work does not fail to get established.

NOTES

1 Charles Rycroft, *A Critical Dictionary of Psychoanalysis*, 2nd edition (London, Penguin Books, 1995).
2 Charles Rycroft, *The Innocence of Dreams* (London, The Hogarth Press, 1979).
3 Charles Rycroft, ed., *Psychoanalysis Observed* (London, Constable, 1966); Charles Rycroft, *Imagination and Reality* (London, The Hogarth Press, 1968); Charles Rycroft, *Anxiety and Neurosis* (London, Allen Lane, 1968); Charles

Rycroft, *Viewpoints* (London, The Hogarth Press, 1991). See also Charles Rycroft, *Reich* (London, Fontana, 1971).
4 Charles Rycroft, *Psycho-Analysis and Beyond*, ed. Peter Fuller (London, Chatto & Windus, 1985), Ch. 22, pp. 214-32.
5 D. W. Winnicott, *Collected Papers: Through Paediatrics to Psycho-Analysis* (London, Tavistock Publications, 1968).
6 Paul Roazen, *Freud: Political and Social Thought* (New York, Knopf, 1968; London, The Hogarth Press, 1969; 3rd edition, New Brunswick, N.J., Transaction Publishers, 1999), p. 176n.
7 Helen Walker Puner, *Sigmund Freud: His Life and Work*, with a new Introduction by Paul Roazen (New Brunswick, New Jersey, Transaction Publishers, 1992).
8 Charles Rycroft, "On Ablation of the Parental Images, or The Illusion of Having Created Oneself," in *Psycho-Analysis and Beyond*, ed. Peter Fuller (London, Chatto and Windus, 1985), p. 214.
9 *Ibid.*, p. 215.
10 Paul Roazen, *Oedipus in Britain: Edward Glover and the Struggle Over Klein* (New York, Other Press, 2000).
11 Rycroft, "On Ablation," *op. cit.*, p. 216.
12 See Paul Roazen, *Freud and His Followers* (New York, Knopf, 1975; New York, Da Capo, 1992), p. 41.
13 Rycroft, "On Ablation," *op. cit.*, p. 220.
14 *Ibid.*, pp. 220-21.
15 *Ibid.*, p. 222.
16 *Ibid.*, p. 223.
17 *Ibid.*, p. 224.
18 *Ibid.*, p. 225.
19 *Ibid.*, p. 227.
20 *Ibid.*, p. 227.
21 *Ibid.*, p. 228.
22 *Ibid.*, p. 229.
23 *Ibid.*
24 *Ibid.*, p. 230.
25 *Ibid.*, p. 230.
26 *Ibid.*, p. 231.
27 *Ibid.*, p. 232.
28 Helene Deutsch, "Absence of Grief," "Some Forms of Emotional Disturbances and Their Relationship to Schizophrenia," "The Imposter," in *Neuroses and Character Types: Clinical Psychoanalytic Studies* (N.Y., International Universities Press, 1965), pp. 226-36, 262-81, 319-38; Helene Deutsch, "Two Cases of Induced Insanity," "On the Pathological Lie," "On a Type of Pseudo-Affectivity (the 'As If' Type)," and "Clinical and Theoretical Aspects of 'As If' Characters," in *The Therapeutic Process, The Self, and Female Psychology: Collected Psychoanalytic Papers*, ed. Paul Roazen (New Brunswick, N.J., Transaction Publishers, 1992), pp. 91-100, 109-21, 193-207, 215-20; and also see Paul Roazen, *Helene Deutsch: A Psychoanalyst's Life* (New York, Doubleday, 1985; 2nd edition, with new Introduction, New Brunswick, N.J., Transaction Publishers, 1992).
29 Helene Deutsch, "Motherhood and Sexuality," in *Neuroses and Character Types, op. cit.*, 193 ff., and Helene Deutsch, *Psychoanalysis of the Sexual Functions of Women*, ed. Paul Roazen (London, Karnac, 1991).
30 Lawrence J. Friedman, *Identity's Architect: A Biography of Erik H. Erikson* (New York, Scribner, 1999), p. 97.

31 See Richard Pollak, *The Creation of Dr. B.: A Biography of Bruno Bettelheim* (New York, Simon & Schuster, 1997) and Nina Sutton, *Bettelheim: A Life and Legacy* (New York, Basic Books, 1996).
32 Judy Cooper, *Speak of Me As I Am: The Life and Work of Masud Khan* (London, Karnac, 1993).
33 Charles Rycroft, "Freudian Triangles: Book Review of *Brother Animal*," *The Observer*, April 26, 1970.
34 Paul Roazen, *Cultural Foundations of Political Psychology*, *op. cit.*, Chapter 1.
35 Paul Roazen, *Meeting Freud's Family* (Amherst, Mass., Univ. of Mass. Press, 1993), p. 201.
36 Roazen, *The Historiography of Psychoanalysis* (New Brunswick, N.J. Transaction Publishers, 2001), p. 87.
37 Charles Rycroft, "Freud's Best Face," *Times Literary Supplement*, July 6-12, 1990.
38 Peter Ackroyd, *Dickens* (New York, Harper Collins, 1990), p. 830.

3
FREUD'S ANALYSIS OF ANNA

The kinds of normal scholarly debates that characterize intellectual history as a whole have never succeeded in being welcomed within the tale of the development of psychoanalysis. This is not just a simple-seeming matter associated with either sectarianism or trade unionism, although both factors have for instance played their part in ensuring that as momentous a conflict in the history of ideas as that between Freud and Jung has still not been adequately surveyed. It has been as if the ideal of science led analytic practitioners to believe that by entertaining a variety of perspectives on the past of the discipline they would be creating a breech in the ranks of those who should be, supposedly, supporting the field by maintaining a monolithic conception of history. Pluralism is more fashionable in theory than practice, and on their own part outsiders and literary critics can be doctrinaire in a way that clinicians, aware of the full complexities of their work, are not. It therefore may come as no surprise if historians of French psychoanalysis have been unaware of the many years in which a "dissident" like Otto Rank practiced in Paris.[1] How the name of Wilhelm Reich, and consequently his key role in Viennese analysis, can be completely ignored might be explained because a discussion of such a controversial figure would be disagreeably painful to have to entertain.[2] Although in academic life in general careers should be able to be made by concentrating on neglected thinkers, the history of psychoanalysis is littered with instances of unconsciously suppressed conflicts.

Given the nature of the work that has failed to be done in this area, it follows that as I look back over all the possible changes that have taken place in the study of the history of analysis during the forty years this subject has interested me, the polarized nature of the controversies that have succeeded in coming up continues to stand out. Even during Freud's lifetime, as a matter of fact pre-dating the outbreak of World War I, people tended to be either passionately favorable to his work or else adamantly antagonistic. Unfortunately both outsiders and insiders have been too easily made angry in this field, at the same time that it has continued to be rather simple to be original, since a little bit of tolerance goes a long way in making one open to the legitimacy of various rival points of view which have been contesting for public allegiance.

These preliminary considerations may help explain, or at least put in perspective, how Freud's analysis of his youngest child Anna (1895-1982) went publicly unmentioned for over four decades; yet that analysis constituted such a striking ethical transgression that I am even today left bewildered about its implications. This violation of his own stated rules for the practice of technique has to leave one questioning what he intended to accomplish with his written recommendations for future analysts. I am inclined to think that Freud's behavior here, and that of Anna too, stemmed from a kind of Nietzschean conviction that the chosen few were entitled to go beyond the normal bounds of conventional distinctions between good and evil.[3] Freud did think of analysis as a source of new moral teachings, and out of this treatment setting he hoped to be able to evolve fresh ethical standards. If the superior few had special entitlements, then lesser beings were to be controlled by a different set of restraints.

It is now over a quarter of a century since I first, in 1969, published a paragraph about Freud's having analyzed Anna.[4] I had some idea ahead-of-time how potentially explosive knowledge of this analysis was capable of being. I was revealing this information in the larger context of the story of Freud's relationship with Victor Tausk, and this reconstruction itself, including Freud's complex reaction to Tausk's suicide, was inevitably going to constitute an upheaval. I have no idea how high a professional price I paid for my forthrightness in going ahead and revealing Freud's analysis of Anna.

For a group of old loyalist analysts this revelation about Freud and Anna was bound to seem debunking. Yet I thought I was proceeding in the spirit of Freud's own idealistic argument in his *The Future of An Illusion*. In that assault on traditional religious faith Freud held out the norm of scientific knowledge, and the precious enlightenment that the truth was capable of bringing. Although I never thought only one set of interpretations could be put on Freud's having analyzed Anna, it did seem to me that the reality of what had happened, taking for granted the context of her achievements, was worth making public.

While Anna Freud was alive, and capable of contesting anything that I wrote, there was a fall-back position for her advocates and defenders. It might be the case that Freud had analyzed her, but then it was commonly said that later she had had a second analysis with Lou Andreas-Salomé.

Presumably that extra therapeutic experience acted as a sort of check on what Anna had experienced with her father; when I think of others who had first been analyzed by Freud, and then by subsequent therapists, it does seem to me that that initial experience of an analysis with Freud had an overwhelming impact that necessarily colored if not overshadowed all later therapeutic encounters. Oddly enough Anna seems to have preferred to think of herself as solely analyzed by her father, as she proceeded to downplay the significance of Lou in her life.

The note at the back of the book, where I first supplied the oral evidence about this then startling bit of information about Freud and Anna, was contrived in that I was deliberately writing while she was capable of reacting to my assertion.[5] Now that I have examined the lengthy letter she wrote to Kurt R. Eissler, who was put in charge of polemically answering me about Tausk, it has to be noticeable that she did not even then discuss the point about her having been analyzed by her father. Presumably Eissler already knew about it himself, since he somehow claimed in print that it was already a "well-known" fact.[6]

I had purposefully left out some key names of my roster of sources, on the grounds that a few of them could not withstand Anna's possible anger at their willingness to discuss such a sensitive matter with me. One of my informants, an old friend and analysand of Anna's (Dr. Anny Katan), waited a period of months before writing to Anna denying that she had ever talked about the subject with me; Anna's official biographer never bothered to check the truth of the matter, and instead chose in 1988 to broaden the possible allegation against me by saying that I had invented interviews with people who supposedly "insisted that they had refused to be interviewed."[7] (Nothing in her text supported that particular broadside against me, and my interview notes record the specific context of Dr. Katan's own analysis in which the subject came up.)

In 1975 I had this time spent several pages discussing the whole subject of Freud's analysis of Anna[8], which had still failed to make its way into the professional psychoanalytic literature. Although I had naively expected that clinicians would have a good deal to contribute to understanding this highly unusual situation, the silence continued pretty much as before. Since some misguided die-hard loyalists have mistakenly sought to give another, usually un-named, the credit for having first put into print the news of Anna's analysis, I returned to the whole issue in a 1993 book.[9]

Finally some public dialogue is getting going on this still sensitive matter. I hope that it proves possible to explore the implications of what went on between Freud and Anna without calling forth outraged wrath. Partisan fervor seems repeatedly to break out in the course of trying to deal dispassionately with the historiography of psychoanalysis. I suppose these sorts of emotions can be attributed to Freud's success in making analysis a powerful secular religion. But moralistic fervor will not accomplish much, other than to discredit the whole tradition of depth psychology at a time when biological psychiatry appears to be as much in favor as before Freud wrote a psychological line. It is unfortunately the case that in the public mind as well as in the historical literature an all- or-nothing approach continues to prevail; and it has been hard to get people to pick and choose what deserves to survive from Freud's teachings, without either completely endorsing everything he wrote or else rejecting analysis root and branch.

Unfortunately the critics who challenged Freud in his lifetime have still by and large not been credited adequately for pointing out the blindspots in Freud's system that they accurately observed. It should always be possible to be respectful of Freud without absorbing his whole outlook, and a substantial literature exists of skeptics who were willing to learn from what Freud had proposed.

Up to now, however, after all these years I can think of only one article in the literature that concentrates on Freud's analysis of Anna; although it was written by an analyst it appeared in a book intended for a general audience concerned with the history of psychoanalysis.[10] My own tentative explorations of the implications of what Freud and Anna cooperated in doing was conceived pretty much in a vacuum, although I did have the benefit of discussing the matter with many who had personally known both the creator of psychoanalysis as well as Anna. If, as I think may have been partly the case, Freud was trying to protect Anna, aware of the damage that any other analyst could do to her, I am not proposing this hypothesis in order to gloss over the negative sides to what he did. Freud's kindliness could sometimes lead him to extend the scope of analysis too broadly; it should be our job, I think, to understand the mixture of motives that went into Freud's actions, even if in the end we assess the analysis to have been one that had consequences that we might not want to see repeated.

I had been gently warned by at least one famous analyst in New York City that I ought not to publish such news of Freud's analysis of Anna, since it was bound to be "miss-used." Although fortunately I did not understand the full force of the fury that would be aroused by my making public a secret that was broadly shared among the oldest analysts, it was never my intention to stack the deck one way or another. Freud was, I believed, a great enough figure in the history of ideas to be able to take the full scrutiny of historical research. Another Viennese analyst told me that Anna, when directly asked whether her father had indeed analyzed her, lied about it in the 1920s. There were many ways of Anna's then rationalizing an evasion of the truth – either that it had not been a genuine analysis, or else that it was nobody else's business. Still a third source told me that when she had, within the confines of old friends, been straightforwardly asked about who her own analyst had been, her response had been silence.

It is hard to know what sorts of meanings to attribute to such reticence, and I want to refrain from undue psychologizing. But it does seem to me, as someone who has had to withstand considerable attack for bringing up a variety of what once seemed unwelcome news, that secrecy can be a powerful political weapon. For example, with certain of the early analysts, when I raised the issue of Anna's own analysis by her father, it was as if I had never said anything at all.

The truth of what had happened was a bit of commonly shared knowledge, even if almost all chose not to want to elaborate on the subject. As an outsider, with a special interest in the history of ideas, I was immediately struck with how various figures in the history of analysis had been unfairly stigmatized as "deviants" if not heretics for daring to propose various technical alternatives to Freud's own written recommended rules of therapeutically proceeding.

I want to suggest now that it seems to me that the impropriety of such an analysis, given the standards of orthodox analysis of a generation ago, meant that all those who shared in such secret information were thereby members of a tightly knit band of true believers who felt themselves able to bear such knowledge, even if the outside world was deemed too weak equally to absorb the burden of insight. I cannot offer any first-hand knowledge of what it may have seemed like to those in the 1920s who learned of the analysis then, although many I met were neither shocked nor upset about what had happened. (I have never been entirely sure, when Ernest Jones brazenly wrote Freud that Anna had been inadequately analyzed, whether Jones knew for certain whom her analyst had been, or whether he was also testing dangerous waters.) At least by the 1960s, when I was most actively pursuing the field work for my research, it was such an impolitic matter to be investigating that I am tempted to think of there then existing some sort of group complicity to blot out an unwelcome aspect of the past.

It would not be surprising if the inevitable negative transferences these pioneers had toward Freud were rarely explored or interpreted. To the extent to which critical feelings were kept under wraps, then it was all the more likely to anticipate the worst possible consequences flowing from historical honesty. In the imaginations of the oldest analysts Freud's stature had still to be achieved; while for those of us who took Freud's standing within intellectual history for granted, it seemed unnecessarily insecure for his followers to be worried about being sure that Freud's contribution was safely established.

To the extent that the inner circle shared in such knowledge, although the outside world remained in the dark, then such hidden complicity was a powerful weapon in explaining how they were all so intimately tied with one another. Of course what I have already referred to as trade unionism, or a desire to protect safe therapeutic turf, ought not to be under-estimated. Analysis in the 1960s was successful in worldly terms beyond the wildest expectations of Freud's early followers, even if by now the tide has turned, at least in America, in a different direction. It would not have been unusual, though, for Freud's own disciples to have thought he had erred, even if some of them went on to analyze their own children. (An explosive chapter to the history of analysis would be an examination of the tale of the relation between the early analysts and their own children.) If it were ever thought that Freud had been capable of being mistaken in having himself treated Anna, then such a belief would have inspired guilt and a desire to cover up the truth.

Defensiveness, however, can only lead historiographically to bad consequences. The best way, I believe, to honor Freud's memory is by accepting him as the daring innovator he was; of course he was capable of making mistakes, even if that has to include his analyzing Anna. (He did succeed in creating a leader who watched over the movement he had founded.) Freud was always his own person, although succeeding generations of analysts have not taken seriously enough Freud's admission that his own way of working as a therapist was simply the procedure that suited him personally best.

Fraudulence arises when analysts are unwilling to accept Freud's limitations as well as their own. Consciously or not, too much idolization has been found necessary. Freud does not need to have been perfect for him to be worthy of immense admiration. Nor need everything he said, wrote or did become sacred writ. It does appear established that he was the greatest writer among twentieth century psychologists, and a great deal of his influence has flowed from his literary prowess. (But a lot of his power also came from the impact of unanalyzed transferences, such as must have been the case with his daughter Anna.) It should not be necessary to lose hold of the possibility of identifying with Freud as a genuine original. The historical cover-ups, including the prettifications of what Freud was like, made it necessary later to unveil the sides of Freud that an earlier generation of analysts might have thought it wise to disguise. I believe he will endure as a thinker and writer long after any particular recommendations that he might have had in mind have evaporated.

Freud was an immensely hard-working clinician, and he sought to generalize from what he encountered. With the advantages of hindsight it is possible to see all sorts of ways in which Freud might have been misguided. Perhaps the analysis of Anna was one of his larger errors, and many will argue that he should have been more cautious in how he tried to implement his insights.

It should almost go without saying that this analysis was something that Anna herself must have wanted very much. I do not think that this was a procedure that was somehow imposed on Freud's youngest child. We do not know at whose initiative the analysis started, but my best hunch would be that it was a collaborative enterprise. For both Anna as well as Freud analysis was the central ethical standard, and in that case whom should she have been expected to turn to for instruction except her father. But to the extent that the future of Freud's "cause" was central to them both, that movement's fortunes could be threatened by the revelation of her analysis.

Even if one bends over backwards in order to appreciate how this tangled situation between Freud and Anna could have come about, there still seems something appalling about what took place. Freud had made privacy and autonomy absolutely central analytic goals, and yet with Anna he was willy-nilly compromising everything he held morally dear. He was, whether he knew it or not, intensifying her attachment to him at the same time that he said he wanted to wean her a bit from her dependence on him. Later he would be proud of her original work as a child analyst, at the same time that he worried about how she would do after his death.

For myself it is gratifying to have had a panel presentation about Anna's analysis at a 1995 New York University conference, and I hope that the different interpretive points of view will continue to be explored as time passes. Occasions have come up, especially over the last Freud-bashing decade, when I have felt a bit like the legendary sorcerer's apprentice who helped unleash forces that he did not anticipate. It should be obvious that it cannot have been my intention to spend so much time on a figure that I did not regard as heroic in terms of intellectual history.

The pendulum has swung against Freud lately, and oddly enough he might be gratified by some of the grounds for analysis getting discarded. All along he had anticipated that it would be possible in the future to found psychology on a modern biochemical basis, and the striking developments that have taken place over the last years have largely been in the area of psychopharmacology. Science inevitably means that one era's point of view will be replaced by a superior subsequent orientation. The biochemistry of dreams has made so many advances that even if Freud's particular theories cannot be confirmed, I think his emphasis on the significance of dreaming has been established as legitimate. Great playwriters, novelists, and poets have long understood this, although there are some scientists now who do insist that we have succumbed to a set of illusions about dreams.

The problem continues to be the extent to which, as I said at the outset, polarities in this area have been allowed to get out of hand. And so there is a danger that the baby will go out along with the bathwater, and all the important humanistic and interpersonal aspects to analytic therapy will be replaced by a strictly organic outlook. Despite the success of the Freudian revolution in the history of ideas that has marked this past century, in some sense we are now more or less back to where Freud was at the outset of his career. A clinical interest in classification exists almost for its own sake, as well as a reluctance to spend an adequate amount of time in getting to know patients. One longs for some common sense middle ground, so that therapeutic ambitiousness does not dominate the latest innovations. Powerful medication can alas be recommended on the basis of premature diagnoses. (Jung once interestingly maintained that a diagnosis could only be made after the conclusion of treatment.) I have already alluded to how small children have had powerful drugs administered to them, before we can understand their long-term effects on developing psyches.

My job is however not that of a therapist or a scientist, but I am working here as a historical witness. I consciously intended that others more knowledgeable than myself would pursue the implications of the therapeutic interaction between Freud and Anna. It has taken a remarkably long time to get this discussion underway, and it may in the end not add to the luster of the myth about Freud that orthodox analysts have liked to entertain. Thirty years ago it was not even a real temptation for me to think of concealing the truth about this analysis of Anna by her father. I do not think I calculated the full consequences of revealing what I did; although I had been warned of the dangers of doctrinal excommunication, and seen how earlier people in the history of analysis had been abused for their daring to be true to themselves, somehow I thought I could get around the worst consequences of being straight-forward.

Analysis, Freud once said, requires three things – courage, courage, and courage. (He was adapting one of Napoleon's sayings about the role of money in war.) I wish it were not so that honesty and attempted integrity stir up so much discontent. The benefits of conventional success often come to those who are more bent on promoting conformist values. But one of the reasons that the history of analysis has attracted so many controversies is that as a field it has drawn to itself those who are dissatisfied with knowledge as it has been bureaucratically defined.

It is still true today, for example in my own field of political science and in particular political philosophy, that Freud has so far failed to become a secure part of the established canon. The concept of the unconscious, no matter how it be construed, is no more widely accepted by political scientists now that it was seventy years ago when Harold Lasswell first wrote his *Psychopathology and Politics*.[11] So the old French political adage still holds: the more things change, the more they stay the same. That maxim applies to much else in intellectual life. For anyone publicly to talk about Freud's analysis of Anna should not, I hope, bring down the anathemas hurled by those who think of themselves as defenders of the faith. There has been enough in the way of ideological warfare in the history of analytic doctrine.

Analysis, despite what Freud sometimes liked to argue, does entail certain moral values and ethical beliefs. Think of what it has been like to try and practice analysis under dictatorial political and social conditions. It is only possible to exclude the philosophic dimensions to analysis by virtue of cutting off the basic lifelines of all genuine clinical endeavors; and analysis is doing better elsewhere in the world wherever philosophy is studied alongside Freud's teachings. How we assess Freud's treatment of Anna is going to depend on our prior moral convictions. Even if we should conclude that analyzing Anna himself was wrong, and at odds with some of Freud's most central principles, historically and ethically it is impossible to pretend that this whole episode never existed.

Aspects to Freud still can take one's breath away. I recall how that was the immediate non-verbal response I got from one of Anna Freud's own patients when I first informally let the news out about who her own analyst had been. Freud felt proud about his ability to think and utter certain shocking thoughts, which takes us back to his identification with Nietzsche that I mentioned at an earlier point. There is no way of successfully shrinking Freud down to fit the practical needs of what we might prefer now the creator of psychoanalysis to have been like. He was a struggling innovator who defied pre-existing categories, and it is only if we appreciate him in the round that we can begin to come to terms with some of the central aspects of the tradition he left us.

Perhaps it is possible to look on Freud's analysis of Anna from a strictly political point of view, in terms of the wielding of power. How different was this one analysis from how other analysts have been trained? Here I am broadening the implications of Freud's treating Anna to question the possibilities of authoritarianism implicit in training analyses in general, a subject I will address further in Chapter 4. Sectarianism has meant that too little debate about the institution of training analysis has been allowed to take place in public. Privately many analysts have reported being unable to tell anything like what they felt as the truth while in training, and that in hindsight it would have enriched their analyses to have been emancipated from the constraints of their formal education. The suppressions of feelings that take place in such a setting are of course all the more powerful for being unconscious at the time.

Although orthodox analysts have rarely understood the point, both Edward Glover in England and Jacques Lacan in France have long ago protested against the effects of training analyses. Outsiders warned all along that training analysis might be an act of spiritual violence. My belief has been that Jung, when he first proposed before World War I that all analysts in the future be analyzed, was implicitly saying that Freud necessarily had not been able to overcome his personal neurosis. Much later Ferenczi was saying something similar in his *Clinical Diary*. When in 1918 it was initially proposed as a rule that analysts undergo analyses, and both Rank and Tausk opposed it, I doubt that they would have done so without the secure inkling that Freud himself was no enthusiast for the idea. In fact it only went into effect after Freud had become ill with cancer of the jaw in the 1920s, after which he could no longer hope to take such personal charge of the future of analysis. (Even analysts today with the greatest private reservations about continuing the institution of training analyses have little knowledge of this whole history.)

It has to remain an open question whether Freud ever thought that Anna could take over as head of the psychoanalytic movement as we know she later did, or whether his analysis of her was part of any such planning on their side. And it is unclear to what extent one can suppose that she was trying to protect her father's creation by undergoing the analysis in the first place. Now I have broadened the issue of Freud's analysis beyond anything I have put in print before, and I hope it will be apparent how tentative and uncertain I remain. It can only serve the "cause" Freud first started if we continue to ask all possible questions, considering nothing as too great a taboo to challenge.

NOTES

1 Roazen, *The Historiography of Psychoanalysis, op. cit.*, pp. 333-37.
2 *Ibid.*, Part VI, pp. 246-47.
3 Roazen, *Political Theory and the Psychology of the Unconscious, op. cit.*, Part I, Ch. 2.
4 Paul Roazen, *Brother Animal: The Story of Freud and Tausk, op. cit.*, 1969; p. 100.
5 *Ibid.*, pp. xiv-xvi.
6 Roazen, *Encountering Freud, op. cit.*, p. 105.
7 Elisabeth Young-Bruehl, *Anna Freud: A Biography* (New York, Summit Books, 1988), p. 433.
8 Roazen, *Freud and His Followers, op. cit.*, pp. 436-40.
9 Roazen, *Meeting Freud's Family, op. cit.*, Ch. 7.
10 Patrick Mahony, "Freud As A Family Therapist," in *Freud and the History of Psychoanalysis*, ed. Toby Gelfand and John Kerr (New York, The Analytic Press, 1992), Ch. 12.
11 Roazen, *Encountering Freud, op. cit.*, pp. 241-44.

4

THE PROBLEM OF SILENCE: TRAINING ANALYSES

One of the special sources of appeal of the history of psychoanalysis for intellectual historians has been the prevalence of an unusual amount of silence. For example, when I started out in the mid-1960s interviewing early analysts who had known Freud personally, I was told by Dr. Rene Spitz how extraordinary it was that Carl Jung had once in talking to Spitz claimed credit for having invented the idea that all analysts undergo themselves personal analyses as part of their training. At the time I was mainly concerned with trying to establish, for the sake of political scientists, the relevance of Freud for political theory. I was surprised in those days to come across a passage in one of Freud's own papers where he explicitly credited Jung (under the rubric of "the Zurich school of analysis") with the exact contribution that Spitz considered so dubious. In 1912 Freud reminded his readers that he had already written about the utility of analyzing one's own dreams as part of becoming an analyst:

> I count it as one of the many merits of the Zurich school of analysis that they have laid increased emphasis on this requirement, and have embodied it in the demand that everyone who wishes to carry out analyses on other people should first himself undergo an analysis with someone with expert knowledge. Anyone who takes up the work seriously should choose this course, which offers more than one advantage; the sacrifice involved in laying oneself open to another person without being driven to it by illness is amply rewarded. Not only is one's aim of learning to know what is hidden in one's own mind far more rapidly attained and with less

expense of affect, but impressions and convictions will be gained in relation to oneself which will be sought in vain from studying books and attending lectures. And lastly, we must not under-estimate the advantage to be derived from the lasting mental contact that is as a rule established between the student and his guide.[1]

Although this essay by Freud has been carefully studied by generations of analysts now, the significance of Freud's reference to "the Zurich school of analysis" continues to be allowed to go unnoticed. I would argue as a matter of fact that many valid points which Jung had to contribute on the subject of analytic technique also today go unmentioned in the literature. (For example, Jung wrote powerfully about the importance of the model of the analyst, and how an emphasis on technique can itself be deadly for therapy.) But it should be enough to underline now how striking it is that today's readers continue to slip by Freud's meaning in connection with "the Zurich school," and also fail to acknowledge the significance of that point in connection with the whole subsequent history of training analyses.

Dates are important here – by 1913 Freud and Jung had had their epochal falling out. Historians should at least wonder whether Jung's suggestion that all future analysts be themselves analyzed did not already imply some possible reproach toward Freud, the unanalyzed leader of his movement. (Jung subsequently maintained that on their 1909 trip to America Freud had refused to provide the associations to a dream, and that that refusal had helped undermine Freud's standing for Jung. Freud also shared his dreams with someone like Otto Rank.) Nonetheless, by the end of his life Freud's might well have questioned the benefits of what he had once called "the lasting mental contact that is as a rule established between the student and his guide."

The next date that counts in this tale is that of the year 1918; for it was then that it was first proposed at a meeting of Freud's International Psychoanalytic Association that training analyses become a requirement for future analysts. As Herman Nunberg remembered it: "At the Congress in Budapest in 1918, I moved that the future psychoanalyst be required to undergo an analysis himself. The motion was rejected because Rank and Tausk energetically opposed it. It was only in 1926 at the Congress in Bad Homburg that this rule was adopted."[2] (In reality the 9th Congress of the IPA in Bad Homburg was held in 1925.) We still know nothing about what objections Otto Rank and Victor Tausk had to Nunberg's 1918 proposal, but I feel certain that when they made them "energetically" they were not countering anything that Freud himself then cherished. But Nunberg was also as of 1918 not putting forward an idea at odds with Freud's own inner preferences, although I suspect that both Rank and Tausk remembered Jung's own advocacy of the idea, and Freud's reluctance to embody it as a rule. The centrally important point about all these dates is that the institution of training analyses only got securely established after Freud had himself fallen ill of cancer of the jaw in 1923. Whatever for example might have been going on at the Berlin Psychoanalytic Institute in the early 1920s, Freud could still imagine that he could keep personal control over who did or did not become an analyst. Only after his illness – which at first was thought might be immediately fatal – did Freud acknowledge the inevitability of a more highly bureaucratic system of training. (Jung would behave similarly in connection with finally institutionalizing his "analytic psychology" only following his World War II heart problems.)

In keeping with my own background as a political theorist, I would like to insist on the central relevance of the asking of questions. It is not a matter of committing oneself to what Freud called "wild analysis" to subject to scrutiny the requirement of training analyses. As a matter of fact, there has been a bit more leeway about the use of the couch by analysts. When I once interviewed Jung's son Franz and saw Jung's Küsnacht consulting room, one question that immediately came to mind was where there had been space for an old-fashioned analytic couch. From those I have asked it seems that Jung, who first started practicing there in 1909, never had had a couch; and there is no sign of Freud's having objected. I would guess that once again it was only the Berlin reliance on the couch which got established in the 1920s that paved the way for Freud's later objecting, for example, to A. A. Brill's sometimes seeing patients sitting-up.

As a field psychoanalysis has allowed itself to become enmeshed in what amounts to pseudo-history. Organizational trade unionist politics too often substitute for genuine scholarship. Papers regularly begin with dates of earlier works, but central features to the real past of the field go unnoticed. Each of Freud's technical essays, such as the one in which he credits "the Zurich school," were written in dialectic relation to other writers. And before World War I Freud was centrally concerned with separating off his field from the practices of those like Alfred Adler or Wilhelm Stekel, whom Freud stigmatized as defectors. Everything Freud ever wrote needs to be placed in historical context, which is rarely ever done within the professional literature. In later years Freud would, usually in an unspoken way, be arguing with people like Rank, Wilhelm Reich, or Sandor Ferenczi. But the silences he could allow himself mainly for tactical reasons, since he did not want to publicize his opponents any more than necessary, have been credulously echoed by later generations as well.

Just as it has become legitimate to question the use of the couch, or at least to understand the pros and cons of that reliance on a specific bit of furniture, so I cannot see why there has not been more sustained understanding, not just of the history of training analysis, but of the advantages and limitations of the practice. For example, we ought to know much more about under what historical circumstances different analytic groups have sought to put restrictions on "the lasting mental contact that is as a rule established between the student and his guide". The literature is remarkably limited on this subject. And even if training analysis once was a thoroughly good idea, what has been the case over the past decades, and is it still so today?

I can again cite two leaders in psychoanalysis who strenuously opposed the use of training analyses, Edward Glover in Britain during the early 1940s and Jacques Lacan later in France. Glover had become convinced, in the course of the struggle over the introduction of Melanie Klein's innovative ideas, that training analyses had become politicized within the British Psychoanalytic Society. And Lacan in France became centrally concerned with the issue of "transmission," and what entitles someone to become an analyst. While in America it would be a taboo to question publicly the institution of training analysis, I do not believe that would be the case in France.

Within university academic life we have become ensnared in what William James once decried as the Ph.D. "octopus," but the potential for the abuse of power within psychoanalysis makes me think that far too little attention has been paid to training analyses. The issue of infantilism among candidates has repeatedly been raised, and some brave souls have been willing to talk about authoritarianism in training. As Freud himself acknowledged, in a warning that has too rarely been repeated, "when a man in endowed with power it is hard for him not to misuse it."[3] The roots of childishness are though powerfully unconscious, which points I think straight at the reliance on training analyses.

The device of supervised analyses was invented in the 1920s, I think, primarily as a check on the force of training analyses, yet within almost no time such supervisions were leading to authoritarian problems of their own. Freud's original reluctance to write on the subject of technique was due I think to a Catch-22 situation; the more one lays down how to proceed, the likelier that such suggestions will get mechanistically codified by naïve beginners too eager for a rule-book. And so Freud tried to restrict himself largely to negative recommendations, examples of where he himself had earlier been tempted to go wrong. His technical papers, though, have rarely been read in the cautious spirit they deserve.

No decent practicing cultural historian believes in progress, or in the idea that teleology is at work insuring that human beings move in a better and better direction. One would think that it would be obvious by now that with every new step there are bound to be losses as well as gains. Yet psychoanalysis continues to talk naively about Freud's "discoveries," as if what were at issue were "facts" rather than new ways of looking at things. And analysts continue to use the image of the "mainstream," as if that metaphor did not communicate disquieting authoritarian implications all its own. For if one is not in the so-called mainstream, then is one in the backwaters of a swamp? Intellectual historians commonly consider marginality a source of creativity.

It has to be puzzling to me that such points so rarely seem to be made. Bibliographies that substantially repeat each other do little to counter the silences that I have been complaining about. Reviewers have been known to avoid touching certain books that raise too many so-called controversial points. And in my own case I can report that only a quarter of a century ago *The Journal of the American Psychoanalytic Association* refused to accept an advertisement for one of my books placed by a thoroughly respectable publisher. So censorship, and inquisition-like heresy hunting, has taken place within our own lifetimes. Erich Fromm was once feared as a malcontent, but once he was securely dead in 1980 his works were allowed to be advertised even in orthodox psychoanalytic publications.

It seems to me that this curious way psychoanalysis has had of dealing with so-called dissidence has been intimately associated with what the late Charles Rycroft called "On Ablation of the Parental Images, or The Illusion of Having Created Oneself," just discussed in Chapter 3. It can be frightening to run the risk of becoming a psychoanalytic orphan, and/or expelled from the future bibliographical references. Such has been the fate of all too many figures from the psychoanalytic past, which is again why intellectual historians can have such a field-day with this subject, as they try to resurrect forgotten thinkers. But I do not believe that this is an antiquarian matter, for not only are genuine analytic lineages fouled up, but it is always too easy to overlook the degree to which just below the surface we find ferocious intolerances still fully capable of becoming operative.

The problem of ethics itself, and not just the issue of training analyses, is one that has traditionally been difficult to establish securely as a legitimate subject within psychoanalysis. Yet Freud, who has been under recent unfair scientific attack in the United States, and also Britain, has been flourishing in countries like France where psychoanalysis has been kept closely allied to philosophy. Freud's effort to demarcate psychoanalytic psychology from ethical thought was taken literalistically in America, instead of absorbing the full implications of all Freud's writings, which certainly included an explicit moral component. The future of psychoanalysis may depend on the extent to which the political, social, and strictly philosophic sides of psychoanalysis continue to be explored. Such an enterprise should make it less likely that clinical practices become rigidified.

It is a psychoanalytic truism that the outsider gains certain key advantages, which has permitted me to believe that someone with a background like mine has a valuable starting point. One of the attractions to this field which has continued to hold my interest has been the conflict between rival conceptions of the good life that get exemplified within the psychoanalytic literature. At the same time that otherwise sophisticated people simplistically accuse Freud of telling "lies," as if he were not capable of self-deception or lacked the capacities to be a great rhetorician, psychoanalysis has run into heavy weather precisely where philosophy and literature have been kept at bay. Diderot once wrote an article "Eclecticism" which has something enduring to teach us.

> The eclectic is a philosopher who, trampling under foot prejudice, tradition, venerability, universal assent, authority – in a word, everything that overawes the crowd – dares to think for himself, to attend to the clearest general principles, to examine them, to discuss them, to admit nothing save on the testimony of his own reason and experience; and from all the philosophies he has analyzed without favor and without partiality, to make one for himself, individual and personal, belonging to him.[4]

Instead of the artificial suppression of dissent, what we need is the examination of all historical quarrels, so that our ethical choices can be made as meaningful as possible.

Training analyses are part of a larger problem of silence. We need I think to ask, for example, under what circumstances do training analysts find their candidates boring. And altogether more attention should be directed to questions of money, power, and prestige. If training analysts find their time consumed in bureaucratic requirements, hopefully they are going to have less incentive to hang on to the advantages of their status. I have always tried to proceed in Freud's own spirit, when first alerted by a medical colleague to the significance of sexuality: "'Well, but if he knows that, why does he never say so?'"[5]

Occasionally there have been critiques of psychoanalytic training, such as those by Siegfried Bernfeld or recently Otto Kernberg.[6] But I have to be struck by the prevalent inattention to the core issue of the original idea that all analysts be themselves analyzed. It should not be considered irresponsible to point out the unexplored historical origins of this idea, or to remind us of the advantages and limitations inherent in the proposal. There are ethical dilemmas inherent in many aspects of any professional training. In 1999 Rene Major issued "A Call for the States General of Psychoanalysis," in which he relevantly pointed out how

> psychoanalytic institutions themselves, created to preserve the Freudian inheritance and to promote psychoanalytic research, have inevitably at times developed rigidities which stand in the way of the aims they pursue. An analytic establishment is necessarily called upon to be conservative since its tasks are to protect basic principles and to establish standards of excellence for teaching and practice, while analytic procedure is called upon to be innovative, and even subversive, always working in inquiry for new and original understandings and insights.

The issue of training analyses seems to me the tip of a large over-all historical subject, which as I say has kept me fascinated as a matter of scholarship for four decades now. Once it was a question of keeping quiet the fact that Freud had analyzed his own daughter Anna. In the future, I hope that Freud's neglected interests in phylogenetics, as well as telepathy, will receive the full attention that they deserve; it is no tribute to his memory to narrow him down to what might be plausibly acceptable today. The whole question of money in the history of psychoanalysis also needs to be adequately explored. I anticipate that the uncensored publication of Freud's various correspondences, which will go on after anyone alive today is still around, will continue to be challenging and instructive. It can never be bad for business to use all the resources of scholarly life to expand our understanding of the history of psychoanalysis. The field is, I think, inherently strong enough to withstand the kind of examination that important subjects all deserve. Silence itself belongs at graveyards, not to the life of the mind.

NOTES

1 "Recommendations to Physicians Practising Psychoanalysis," *Standard Edition*, Vol. 12, pp. 116-17.
2 Herman Nunberg, Introduction, Vol. I, *Minutes of the Vienna Psychoanalytic Society*, ed. Herman Nunberg & Ernst Federn, translated by M. Nunberg (New York, International Universities Press, 1962), p. xxii.
3 "Analysis Terminable and Interminable", *Standard Edition*, Vol. 23, p. 249.
4 A. W. Wilson, *Diderot: The Testing Years, 1713-1759* (New York, Oxford University Press, 1957), p. 237.
5 "On the History of the Psychoanalytic Movement," *Standard Edition*, Vol.14, p. 14.
6 Siegfried Bernfeld, "On Psychoanalytic Training", *Psychoanalytic Quarterly*, Vol. 31 (1962), pp. 453-82; Otto Kernberg, "A Concerned Critique of Psychoanalytic Education", *International Journal of Psychoanalysis*, Vol. 81 (2000), pp. 97-120. See also the story of the A.P.F. in Jean Laplanche, "Une revolution sans cesse occultee", *Revue Internationale d'Histoire de la Psychanalyse*, Vol. 2 (1989), pp. 393-402.

5
THE EISSLER PROBLEM

Writers are not usually known for being able to sustain self-criticism about their prior works, and I am afraid that a normal amount of the vanity to be expected in an author may becloud my judgment. Even in the face of the multiple criticisms that have been directed at *Brother Animal: The Story of Freud and Tausk*,[1] especially by Kurt R. Eissler, I remain convinced that the encounter between Freud and Tausk was a story that needed to be told. At the time I was working on *Brother Animal* in the late 1960s the tale seemed to tell itself. Even now I have the feeling that my own role was that of a distant communicator of a historical discovery that it had been my good fortune to stumble upon. Tausk's fate, almost from the earliest inklings I had of the outlines of his life history, seemed to me a moving human tragedy, and I was aware that by the close of the book, in the "Afterward," I had left the stage of the drama littered with human bodies. (At least two scripts of plays, one off-Broadway, have been performed about *Brother Animal*.)

The only happy ending one could take away from the book is the exhilaration that comes from finding out something new. It is over thirty years since the book first appeared, and the name of Victor Tausk, even in well-educated circles, is still hardly a household word. Within the profession of psychoanalysis *Brother Animal* has not, I think, got the respectful attention that it deserves. Yet among a select group of people it has brought me rewards unlike that of any other book I have written. D. M. Thomas, for example, published a four-page poem titled "Fathers, Sons and Lovers" that is derived from a sensitive reading of *Brother Animal*[2]; in his *White Hotel* Thomas imaginatively reworked the theme, first broached in *Brother*

Animal, of an affair between a Freud son and a Freud patient. And David Salle did a large painting, "Brother Animal", that hangs in the Museum of Contemporary Art in Los Angeles.

Although the research for *Brother Animal* took place in the mid-1960s, the book itself appeared only in 1969. It is important to try to understand what conditions were like then in the field of the history of psychoanalysis because it would be misleading for others to take for granted an earlier generation's struggles. Despite all the public recognition Freud had achieved, things were still on such an amateur basis that even Freud's apartment and office in Vienna had not yet been made into a museum. More important, a number of the key participants in the story of Freud and Tausk were still alive, and able to be witnesses to what had happened; I thought it vital to publish while they were still able to contradict or confirm what I said. I regret that I missed out on knowing at the time that a number of Tausk's many former lady friends were still living. Two of them contacted me after the book came out,[3] but when one of the others died in 1972, her executrix took the initiative in destroying Tausk's love letters to her.

If I inevitably failed to achieve the ideal of historical omniscience, *Brother Animal* still contains a number of breakthroughs. It remains the first and still most central account of Tausk's life and struggles. But I had hoped that *Brother Animal* might also help change people's minds about early psychoanalysis; it was my perhaps mistaken aspiration that the book would be read as an attempt to put Tausk into the history books rather than as an effort to detract from Freud's reputation. *Brother Animal* appeared before the 1974 publication of the Freud-Jung correspondence, and hence many people in 1969 did not yet appreciate some of the tougher aspects of Freud's character. Freud was, like Karl Marx before him, a battling innovator who led a movement that exerted an extraordinary impact on how we think about ourselves; and the warrior side of the founder of psychoanalysis has to be appreciated if we are to make any sense at all of his career.

At the time *Brother Animal* first appeared, it packed a wallop that may not as easily be understood now. Hugh Trevor-Roper articulated a relevant ideal of the best kinds of research: "The water must be fresh, cold and stimulating; it must flow from outside sources, and its impact must be perceptible, causing sudden shock, gradual adjustment, and the pleasant gurgle of controversy."[4] In 1968 I had mentioned in my *Freud: Political and Social Thought* two instances of the censorship of Freud letters that had appeared in print; I was even bold enough to put in the index, under the heading "censorship, by Freud family" the two points in my text where I had touched on the matter of the hanky-panky with Freud's correspondence.[5] No one had ever raised this sensitive issue in public until I did. But the sentence in Freud's letter to Lou Andreas-Salomé after Tausk's suicide, which had been cut out of Freud's correspondence until I raised the point in *Brother Animal* and then got restored, was far more disturbing. With the appearance of *Brother Animal* people knew about the censorship in a decisive way that they had not before.

As we saw in Chapter 3, *Brother Animal* was the first time anyone had put in writing the fact that Freud had himself psychoanalyzed his youngest child, Anna. The footnote in which I indicated my sources for this matter was contrived with deliberation; I left out more than one of my informants on the grounds that they were not in a position to be able to withstand the criticism they might face for having helped me understand this crucial point. The contemporary reader should try to realize that in 1969 Anna Freud was not only still alive and well but capable of wielding her considerable power vengefully. (In 1970 a book appeared containing a letter of Freud's, which I had heard about at length, concerning his analysis of Anna.[6]) Reconsidering *Brother Animal*, I am struck by how much of what I reconstructed then has gone uncontested.

Anna Freud did try to deny that she had ever been analyzed by Lou Andreas-Salomé, although several people I interviewed were adamant that it was true. She could "get out of it," I was told by one insider, by arguing that it had not been a proper analysis; but then the one she had had with her father had also violated the known rules for any technical analytic procedure. It turns out that after a 1921 visit that Lou paid to Freud's household, he wrote to one of his sons and a daughter-in-law: "She was a charming guest and she is altogether an outstanding woman. Anna worked with her analytically; they visited many interesting people together, and Anna very much enjoyed her company."[7] Freud's comment that Anna had "worked with" Lou analytically seems to me to cast doubt on Anna's own later denial, and we know that Freud discussed with Lou some of Anna's emotional problems. As I already mentioned, even after all these years it is still only starting to be possible to get a dialogue going on the significance of Freud's having analyzed Anna. In 1969 I knew that I was violating a taboo by opening up this issue, but I never realized, even in 1975 when I discussed it at greater length in my *Freud and His Followers*,[8] that the silence over what Freud had done would persist. No psychoanalytic journal, as far as I know, has ever allowed the subject to get interpreted or explored further. Anna Freud's official biographer in 1988 handled the matter with diplomacy.[9]

To continue listing some of the glass *Brother Animal* shattered, it is also true that the book was the first occasion when anybody had mentioned in print the fact that Carl G. Jung had had a long-standing extra-marital affair with a woman who became a loyal student of his, Antonia Wolff. When a comprehensive biography of Jung finally appeared in 1976, which cited in its preface this key information gleaned from *Brother Animal*, I wrote the author to inquire whether my book had made it easier or harder to get further biographical information from the Jung family.[10] I was delighted to discover that the biographer had found the Jungs more, rather than less, forthcoming thanks to what I had earlier written.

Among orthodox Freudians, however, I found deep resentment for my having betrayed "the cause" through publishing *Brother Animal*; my *Freud: Political and Social Thought* had earlier been warmly received by them. For a remarkable number of people, the only legitimate way to write about Freud is by composing propaganda that not only idealizes the first psychoanalyst but simultaneously serves to promote the business of contemporary analysis. The historical Freud must be, from their point of view, presented in such a way that in our time he buttresses the self-image of today's practicing analysts. But this means we are deprived of Freud as a model of originality and daring who should, I think, be used to challenge rather than support our preconceptions. (One point in *Brother Animal* was particularly difficult for pious believers in the myth about Freud's technical orthodoxy as an analyst; whatever his own recommended rules that appear in his writings, in the late 1920s when he had five regular analytic patients three of them were close relatives of one another.)

Over the past thirty years a good deal of new information about Tausk has come to light. It is now known, for example, that the expression "Brother Animal" appears not only in Lou Andreas-Salomé's diary, quoted as the epigraph to my book, but also in a letter she wrote to Tausk. He commented, "I thank you for the Brother-Animal, dear Brother-Animal." She had meant to describe him as a fellow human being, in contrast to the egotist whose mind is only on himself. (Even the title of my book was attacked by Kurt R. Eissler as "offensively coarse, if not down-right vulgar."[11])

To move from the meanings associated to the title to another central thesis of the book, it turns out that Ludwig Jekels, a Polish analyst in Vienna, had supported Tausk's efforts to get analyzed personally by Freud. According to Jekels: "Freud thought very highly of Tausk's analytic talents yet refused firmly to analyze him although Tausk had asked him repeatedly to do it; I, too, asked Freud to do that, but he replied: 'He is going to kill me.'"[12] And as a partial confirmation of these extraordinary feelings on Freud's part, within a few weeks after Tausk's suicide in 1919 Anna Freud, already thoroughly identified with her father, dreamt that Tausk's fiancée had rented an apartment across the street from the Freud family in Vienna for the sake of killing Freud with a pistol shot.[13] Such fears bear on Freud's development of theories of a death drive and suicide that I outlined in *Brother Animal*.

Although it took me exactly two decades to find it out, it seems that Anna Freud herself was the chief opponent I had over *Brother Animal*. This was not easy, at least for me, to see, and when I was attacked in a long 1971 book by Eissler, he made no specific mention of her help to him, although he did thank her intimate friend Dorothy Burlingham for having read his manuscript.[14] When I finally and with great effort succeeded in getting a journal brave enough to publish my brief reply to Eissler's lengthy assault, he privately protested to an ally, who contacted the editor, and then

Eissler wrote an article against me. I in turn answered his peculiar charges, this time having less trouble finding a forum. Eissler then launched still a further piece assailing me, and once again I did not leave his attack unanswered.[15] I should point out that in those days it looked to me like a match between David and Goliath because Eissler was not only a well-known psychoanalytic author but a watchdog in behalf of orthodoxy who denounced anyone who threatened to shake a narrow establishment view of Freud. He was in a position to exert substantial power as the founding head of the Freud Archives in New York City, the chief donor of the material that now resides in the Sigmund Freud Collection at the Library of Congress in Washington, D. C. Although Eissler had easy access to documents that he had decided to close to others, and sometimes used sealed items himself or allowed others special privileges, he did not initially pursue the vexing question of what Freud might have written after Tausk's death to correspondents besides Lou Andreas-Salomé. (Although Freud was harsher to Lou than to Karl Abraham, Freud told Abraham too that he thought Tausk was "of no use to us."[16])

In 1983, however, Eissler published still one further book on what Lou had long ago called the "Tausk problem." Here again he claimed to be exercised over the supposed contention on my part that Freud was somehow Tausk's murderer; at the same time Eissler continued to ignore almost all the general conclusions I hypothesized in the chapter "Free Associations." Eissler built his new book around the letter written to Anna Freud by a physician who said she had special knowledge about Tausk's having impregnated his fiancée, which Eissler woodenly seized upon as a special "proximate cause" of the suicide. At the same time Eissler blithely paid no attention to the oddity of Tausk's double suicide, by a shooting and a hanging, which I tried to trace to the two sides of his conflicts with both love and work.

Yet what Eissler never told any reader, in all his numerous assaults on me, was that Anna Freud had originally in 1969 sent him a seven-page typed letter with her own detailed objections to *Brother Animal*. The document is of interest mainly to me, rather than to general readers, because I am acutely aware of what she failed to challenge in my book, as well as the specific biases and weaknesses of her own lengthy catalogue. Oddly enough, most of her specific points did not match those that Eissler eventually put into print. Unlike Eissler, she was ready to concede that Freud's having sent Tausk to Helene Deutsch for an analysis in 1919, while Deutsch was herself in treatment with Freud, was clinically "unwise." (Although I had feared that Deutsch might "hit the roof" over what I wrote about her own involvement in Tausk's failed analysis, she never seemed to be defensive about, or even to absorb, my interpretive indictment.) But importantly, not once in Anna Freud's letter did she lend support to Eissler's own later peculiar claim to believe that I had alleged that my story was "not of a suicide, not even of a manslaughter, but of a murder in which Freud is unmasked as the culprit."[17] Marius Tausk, the surviving son, wrote such a restrained and intelligent response to Eissler's weird constructions that at the time no further rebuttal by me seemed necessary.[18]

We now know that Freud could write acknowledging how jealous he could be of one of his male pupils for having an affair with the Princess George, Marie Bonaparte, a leading disciple in Freud's last years. So it was not, I think, so speculative of me to have suggested that Freud might have envied Tausk's opportunity to have an affair himself with Lou Andreas-Salomé, who earlier had been closely involved with both Nietzsche and Rilke.

I think there are now two stories about Freud and Tausk – the first refers to the events that took place historically between the two men, and the second has to do with the cover-up to counteract *Brother Animal* that Eissler, with Anna Freud's full backing, undertook in the early 1970s. Had Eissler not performed his polemical tasks, others would doubtless have undertaken the battle instead. Psychoanalysis has continued to attract zealots who take upon themselves the task of being defenders of the faith. Independent historians, however, will not be impressed by partisanship that seeks to uphold certain idealized views of Freud that may suit short-run organizational needs.

In writing *Brother Animal* I had assumed that a mystery would always remain about the explanation for Tausk's suicide. One of the most intriguing aspects of Tausk's suicide note to Freud is that he did not tell him why he was killing himself. Although it took Eissler years to get around to asking Anna Freud for the evidence, we now find out that Freud had written to Sandor Ferenczi that the origin of the suicide was "obscure"; Freud then alleged impotency in Tausk but also conceded, "despite acknowledgement of his endowment, no adequate empathy in me."[19] This coldness admitted by Freud is consistent with the narrative I had originally put together, which relied heavily on several eyewitness accounts of what had happened in 1919. Freud confessed to Lou that he did "not really miss" Tausk. Freud, like Nietzsche, went further beyond good and evil than some of today's devotees might like to think; Peter Gay, for example, likes to argue of Freud that despite a story like *Brother Animal*, he "did not invite the world to discard the responsible conscience, let alone good manners."[20] But Freud's speaking ill of the newly dead was part of his defiance of traditional Western morality.

I had been trying to put the story of Freud and Tausk in the context of intellectual history; one of my chapter headings was "More than a Chinese Puzzle," quoting Kafka, and I still want to be cautious when imputing motives to the personalities involved in Tausk's being, as I put it early on *Brother Animal*, "overwhelmed by his contact with Freud." I had thought it obvious that Tausk "had tremendous yearnings for dependency, if not victimization." One of the strangest aspects of the whole post-*Brother Animal* tale is the contention of Eissler that my account of the struggle between Freud and Tausk was an invention; he subtitled his first book against me "The Fictitious Case of Tausk Contra Freud." Additional evidence has appeared to support and expand understanding the full difficulties between Freud and Tausk, and the degree of rancor that built up.[21] And it should almost go without saying that other analysts have not necessarily agreed at all with Eissler's polemics,[22] so that by now he is increasingly regarded as having been something of a crackpot. It is therefore all the more interesting to discover, with Anna Freud's lengthy 1969 letter, that Eissler was then just the tip of the establishment iceberg. A French analyst, François Roustang, has on the other hand written a subtle and interesting chapter about the nature of the tensions between Freud and Tausk.[23]

If I were able magically to rewrite *Brother Animal*, there are many details that I would change, although I think the story may appear almost as shocking to some now as it did in 1969. Over the years I have repeated key aspects of the narrative, first at the insistence of the publishers of my *Freud and His Followers*, and later as a chapter in my biography of Helene Deutsch, when thanks to new material, I could see the tale in a fresh light. Each time I have written about Tausk and Freud I have worked in new aspects of my understanding of what had gone on. On the one hand it is necessary not to overdo Tausk's psychopathology, nor how "callous"[24] Freud could be, for the situation was such, as I originally put it in *Brother Animal*, that the "cruelty was so built into the situation that none of the participants had to realize what had happened."

But what I come away with now is renewed hope that I may have succeeded in my objective of helping to bring Tausk back to life. My own central interest lies in the history of ideas, and from the point of view of the intellectual historian it remains fascinating how a figure like Tausk could have for fifty years been so left out of the history books. But an interesting story is now also at hand, as I try to find out, based on new historical evidence that has just become available, the exact steps surrounding the origins of the polemical controversy associated with the initial publication of *Brother Animal*. I have often wondered whether people have been so exercised by the story of Freud and Tausk because if Tausk had been psychotic, he should have received different treatment, and if Tausk had been neurotic, he should not have ended up a suicide.

No matter how much the story of Freud and Tausk may clash with the need some people have to mythicize Freud, glamorizing the romance of early psychoanalysis, I trust that in the long run Lou Andreas-Salomé's own judgment will be sustained: she held that during the time of her 1912-13 stay in Vienna, Tausk was "the most prominently outstanding"[25] of Freud's immediate circle. And despite the polemics launched by Eissler on behalf of Anna Freud, I hope Freud's own considered judgment will triumph in the future. As Freud put it so memorably in his 1919 obituary of Tausk, the longest one Freud ever wrote:

All those who knew him well value his straight-forward character, his honesty towards himself and towards others, and the superiority of a nature which was distinguished by a striving for nobility and perfection. . . . No one. . .could escape the impression that here was a man of importance. . . . He is sure of an honorable memory in the history of psychoanalysis and its earliest struggles.[26]

Even Eissler suggests that Freud "considered Tausk to have been a great man."[27] The fact that Freud's private judgment, as expressed in his relief to correspondents that Tausk was gone, could be so at odds with his obituary of Tausk leaves us with a troubling enigma (which would also be true of the contrast between Freud's letter-writing as opposed to his public obituary in the case of Ferenczi). Even as a young man Freud thought of the possibility that his letters might be saved[28], so it remains a mystery what he thought he was doing when he gave such different versions of the fate of one of his most devotedly loyal students, who in the end could not survive in Freud's world. It may be hard to over-emphasize the hypocrisies (and tact) of Old World manners, which stand in such sharp contrast to the North America allegiance to the value of sincerity; authenticity, though, can be readily manipulated for fresh hypocritical purposes.

Dr. Kurt R. Eissler was the founding Secretary of the Sigmund Freud Archives, Inc., which deposited a large collection at the Library of Congress. The original 1951 agreement was one which the Library of Congress should not, I think, have undertaken; for they did not anticipate that despite the restrictions on access to others, Dr. Eissler made copies of material, felt free to send these around (for instance to Ernest Jones), and cited what he chose in behalf of his efforts to idealize Freud.

In 1971 Eissler initiated his first assault on my *Brother Animal*, and in so doing cited details from an unpublished letter Freud wrote in 1934. Eissler then put it the following footnote: "The letter is contained in the collection of the Sigmund Freud Archives. It is the Archives's policy not to make its collection accessible, for the time being, to the public. The Board of Directors has given me special permission to deviate in this instance from this policy."[29] Later, after my article of rebuttal to *Talent and Genius*, "Reflections on Ethos and Authenticity in Psychoanalysis,"[30] challenged Eissler's use of archival material, he wrote in connection with his reliance on that 1934 unpublished letter:

In my quotation from this document, which is contained in the collection of the Sigmund Freud Archives, the same facts that are known from other sources are presented. The Board of the Archives thought, I think rightly, that under these circumstances the exception is not a breach of the general rule that governs the administration of the Archives. This is the only instance where I have made use of a document from the Archives's collection.[31]

Eissler did not state why, if "the same facts" were indeed available elsewhere, he chose to rely on the Sigmund Freud Archives. It is not true that that was the "only instance" where he made use of a document from the collection. He has acknowledged in print the use of interview material, supposedly at the request of donors. But according to the Library of Congress, the Sigmund Freud Archives, Inc. is the donor of interviews conducted by Eissler. The Library of Congress justifiably kept referring to the Sigmund Freud Archives, Inc. as Eissler's organization. Independent scholars were trapped in a frustrating situation as far as the most important material in the Sigmund Freud Collection at the Library of Congress. "As matters now stand," Eissler wrote in 1974, "the bulk of the documents will be open to scholars after the year 2000."[32]

This background may help prepare the reader to appreciate a discussion of the issues Eissler proceeded to make so much of, but which appear to me small potatoes. As time passes it is inevitable that one re-thinks earlier books. For instance, now that I have two sons, I am more acutely aware of how selfish a suicide can be; and I also think that Tausk's feelings about Henrik Ibsen may have reflected uncertainties about whether his creativity should have been directed to art rather than science. But I do not believe in re-writing old books, and instead have published fresh ones; but Eissler kept on berating me for *Brother Animal*.

In my defense I will restrict myself to answering the specific points Eissler raised this time around. I will not discuss the multiple errors Eissler committed in the course of his many differing attacks on my book. The bare bones of the Freud-Tausk story, as Eissler presented them now, are not too far afield. His account omits, however, the circumstances under which Helene Deutsch terminated Tausk's treatment (Freud's injunction that she had to choose between continuing with Freud or Tausk), as well as Freud's reaction, both public and private, to Tausk's death. The chronology at the back of my book is less confusing that Eissler's sloppy set of dates.

I will confine my discussion to the seven illustrations of the "basic errors of fact" Eissler alleged my book contains. The feebleness of his argument is, I believe, betrayed by the clumsy stylist device of numbering his points, which are otherwise unconnected. But since I want to show that they are wrong, I too will use numbers for the sake of making it easier for neutral observers to weigh my evidence against Eissler's.

First, it was peculiar of Eissler to spend so much time over a Nov. 12, 1912 letter of Freud to Lou Andreas-Salomé, written early in her stay in Vienna, which Eissler said was "the only support for the claim that Freud was in love with Lou Andreas-Salomé and jealous of Tausk. . . ." On March 2, 1913 Freud wrote a similar letter, with affectionate passages, in which he also regretted her absence at one of his lectures: "I was deprived of my fixation point and spoke falteringly."[33] Anyone carefully reading Lou's diary would know of both passages. Why all the fuss about the Nov. 12,

1912 date? Perhaps Eissler could have benefited from re-reading his own writings; for he once knew about the later letter of Freud's.[34] Eissler sometimes argued that those who disagreed with him suffered from imprecise recollections due to the passage of time. Whether Lou was or was not with Tausk on either occasion might have been a question, conscious or unconscious, in Freud's mind. It is not possible to prove where Tausk was the night of Freud's lecture in early March.

It is possible to establish, however, that when Eissler corrected me in saying it was 1:30 in the morning, not 2:30, when Freud walked Lou home, Eissler was mistaken. Evidently he forgot that Lou mentions both times on different evenings.[35] What can account for such slovenliness? Eissler mentions the question as a "triviality" which nonetheless he felt compelled to correct. But since he once argued that my own supposed "errors...are always tendentious,"[36] I feel like the kettle who has been called a name by a pot.

Eissler's apparent precision could mislead the unwary. For example, he says that only on two occasions did Freud refuse to see someone with whom he was angry. Eissler may or may not be right. But he omits to mention occasions when former colleagues of Freud's tried to re-establish ties with him and were rebuffed. This is a more significant point that the source of the flowers Lou received from Freud. Did he perhaps order them specially to give them to her? Does it really matter? Freud's death anxieties, which interfered with his relation to Tausk and other disciples, do make a difference in how one understands the creator of psychoanalysis.

Eissler objected to the words "devilish arrangement" that I used to describe Freud's sending Tausk to be analyzed by Helene Deutsch while she was undergoing analysis with Freud. Eissler says that I have built my "theory of the 'devilish arrangement' exclusively on insinuations." The precise words "devilish arrangement" were, though, Helene Deutsch's; she used them when recounting to me the difficult position she found herself in.

Eissler had already bitterly attacked Dr. Charles Rycroft. Eissler was wrong in his ironic reference to my own "original" idea that Freud was jealous of Tausk over Lou. I am grateful to Dr. Rycroft for raising the question, for I then repeated it to Dr. Deutsch in the course of my research. She believed that once the question was asked it was impossible to dismiss it. And although she had not thought of it while Tausk was in analysis with her, she concluded that jealousy must have played a part in the difficulties between Freud and Tausk. It should obviously be possible for jealousy to exist before, as well as after, an affair exists. And Freud could have been jealous of Tausk without being in love with Lou himself.

Secondly, Eissler had been upset because I have mentioned Freud's sensitivity about his height, especially in relation to Jung. He claimed that the photograph of Freud standing on a box in the midst of his followers at the Weimar Congress in 1911 fails to support my point. I can only suggest that others look at the photograph, noting Jung's crouching posture. Eissler was wrong when he asserted that no "other evidence" assists my contention. When I interviewed Theodor Reik, among other questions I asked was one about the nature of Freud's neurosis.[37] He replied by discussing Freud's height in relation to Jung. Later Reik also commented on the matter in a book of reminiscences: when asked about Jung, Reik mentioned that he was "blond and tall"; in being questioned about Freud's liking for Jung, Reik replied: "I think he was attracted to him originally, because Freud was small, you know, and Jewish-looking, don't forget."[38]

Eissler assumes it is somehow miraculous that Jung failed to mention the episode at Weimar. Professor Henry A. Murray, a well-known student of Jung's, first told me the story about the photograph. The existence of other photographs of Freud standing next to Jung underscores, for me, the Weimar one. But there is at least one photograph at Worcester where Freud, Jung, and Hall are seated – not standing – in the front row, and once again it is hard to assess their respective heights.

Thirdly, Freud had a problem with doubles. I do not pretend to have gotten to the bottom of it, but I believe his difficulty had both libidinal and ego components. Those who are experienced at untangling double complexes can, I hope, help to appreciate the rich complexities to Freud's character. But they have to anticipate that to Eissler they would have appeared to be maligning Freud. Partly due to his problem with doubles, Freud found he could not tolerate Tausk. Eissler had earlier maintained that "originality was never an irritant for Freud."[39] In *Brother Animal* I had discussed a few of Freud's concerns with priorities. The chapter called "Plagiarism," like the rest of the book, is largely a narrative of events. But since Eissler's latest criticism of my book relied on Lou's diaries, let me quote some passages he did not mention. She had noted Freud's "conflict with independent, or temperamental, characters," and also that

> Freud acts with complete conviction when he proceeds so sharply against Tausk. But along with the "psychoanalytic" fact (that is, bearing in mind Tausk's original neurotic disposition), it is also clear that any independence around Freud, especially when it is marked by aggression and display of temperament, worries him and wounds him...forcing him to premature discussion....[40]

Elsewhere Eissler chastised me for what I take to be clarity of expression. As far as I can unpack his sentences the material he offers under #3 undermines his own position. It was legitimate for Freud to fear that Tausk might steal one of his own ideas and develop it prematurely. Tausk shared many of Freud's traits, and it also was appropriate for him to fear Freud's genius for using the world around him for his work. Part of Helene Deutsch's fascination with Tausk came from the similarities she perceived between Freud and Tausk; she thought there was truth on both sides.

Fourthly, Eissler somehow believed that I had argued that Tausk's paper on artistic inhibitions was not founded on Freud's earlier thoughts. How can it be made plainer than this — Freud was the first psychoanalyst, and Tausk was a disciple of Freud's. To repeat: one of Eissler's central objections to my book was that my account of a struggle between Freud and Tausk was fictitious. Yet let us read Lou's report of Freud's reaction to Tausk's paper on artistic inhibitions: "Freud's rejoinders were more severe than usual and yet no other person presents his papers to him with such evident reverence. I think that Tausk is of all the most unconditionally devoted to Freud and at the same time the most prominently outstanding."[41] Could it not be that the rivalry between the two men can partly be explained by Freud's genuine (as well as neurotic) concern over priorities? Tausk had an uncanny need to work on issues that were preoccupying Freud, and Lou perceived the potential destructive element in this for Tausk. The problem of art was not one Freud thought settled, and therefore he preferred to work on it alone; illustrations for future editions of *The Interpretation of Dreams* would be another matter. Paul Federn's letter, written after Tausk's suicide, documents the extent of the final split between Tausk and Freud.[42]

Fifthly, Dr. Edoardo Weiss was in a tough spot with Eissler. He knew that Eissler was a denouncer of "deviants" in psychoanalysis. Is Weiss's failure to "recall" in a letter to Eissler (now locked up at the Library of Congress) really identical with a "denial", as Eissler's reasoning would have it? Despite the appearance of erudition in his books Eissler was not a good scholar. Eissler has called me "a negligent author"; if he could have turned from my *Brother Animal* to my *Freud and His Followers* (a book Eissler never discussed) he would have found the following sentence: "Other pupils of Freud's last years, such as Edoardo Weiss, felt that Freud had lifted concepts from them without acknowledgement."[43] A note at the back of the book indicates a passage in one of Weiss's books which begins to answer Eissler's reproach that I supposedly invented an imaginary complaint of Weiss's. So much for Eissler's latest certainty that if I had know what I was talking about I "would have made more of it than to banish it into a mere footnote" in *Brother Animal*.

I interviewed Weiss at some length, and read the transcript of the interviews (which Eissler tried to lock up until the year 2057) Weiss had given to Eissler. This is not the time or place to publish an account of my interviews with Weiss. I did follow up on all Eissler's questions, and had a number of my own as well. But Eissler could hardly expect scholars, or even early analysts, to share their knowledge with him freely, given his history of polemicizing. The man who presided over the Freud Archives was hardly in an ideal position to criticize others for failing to make "an honest contribution to the history of psychoanalysis."

Oddly enough Eissler accused one of Freud's patients, Albert Hirst, of a "paramnesia" (false memory). A copy of Eissler's transcript of his interviews with Hirst was in the Jones Archives in London. (I also interviewed Hirst in New York City.) What is especially interesting in the interviews Eissler conducted is the contrast that emerges between Hirst's view of Freud as a therapist and Eissler's. Hirst stoutly maintained that had Freud operated on Eissler's principles, the therapy would not have been a success.[44]

I also had notes from Hirst's letter to Anna Freud (it did not go to Jones, as Eissler recalled it). If Eissler had reread Hirst's letter to Anna Freud he would have found himself guilty of what he accused Hirst of, false recollection. For by no means was Hirst writing because Jones had "lessened Freud's contribution," as Eissler maintained, but rather to make clear that Freud as late as 1909-10 had laid some claim of priority to the discovery of the uses of cocaine. Eissler also invented uncertainties in Hirst that cannot be borne out by the documents. When Eissler stressed Hirst's age of sixty-six, and what "most people" think about age and forgetfulness, was Eissler suggesting a principle that would lead one to conclude that because I was younger than Eissler my memory was necessarily superior? Perhaps it was Eissler's idealization of Freud that led him to overlook genuine evidence, and also to see detractors of Freud behind every tree and beneath every bed.

Sixthly, Fritz Wittels's first book about Freud presents him as a live human being, an interesting person fully capable of having created psychoanalysis. Eissler pointed out that Wittels later "recanted" that first biography of Freud. It is impossible, I think, to be a member of a religious sect and also succeed in approaching the ideal of historical objectivity.[45]

Seventhly, both Paul Federn and Weiss believed, despite what Eissler argued was the case, that Tausk advocated changes in analytic technique to cope with psychoses. As we know, Tausk was a psychiatrist and Freud was not. Earlier Eissler accused me of "not knowing that Freud was no psychiatrist and never did consider himself to be a psychiarist."[46]

Eissler's lengthy quotation from Freud on the practicality of studying psychoses psychoanalytically can establish little by itself. As I read the passage Eissler selected, placing it in the context of Freud's stage of life when he wrote it, he was proceeding more as a scientist than a healer. Partly out of disappointment at earlier therapeutic failures Freud could sometimes expect too much of psychoanalysis as a science. The key sentence, at least as I saw it at the time, is Freud's saying: "There are nevertheless a number of methods of approach to be found." Freud appeared, to me, to be contrasting analytic technique to alternative methods, and the former seemed to me to be in Freud's view less than ideal for studying psychosis. Eissler himself had a strict view of what was and what was not properly psychoanalysis,[47] and so did Freud in old age.

But Eissler offered evidence that weakened what he was purporting to support. For he once quoted a letter of Freud's which confirms what many feel about his attitude toward psychosis. Freud wrote of insanity: "I do not like these patients. . . . I am annoyed with them. . . . I feel them to be so far distant from me and from everything human. A curious sort of intolerance, which surely makes me unfit to be a psychiatrist."[48]

The journal *Contemporary Psychoanalysis* properly allowed Eissler to reply (1977) immediately to my article there defending myself against his 1974 article in the *International Review of Psycho-analysis* criticizing my 1972 defense of myself in *The Human Context*.[49] Instead of replying, Eissler made the wistful suggestion that my earlier remarks about him constituted "slander," which can best be assessed in the light of his own scarcely temperate attacks on me. At that time he stuck by his earlier statement that he would not further continue the debate he had started. Later, however, Eissler sent a letter to the editor of *Contemporary Psychoanalysis* asking me to agree for a committee to be set up to find out if Eissler's own "reasoning capacity" had led him "astray."[50] Eissler's need for reassurance on that score still sounds to me like an unintentional joke. If he could isolate passages from *Brother Animal* as he did in that letter he could be confident that "the reasoning capacity nature gave" him was being misdirected.

Here is the letter of mine that I asked to be published in the *International Review of Psycho-analysis* in 1976.

> Dear Sir,
> My reply to Dr. Eissler's "On Mis-statements of Would-Be Freud Biographers with Special reference to the Tausk Controversy," *International Review of Psycho-analysis*, Vol. 1, Part 4 (1974), which belatedly came to my attention in Canada, will appear as an article, "Orthodoxy on Tausk" in *Contemporary Psychoanalysis*, Vol. 13, No. 1, January 1977.
>
> In his inaugural editorial Dr. Sandler stated that the *International Review of Psycho-analysis* should be "a sister Journal to the *International Journal* which, when it was first published in 1920, had as one of its functions 'the defence of the pure science of psycho-analysis against various forms of direct or indirect opposition.' Psychoanalysis does not now need defending in the same way as then, nor does its 'purity' have to be guarded so vigorously."
>
> Dr. Sandler's principle seems to me a sound one. It is therefore to be regretted that although the editor of *Contemporary Psychoanalysis* offered Dr. Eissler the space for a rejoinder, the *International Review of Psycho-analysis* did not display the same commitment to the free and open expression of ideas by extending to me the identical courtesy.

The *International Review of Psycho-analysis* refused to print my letter. The level of competence or partisanship can be inferred from the subsequent publication in that journal of an article which was unaware of my "Orthodoxy on Freud: The Case of Tausk."[51]

Writing in *Contemporary Psychoanalysis* (1978) once again Eissler was more cautious than elsewhere. But why was he still so exercised by the story of Freud and Tausk? Was it, as I have already proposed, because if Tausk had been psychotic, he should have been approached differently; and if Tausk had been neurotic, he should not have ended up a suicide? I think Eissler needed to see Freud as perfect.

Eissler chose to make a battleground with printed words. He then claimed in his "A Challenge to Professor Roazen" in *Contemporary Psychoanalysis* that "in print one can escape issues." I think that that is so only if one has difficulties with reading and writing, as well as a faulty memory. The future of psychoanalytic psychology cannot be enhanced by the various crusades of Eissler. (Lest the reader think I have been overdoing Eissler's general importance, after his death in 1999 the *New Yorker's* Janet Malcolm published in the Sunday *New York Times Magazine* section a tribute to him, "Keeper of Freud's Secrets."[52])

Answering Eissler, as in my attempt to deal with his specific allegations in his 1978 *Contemporary Psychoanalysis* article against me, represented one way of handling him. And not answering him, for example when it came to his second book against me, seemed to me increasingly an attractive alternative. So that when Eissler's further full-length book criticizing how I had dealt with "the Tausk problem" came out in 1983, I did not reply publicly in any way to him. But I did write privately to Dr. Marius Tausk, who had been helping me write about his father for some years, but had all along advised me against tangling with Eissler in print.

May 17, 1983

Dear Dr. Tausk,
I have now finished reading *Victor Tausk's Suicide*. Before I send you my reactions, I want to congratulate you on your "Comments." They are restrained and dignified, yet cut through to the central weaknesses in Eissler's approach.

I don't know how relevant it is, but Dr. Deutsch once told me that Olga Knopf [whom Eissler cited about Victor Tausk's last days] had been involved in a fake kidnapping in New York, staged by Fritz Wittels, which was designed to establish her as a psychoanalyst. If I have a chance, I will look it up in back New York newspapers.

On the issue of sexuality not being able to provide full gratification, that might have well been a legitimate problem of priority between your father and Freud. At any rate, in *Civilization and Its Discontents*, written later, Freud developed the idea.

Although I started out by going through the book point by point, I want now to jump ahead to pages 140-41, and Freud's letter to Ferenczi; it seems to me you are quite balanced in what you say about it. Eissler's paragraph at the top of page 141 is a stunning bit of reasoning – based on absolutely nothing.

Eissler could find out what Freud wrote to Abraham on your father's death; he has that material under his control in the Library of Congress. It might be worth your asking him for it, since it has taken him so long to come up with this passage to Ferenczi.

Does it seem strange that Freud writes your father "shot" himself, when the facts were more appalling? Later on he wrote Lou with a phrase that indicated your father had made a thorough end of things, without specifying the means. But Freud's interpretations are really a way of distancing himself from what happened. You are entirely correct to question the impotency; it was a hypothesis of Freud. Eissler's notion that (p. 139) your father "rushed home" afterwards is a familiar bit of mechanistic reasoning. Anyone experienced knows how to tolerate impotency, with its many causes; in this instance, your father's understanding was communicated in what he wrote early on July 3rd. In any event, the suggestion of impotency is demeaning, and notice that Eissler scarcely follows up the [phrases] "last act of his infantile fight with the father ghost." Nor does Eissler pursue what Freud meant by "no adequate empathy in me."

By the way, would you like Dr. Winnik's address in Israel? I cannot believe that that is all Lea Rosen thought of your father, otherwise why should she have saved all his love letters until her death.

Eissler, as you say, finds "brutal" "traumas" to women where they claim none. Quite the opposite, in their view.

(Incidentally, it is grimly amusing how I am described by Eissler as "Roazen," whereas you are "Prof. Dr. Tausk"; even Ernst Federn gets awarded a professorship, while as far as I know he is retired, and used to be a social worker.)

Did you show Eissler your father's letter to Lou about the Budapest Congress? The one in which he complains that Freud had left him out as a speaker on war neuroses. Or has Eissler just decided to omit that evidence, since it supports the notion of a conflict between them.

I hope you notice that now Eissler has tossed in the towel, and says Freud "arranged" for Tausk's treatment by Dr. Deutsch. Dr. Deutsch repeatedly mentioned your father's grieving over Freud's attitude toward him, but Eissler has ignored this point.

What on earth is the evidence for the allegation on page 69 that your father practiced "wild analysis"? He was a solidly respected analyst, which is one reason Dr. Deutsch looked up to him so.

On one point I can be critical of what you failed to bring out: the sentence from Freud's letter to Lou about your father's "uselessness" is translated differently by Eissler, and for once in this book he fails to give the reader the German. I suspect him of tendentiously twisting the words to cushion the impact of what Freud wrote.

I was amused by Eissler calling the obituary [by Freud] "meandering" (p. 158); as I indicated in my replies to Eissler before, that obituary stands in the way of Eissler's attempt to discredit your father.

Have you any idea why Hilde [Tausk's fiancée] was so "bitter" about her interview with Freud? I assume that it had to do with Freud's self-declared lack of empathy. (Helene traced that to guilt feelings in Freud.)

Medically I am ignorant about abortions in that time; why, if Hilde was pregnant, couldn't something more have been done about it? Why should she wait so long to go back? (Dr. Deutsch once had what she delicately called a "planned miscarriage," and there seemed no special hardship, especially away from Vienna.)

It goes without saying that the "secret" Dr. Deutsch and other early analysts knew about in connection with your father had to do with the struggle with Freud preceding the suicide, not the alleged pregnancy [which Olga Knopf proposed].

Somewhere or other Eissler states that Freud intervened in the Federn marriage because of your father's attraction to Federn's wife; that is completely unsubstantiated. Freud did intervene, and your father was supposedly attracted to her; but the two points are independent of each other.

I too was struck by the bit on page 114 about "morale" and "nagging." In general, I think your "Comments" highlighted what will be most striking to a general reader.

Now that I have published Jekels's comments about Freud's fears of being murdered, I wonder whether Eissler will cite Jekels approvingly again, as he does on p. 115. (Incidentally, I heard that Eissler was so upset about my letter in retort to him that he wrote lots of letters of his own to that journal, and then, fearing a law suit, flew to London to retrieve his letters. So his health cannot be so very bad.)

Eissler does not seem to realize that leaving Vienna would have been the best thing your father could have done under the circumstances. I was, by the way, tremendously moved by your translation of the Spinoza-Dialogue. Is my memory accurate, that it has so far appeared only in French? Would it be worthwhile trying to publish it in English?

I am struck how Eissler has it that Freud "preferred to pretend ignorance of the precipitating factors" of your father's suicide, while Eissler has no doubts of his own; I don't think Freud was pretending, he might have had guesses but he didn't allow himself to know more.

Ch. 7 is so loosely constructed that I wonder if many will plow through it; nonetheless, the comparison of your father and [Otto] Gross is an insulting one.

The suggested comparison between Adler and your father (p. 197) is laughable; Freud had the utmost contempt for Adler, and did not at all wish him well in anything.

You have every right to be pleased by your "Comments." There is certainly no need, even if I had felt so inclined, to write a reply to Eissler this time. If a choice place offered me a book review, I might take it on. But I am content.

I am enclosing a copy of a review of mine which recently appeared in the *TLS*.

As ever,

Paul

I hope you will treat this letter as written solely for yourself.

The historiography of psychoanalysis has been an odd tale. Although an abundant amount of material has been appearing at an accelerating rate in connection with the story of Freud and his school, certain taboos still remain in place. Just over one hundred years have passed since Freud published his most distinctive psychological contributions; still, some of the most elementary questions about his life and ideas, as well as the movement he founded, have only now begun to be asked. Freud's name has been so hallowed with religious reverence, and at the same time smeared with vilification, that it has been hard for independent observers to evaluate his proper standing in intellectual history.

Looking back on the earliest reception of Freud's work at the turn of the century, some of his critics were capable of being surprisingly perceptive and trenchant.[53] And that first biography ever written of Freud, by Fritz Wittels in 1924, is still well worth reading today.[54] On the whole, however, most of what has appeared in connection with Freud has been composed for partisan, if not public relations, purposes. I regret to say that almost all the psychoanalytic journals, however often Freud's name may have appeared in them, have done almost nothing to advance the cause of understanding the early days of psychoanalysis in a way which could approach what one would expect of a proper academic inquiry.

It is in this context that Helen Walker Puner's early book is so outstanding.[55] Its original appearance was one of the reasons that moved Freud's daughter Anna to proceed, against her father's wishes, in authorizing an official biography, which was carried out by Ernest Jones in the 1950s. I do not know how Puner, working in the relative vacuum of knowledge available as of the mid-1940s, could have come up with what she did; but Jones's references to her in volumes I and II of his biography constitute testimony of the need he felt to counter her influence.

Re-reading her book recently, I found that Puner's book still stands up and has much to teach, which helps to explain why it has been rarely out of print since its first appearance in 1947. To cite my own initial reaction to her work, her *Freud* was the first place in print that, in the 1960s, I had ever noticed a reference to his being capable of making the diagnostic mistake of calling a physical illness a psychogenic one; and she did so with sure-footedness, since she was able to quote Freud himself admitting having committed exactly such an error of thinking a problem was psychological when it turned out not to be so at all. Freud was a better critic of himself than many of those who afterwards chose to claim his mantle of authority could tolerate. Puner was exceptionally sensitive in connection with the important problem of Freud and religious belief. As she put it in writing about Freud's *Totem and Taboo*:

> This view of the religious impulse, which Freud was never to relinquish but only to augment and embroider, left no room for the inclusion of any of the positive elements which have entered into man's need for religion. Freud saw the religious impulse as a purely negative and fear-driven drive, based not on love but on guilt; not on faith but on the need to atone; not on communion with a loved figure but an anxious pacification of a hated figure.

Insights of hers still retain their acuteness; for example, she writes:

> Because Freud wanted to fight against the stern, commanding voice of his father within himself, just as he had wanted to fight the actual voice of his childhood, his conscience, stiffened by opposition, became an unyielding tribunal before which all the less stern, more pleasurable aspects of life were tried and found wanting.

Her Freud was a complex one: "He was a kind, a benevolent, a good man, but he was kind without softness, benevolent without compassion, and good without mercy."

The reader can expect to find extraordinary nuggets of insight from Puner. In order to establish the role of her book in the history of the literature about the creator of psychoanalysis, I would like to quote from a letter she sent me after Eissler invited her to dinner in New York City some thirty years after the publication of her *Freud*. Her independent insights help complement my own more distant relation to him. (Although we had exchanged a few letters, I only formally interviewed him once.) The expressiveness of Puner's writing gives an added dimension to her literary capacities, as well as helps to establish the enduring affront to received wisdom about Freud that her book constitutes.

My dinner at Eissler's was loathsome – nine courses all covered with cream sauce; clicking of the heels and kissing my hand as he greeted me at his door – looking, it seemed to me, like the rigid, jerky death figure in the Jooss ballet *The Green Table*.

With his last sip of coffee – desperately needed to counteract the *schlagober* [whipped cream] – he arose and said it was time for "the debate." I said what debate? But he ignored my remark, and led me to his study. I asked, entering, "Is this room bugged?" (In addition to the man's being a lunatic, he has no sense of humor.) He blanched a deeper putty color and mumbled, "Mmm, ha...I had thought to tape record this conversation but hmm...ah... decided not..."

He then proceeded to point out to me for about two hours the many "mistakes" I had made in my book. These boiled down to a wrong date and what were, in truth, differences of interpretation, let alone the vast difference of vision that exists when one person is a mensch and the other a whited simulacrum of same. (He is indeed, as I believe you said, an odious combination of obsequiousness and grandiosity.) He was particularly exercised over my treatment of Freud as a Jew, and went on for a long time about how happy or well-adjusted Freud was to be a Jew. He also said that geniuses were not human beings – that humans had evolved by adapting to the environment and geniuses stood out against the environment and therefore Freud wasn't human and I had made a big booboo in treating him as a human being. When I asked him if he found anything valid about my book, he started mumbling again. From what I could make out of the mumble, he was saying that he hears from "professors" here and there with some regularity who write him, "But Helen Puner says this," or "Helen Puner put it this way." I said, "You mean my book is still being taken seriously?" He mumbled sadly, "Very seriously indeed." When I told him I had heard that there was correspondence about my book in the archives, he said loudly, "No." I said my source was informed and reliable. He then said, "I don't know. I get this mate-

rial all the time and I send it down to the Library of Congress."
In other words, he doesn't read it – a liar, the man is also a liar ...

The sequel is that he hasn't stopped writing me since I left his house...Basically, he is bombarding me with obsessive material and I am responding with wit and humor – he doesn't know what to make of my answers...

In one of my replies to one of his letters, I thanked him for the rare experience he had afforded me of putting me down while kissing my hand. His reply to this was agitated.

I am citing this letter of Helen Puner's due to the inherent interest of her encounter with Eissler, who later became celebrated because of Janet Malcolm's portrayal of him in connection with Eissler's having hired, and then fired, Jeffrey M. Masson as Projects Director of the Freud Archives. This quotation also demonstrates Puner's artistic talents and spiritual quality. In writing to me she knew that as objects of Eissler's ire she and I were kindred spirits. In certain orthodox psychoanalytic quarters Eissler is still a "revered"[56] figure. Following Eissler death in 1999, a web-page was set up for him on the internet. (His strange books on Goethe sold surprisingly well in hard-cover in Germany.) Anna Freud and Eissler were the closest allies right up until her death in 1982. But in the history of those who have tried to approach Freud's life and mind with appreciative detachment, as opposed to worshipful religiosity, Puner's book deserves to be remembered and studied by a new generation of students, who are able to approach his life and struggles without the blinders and prejudices of an earlier time. One hopes that with Eissler's passing there will be an end to the special kind of religious warfare that he became so intimately associated with.

NOTES

1 Roazen, *Brother Animal: The Story of Freud and Tausk*, op. cit.
2 D. M. Thomas, *Selected Poems* (New York, Viking, 1983), pp. 14-17.
3 See *Encountering Freud*, op. cit., pp. 104-05.
4 Hugh Trevor-Roper, *The Times Literary Supplement*, November 20, 1981, p. 1348.
5 Roazen, *Freud: Political and Social Thought*, 3rd edition, op. cit.
6 Edoardo Weiss, *Sigmund Freud As A Consultant: Recollections of a Pioneer in Psychoanalysis* (N.Y., Intercontinental Medical Book Corp. 1970; 2nd edition, with a New Foreword by Emilio Weiss and a New Introduction by Paul Roazen, New Brunswick, N.J., Transaction Publishers, 1991), p. 81.
7 *Sigmund Freud and Lou Andreas-Salomé: Letters*, ed. Ernst Pfeiffer, translated by William and Elaine Robson-Scott (London, Hogarth, 1972), p. 231.

8 Roazen, *Freud and His Followers*, op. cit., pp. 438-40.
9 Young Bruehl, *Anna Freud*, op. cit.
10 Barbara Hannah, *Jung: His Life and Work: A Biographical Memoir* (New York, G. P. Putnam's Sons, 1976).
11 Kurt Eissler, *Talent and Genius: The Fictitious Case of Tausk Contra Freud* (New York, Quadrangle Books, 1971), p. 42.
12 Ludwig Jekels, "Early Psychoanalytic Meetings," p. 8. (Library of Congress, Bernfeld papers) I remain grateful to Peter Swales for first bringing this passage to my attention.
13 Peter Gay, *Freud: A Life For Our Time* (New York, Norton, 1988), p. 439.
14 Eissler, *Talent and Genius*, op. cit., p. 267.
15 Roazen, *Encountering Freud*, op. cit., Chapter 6.
16 *The Complete Correspondence of Sigmund Freud and Karl Abraham 1907-1925*, ed. Ernst Falzeder, translated by Caroline Schwarzacher (London, Karnac, 2002), p. 400.
17 K. R. Eissler, *Victor Tausk's Suicide* (New York, International Universities Press, 1983), p. 3.
18 Marius Tausk, "Comments," *Ibid.*, pp. 299-322.
19 *Ibid.*, p. 140; see also *The Correspondence of Sigmund Freud and Sandor Ferenczi, Vol. 2, 1914-1919*, ed. Ernst Falzeder and Eva Brabant, translated by Peter T. Hoffer (Cambridge, Harvard Univ. Press, 1996), p. 363.
20 Peter Gay, "Introduction," *Sigmund Freud and Art: His Personal Collection of Antiquities*, eds. Lynn Gamwell and Richard Wells (Binghampton, State University of New York, 1989), p. 17.
21 Roazen, *Helene Deutsch*, op. cit., Part II, Chapter 9.
22 B. M. Robertson, "Book Review of Eissler's *Victor Tausk's Suicide*," *International Journal of Psychoanalysis*, Vol. 16, Part 2 (1989), pp. 253-57.
23 François Roustang, *Dire Mastery: Discipleship from Freud to Lacan*, translated Ned Lukacher (Baltimore, Johns Hopkins University Press, 1982), Chapter 5.
24 Gay, *Freud*, op. cit., p. 391.
25 Lou Andreas-Salomé, *The Freud Journal*, translated by Stanley A. Leavy (New York, Basic Books, 1964), p. 57.
26 "Victor Tausk," *Standard Edition*, Vol. 17, p. 275.
27 Eissler, *Victor Tausk's Suicide*, op. cit., p. 169.
28 *Letters of Sigmund Freud, 1873-1939*, ed. Ernst L. Freud, translated by Tania and James Stern (London, Hogarth Press, 1961), p. 22.
29 Eissler, *Talent and Genius*, op. cit., p. 156.
30 Paul Roazen, "Reflections on Ethos and Authenticity in Psychoanalysis," *The Human Context*, Vol. 4: 3, pp. 577-87; see Roazen, *Encountering Freud*, op. cit., Ch. 6.
31 Eissler, "On Mis-statements of Would-be Freud Biographers with Special Reference to the Tausk Controversy," *International Review of Psycho-analysis*, Vol. 1, Part 4 (1974), p. 404. See, earlier, Eissler, *Talent and Genius*, op. cit., pp. 156-57.
32 Eissler, "On Mis-statement of Would-be Freud Biographers with Special Reference to the Tausk Controversy, op. cit., p. 403.
33 *Sigmund Freud and Lou Andreas-Salomé: Letters*, ed. Ernst Pfeiffer, translated William and Elaine Robson-Scott (London, The Hogarth Press, 1972), p. 13.
34 Eissler, *Talent and Genius*, op. cit., p. 31.
35 *The Freud Journal of Lou Andreas-Salomé*, op. cit., pp. 114, 97.
36 Eissler, *Talent and Genius*, op. cit., p. 206.
37 Interview with Theodor Reik, April 4, 1967.

38 Erika Freeman, *Insights: Conversations with Theodor Reik* (Englewood Cliffs, N.J., Prentice Hall, 1971), p. 116.
39 Eissler, *Talent and Genius*, op. cit., p. 34.
40 *The Freud Journal of Lou Andreas-Salomé*, op. cit., pp. 58, 97.
41 *Ibid.*, p. 57.
42 Roazen, *Brother Animal*, op. cit., pp. 153-54.
43 Roazen, *Freud and His Followers*, op. cit., p. 474.
44 Paul Roazen, *How Freud Worked*, op. cit., Ch. 1.
45 Eissler, *Talent and Genius*, op. cit., p. 210.
46 *Ibid.*, p. 201.
47 *Ibid.*
48 *Ibid.*, p. 319.
49 Paul Roazen, "Orthodoxy on Freud: The Case of Tausk," *Contemporary Psychoanalysis*, Vol. 13:1 (1977), pp. 102-15. See also Roazen, *Encountering Freud*, op. cit., Ch. 6.
50 Kurt R. Eissler, "Comment and Criticisms," *Contemporary Psychoanalysis*, Vol. 13:3 (1977), pp. 426-28.
51 Paul Neumarkt, "The Freud-Tausk Controversy: A Symphony of Disharmonies," *International Review of Psychoanalysis*, Vol. 4 (1977), pp. 363-73.
52 *The New York Times Magazine*, Jan. 2, 2000, p. 33.
53 Roazen, *The Historiography of Psychoanalysis*, op. cit., pp. 429-34.
54 Fritz Wittels, *Sigmund Freud: His Personality, His Teaching, & His School*, translated by Eden and Cedar Paul (New York, Dodd, Mead & Co., 1924, reprinted Freeport, New York, Books for Libraries Press, n.d.).
55 Helen Walker Puner, *Sigmund Freud: His Life and Mind* (New York, Howell, Soskin, 1947, reprinted, New Brunswick, New Jersey, Transaction Publishers, 1992).
56 See Chapter 8, p. 162.

6

CHARLES DICKENS'S *DAVID COPPERFIELD*

The history of psychoanalysis has given birth to a number of orphans. The striking tale of how Freud's movement spread, which by now seems a secure part of intellectual history, has nonetheless been marked by a series of notable lacunae. For example, although the literature about Carl Jung has been extensive, it is still only relatively recently that Jung studies have started to be pursued with historical professionalism. The bulk of my own writing career has in fact been devoted to trying to correct a bundle of unfortunate discontinuities that for one reason or another have marred the record of the past. And so I have tried also to restore the proper standing of such different figures, besides Jung, as Victor Tausk, Otto Rank, Ruth Mack Brunswick, Helene Deutsch, Edward Glover, Erik Erikson, and Sandor Ferenczi. The reputations of other people too have been unfairly abandoned within the record we know of as history, and I hope that by my not specifically mentioning their names now I am not unnecessarily adding to their neglect. As I have already alluded to, especially in Chapter 4, too many silences are still attached to the story of the revolution in ideas that Freud and his followers initiated.

As I look back over the last forty years, Ferenczi is the one most notable success story that it is possible to point to within the historiography of psychoanalysis. His reputation, when I first started out working in this field, was at a low point. Ernest Jones's biography of Freud had, at least within the general reading public, succeeded in branding Ferenczi as a madman whose ideas, theoretical as well as clinical, could be ignored as an outgrowth of mental illness. Although all along psychoanalytic insiders had privately brushed aside Jones's account of Ferenczi as slanderous, even a generation ago it seemed an uphill battle to try and get recognition for the fact that Ferenczi had been unfairly victimized.[1] The Hungarians within psychoanalysis may have had intense personal rivalries among themselves, but they were nonetheless united in their admiration for Ferenczi as their national pioneer. The power and range of Ferenczi's writings supported the resiliency of his name. And by now the old canards that Jones did so much to popularize have largely been overcome, and Ferenczi's genuine contributions have been more and more widely recognized.

It should not be a matter of much controversy that Freud, and the whole transformation of thought that his system of thought succeeded in bringing about, deserves special credit for alerting us to the special significance of childhood. Ferenczi's last period of work, such as his rich "Confusion of Tongues between Adults and the Child" paper, served to highlight an essential aspect of Freud's teachings: for there is an altogether surprising gulf between what adults see and experience as opposed to what children appear to feel.[2] The poet in Ferenczi enabled him to recapture for science something essential of the imaginative life of the child.

Perhaps only great artists can hope to overcome the inevitable gulf between adulthood and childhood. On more than one occasion Freud acknowledged the general superiority of art; in writing about Dostoevsky, for example, Freud maintained:

> Dostoevsky's place is not far behind Shakespeare. *The Brothers Karamazov* is the most magnificent novel ever written; the episode of the Grand Inquisitor, one of the peaks in the literature of the world, can hardly be valued too highly. Before the problem of the creative artist analysis must, alas, lay down its arms.[3]

An adequate account of all Freud's literary involvements remains to be written. He could, in a buoyant moment, claim that Melville's *Moby Dick* was his favorite American novel.[4] Although the name of Charles Dickens, who wrote so notably about childhood, does not come up in the Index to the *Standard Edition* of Freud's works, we know that Freud gave his copy of Dickens's *David Copperfield* to his Viennese follower Ernst Kris. In 1874 Freud forwarded a volume of the *Pickwick Papers* to his friend Silberstein; Jones reports that Freud sent his fiancée a copy of *David Copperfield*, which Jones said was "Freud's favorite Dickens". (He also commented to Martha about *Bleak House, Hard Times*, and *David Copperfield*, and his letters to her also indicate his reading of *Little Dorrit*.[5])

Two anecdotes in connection with psychoanalysis and the traumas of childhood come to mind, both of which I think illustrate the problem of how we tend as adults to live in a universe separate from childhood. One has to do with a story that Erik Erikson evidently regularly recounted to his Harvard undergraduates "about a little boy who asked his mother where people went when they died. 'Well,' she told him, 'your body goes into the ground and your soul goes up to heaven.' To this, the boy matter-of-factly replied: 'I'd just as soon keep all my stuff together.'"[6] Children do think in ways that defy an adult's sort of rationality.

But everything modern psychology has taught still has a long way to go before it seeps into everyday consciousness. In 1952, during an interview at the White House in which President Harry S. Truman was trying to persuade Adlai Stevenson to run for the presidency on the Democratic ticket, the then Governor of Illinois protested that he was, for the time being at least, not suitable for the job, since he had recently gone through a divorce that had been traumatic for him. Truman brushed aside Stevenson's doubts about his capacities and continued to hector his chosen successor in a manner that was in itself traumatic. After Stevenson, a shaken man, had left Truman's office, the president exhibited a kind of insensitivity characteristic of broker-politicians; he was reported to have turned to an aid and asked: "What the hell's a 'trauma' anyway?" It would be hard to overemphasize the gulf between the respective orientations of the political scientist, with a typical interest in power, influence, and status, and that of the depth psychologist possessing a humanistic concern with the inner dimension of political and social events.[7]

But the inevitable gap between the world of adulthood and that of the child is so great that it requires a continuous imaginative leap for grown-ups to try and keep in touch with what it going on in any child's way of thinking. For example, children's conceptions of time, space, and immortality are not necessarily what we might expect them to be. When it comes to a modern problem like divorce, or parental separation, our court systems have been eager to learn what psychologists have to teach; unfortunately the law has been too credulous, and for example one version of thinking associated with Anna Freud's name has maintained that joint custody has to be bad psychologically for the child, and this school of thinking has been in my view too readily accepted.[8] Continuity for the child is an important value, but so are the legitimate claims of both parents themselves.

Dickens has to be considered as outstanding among the writers who have gone to pains to present the child's outlook on reality. In his *Oliver Twist, Great Expectations, Little Dorrit, Nicholas Nickleby*, as well as *Dombey and Son*, Dickens made a sustained case in behalf of the easily overlooked perspective of the child. (The poetics associated with the death of the child Paul Dombey[9] is said to have driven Dickens's rival William Thackeray to competitive distraction: "Thackeray is supposed to have thrown that number upon [a] ...desk...and to have cried: 'There's no writing against such power as this...it is stupendous!'" In a note to himself about Paul Dombey's death Dickens had simply said: "His illness only expressed in the child's own feelings – Not otherwise described."[10])

But it is Dickens's *David Copperfield* that ranks as his acknowledged masterpiece about childhood. As he himself wrote in his 1869 Preface,

> Of all my books, I like this the best. It will be easily believed that I am a fond parent to every child of my fancy, and that no one can ever love that family as dearly as I love them. But, like many fond parents, I have in my heart of hearts a favorite child. And his name is DAVID COPPERFIELD.[11]

Chapter I, entitled "I Am Born," famously starts: "Whether I shall turn out to be the hero of my own life, or whether that station will be held by anybody else, these pages must show." Dickens begins with what David Copperfield has been told about the circumstances of his birth. He was, he tells us, "a posthumous child," meaning that his father had died before his birth; and Dickens moves on from that to David Copperfield's child-like reactions to his father's grave:

> My father's eyes had closed upon the light of this world six months, when mine opened on it. There is something strange to me, even now, in the reflection that he never saw me; and something stranger yet in the shadowy remembrance that I have of my first childish association with his white grave-stone in the church-yard, and of the indefinable compassion I used to feel for it lying out alone there in the dark night, when our little parlor was warm and bright with fire and candle, and the doors of our house were – almost cruelly, it seemed to me sometimes – bolted and locked against it.[12]

David's mother gets described by his aunt Betsy Trotwood as "a childish widow" destined to become "a childish mother if she lived." Dickens describes nature itself from the point of view of a child; as his mother and aunt talked, the wind went through the trees:

> As the elms bent to one another, like giants who were whispering secrets, and after a few seconds of such repose, fell into a violent flurry, tossing their wild arms about, as if their late confidences were really too wicked for their peace of mind, some weather-beaten ragged old rooks'-nests, burdening their higher branches, swung like wrecks upon a stormy sea.[13]

Dickens had succeeded in *David Copperfield* in having written a powerful fairy-tale-like saga, one that intensifies our sense of reality. David's mother had also been an "orphan"; when it turns out, to David's aunt Betsy's acute disappointment, that he was born a boy and not the girl she had wanted, Betsy "vanished" from the house "like a discontented fairy; or like one of those supernatural beings, whom it was popularly supposed

I was entitled to see; and never came back any more."[14] (David was born with a caul, as was Freud, which was supposed to be a sign of good luck.)

David Copperfield presents his earliest impressions, including his memories of his mother and nursemaid Peggotty, and comments about them:

> This may be fancy, though I think the memory of most of us can go further back into such times than many of us suppose; just as I believe the power of observation in numbers of very young children to be quite wonderful for its closeness and accuracy. Indeed, I think that most grown men who are remarkable in this respect, may with greater propriety be said not to have lost the faculty, than to have acquired it; the rather, as I generally observe such men to retain a certain freshness, and gentleness, and capacity of being pleased, which are also an inheritance they have preserved from their childhood.[15]

Freud was, in *The Future of An Illusion*, echoing a similar idea to Dickens's when Freud wrote: "Think of the depressing contrast between the radiant intelligence of a healthy child and the feeble intellectual powers of the average adult."[16] David Copperfield recalls from his childhood an empty pigeon-house, as well as

> a great dog-kennel in a corner, without any dog; and a quantity of fowls that look terribly tall to me, walking about, in a menacing and ferocious manner. There is one cock who gets upon a post to crow, and seems to take particular notice of me as I look at him through the kitchen-window, who makes me shiver, he is so fierce. Of the geese outside the side-gate who come waddling after me with their long necks stretched out when I go that way, I dream at night: as a men environed by wild beasts might dream of lions.

David can still recall distinct household smells. Since he has been told about his father's funeral, when his mother at night reads "how Lazarus was raised up from the dead...I am so frightened that they are afterwards obliged to take me out of bed, and shew me the quiet churchyard out of the bedroom window, with the dead all lying in their graves at rest, below the solemn moon." David's childhood self expresses its inventiveness at the Sunday service, and imagines of the local church pulpit what "a castle it would make".[17]

David had somehow intuitively asked his nursemaid, Peggotty, whether she was married, which directly leads in the novel to his introduction to Mr. Murdstone, a gentleman with "black whiskers". "I didn't like him or his deep voice, and I was jealous that his hand should touch my mother's in touching me – which it did. I put it away, as well as I could." To David, Murdstone had "ill-omened black eyes". Peggotty shared his gut distrust of Murdstone, which led to words between his mother and Peggotty.

> Gradually, I became used to seeing the gentleman with the black whiskers. I liked him no better than at first, and had the same uneasy jealousy of him; but if I had any reason for it beyond a child's instinctive dislike, and a general idea that Peggotty and I could make much of my mother without any help, it certainly was not the reason that I might have found if I had been older. No such thing came into my mind, or near it. I could observe, in little pieces, as it were; but as to making a net of a number of these pieces, and catching anybody in it, that was, as yet, beyond me.[18]

It is through a visit to Peggotty's brother at the seashore, again related through the poignant eyes of David as a child, that he comes to visit a second family that will link him tragically with Steerforth. When Peggotty's brother goes to wash his face, David recalls that it "had this in common with the lobsters, crabs, and crawfish, — that it went into the hot water very black, and came out very red." Peggotty has an orphaned nephew and niece, with whom David played. As David recalls of the niece, Little Em'ly:

> The days sported by us, as if Time had not grown up himself yet, but were a child too, and always at play. I told Em'ly I adored her, and that unless she confessed she adored me I should be reduced to the necessity of killing myself with a sword. She said she did, and I have no doubt she did. As to any sense of inequality, or youthfulness, or other difficulty in our way, little Em'ly and I had no such trouble, because we had no future. We made no more provision for growing older, than we did for growing younger.

It was after this visit, arranged to coincide with his mother's secret marriage to Murdstone, that Peggotty tells David that he now had "a Pa!" David reacts: "I trembled, and turned white. Something – I don't know what, or how – connected with the grave in the churchyard, and the raising of the dead, seemed to strike me like an unwholesome wind." Only then was it explained to David that it was a "new" father that he had.[19]

It is of the essence of Murdstone and his sister that "the gloomy theology of the Murdstones made all children out to be a swarm of little vipers . . . ." David fell into "disgrace" as he bit Murdstone's hand holding him for a beating. David was afflicted with "guilt" over his wickedness for having done such a thing, as he was "imprisoned" for five days as a punishment.

> The length of those five days I can convey no idea of to any one. They occupy the place of years in my remembrance. The way in which I listened to all the incidents of the house that made them-

selves audible to me; the ringing of bells, the opening and shutting of doors, the murmuring of voices, the footsteps on the stairs; to any laughing, whispering, or singing, outside, which seemed more dismal than anything else to me in my solitude and disgrace – the uncertain pace of the hours, especially at night, when I would wake thinking it was morning, and find that the family were not yet gone to bed, and that all the length of night had yet to come – the depressed dreams and nightmares I had – the return of day, noon, afternoon, evening, when the boys played in the churchyard, and I watched them from a distance within the room, being ashamed to show myself at the window lest they should know I was a prisoner – the strange sensation of never hearing myself speak – the fleeting intervals of something like cheerfulness, which came with eating and drinking, and went away with it – the setting in of rain one evening, with a fresh smell, and its coming down faster and faster between me and the church, until it and gathering night seemed to quench me in gloom, and fear, and remorse – all this appears to have gone round and round for years instead of days, it is so vividly and strongly stamped on my remembrance.[20]

Dickens had an acute sense of the powerlessness of children, and how childhood's terrors can as well be a model for later victimization.

Ever since the original biography of Dickens that he authorized his friend John Forster to write we have known how much of himself Dickens put into *David Copperfield*, and in particular the incident about how he had been sent to a blacking- warehouse at the age of ten or eleven.[21] As Forster reported about how he had stumbled upon Dickens's childhood secret:

> He was silent for several minutes; I felt that I had unintentionally touched upon a painful place in his memory. . . .It was not, however, then, but some weeks later, that Dickens made further allusion to my thus having struck unconsciously upon a time of which he never could lose the remembrance while he remembered anything, and the recollection of which, at intervals, haunted him and made him miserable, even to that hour.
>
> Very shortly afterwards I learnt in all their detail the incidents that had been so painful to him, and what then was said to me or written respecting them revealed the story of his boyhood. The idea of *David Copperfield*, which was to take all the world into his confidence, had not at this time occurred to him; but what it had so startled me to know, his readers were afterwards told with only such change or addition as for the time might sufficiently disguise himself under cover of his hero. For the poor little lad, with good

ability and a most sensitive nature, turned at the age of ten into a "laboring hind" in the service of "Murdstone and Grinby" and conscious already of what made it seem very strange to him that he could so easily have been thrown away at such an age, was indeed himself.

Dickens wrote an eloquent essay about his own autobiographical experiences for Forster.

> It had all been written, as fact, before he thought of any other use for it; and it was not until several months later, when the fancy of *David Copperfield*, itself suggested by what he had so written of his early troubles, began to take shape in his mind, that he abandoned his first intention of writing his own life...What already had been sent to me, however, and proof-sheets of the novel interlined at the time, enable me now to separate the fact from the fiction, and to supply to the story of the author's childhood those passages, omitted from the book, which, apart from their illustration of the growth of his character, present to us a picture of tragical suffering, and of tender as well as humorous fancy, unsurpassed in even the wonders of his published writings.[22]

In the autobiographical fragment itself Dickens had written:

> It is wonderful to me how I could have been so easily cast away at such an age. It is wonderful to me that, even after my descent into the poor little drudge I had been since we came to London, no one had compassion enough on me – a child of singular abilities, quick, eager, delicate, and soon hurt, bodily or mentally – to suggest that something might have been spared, as certainly it might have been, to place me at any common school...My father and mother were quite satisfied. They could hardly have been more so if I had been twenty years of age, distinguished at a grammar school, and going to Cambridge.[23]

Dickens had a ragged little colleague, an orphan, whom he remembered as "Bob Fagin":

> No words can express the secret agony of my soul as I sunk into this companionship...and felt my early hopes of growing up to be a learned, distinguished man, crushed in my breast. The deep remembrance of the sense I had of being utterly neglected and hopeless; of the shame I felt in my position; of the misery it was to my young heart to believe that, day by day, what I had learned,

and thought, and delighted in, and raised my fancy and my emulation up by, was passing away from me, never to be brought back any more; cannot be written. My whole nature was so penetrated with the grief and humiliation of such considerations, that even now, famous and caressed and happy, I often forget in my dreams that I have a dear wife and children; even that I am a man; and wander desolately back to that time of my life.[24]

No matter how often these words have been quoted, they still bear repeating:

> I know that, but for the mercy of God, I might easily have been, for any care that was taken of me, a little robber or a little vagabond...That I suffered in secret, and that I suffered exquisitely, no one ever knew but I. How much I suffered, it is, as I have said already, beyond my power to tell. No man's imagination can overstep the reality. But I kept my counsel, and I did my work.[25]

Dickens's father was meanwhile imprisoned for debt in the Marshalsea, which played such an important role in *Little Dorrit*. (Both Dickens and Freud had fathers who resembled Mr. Micawber.) Thanks to an inheritance his father was finally able to be released. But only a quarrel, over himself, between his father and the relative who had found the blacking-warehouse became the occasion for his release from his "servitude." As Dickens said, from then until he wrote his autobiographical piece for Forster: "I have never, until I now impart it to this paper, in any burst of confidence with any one, my own wife not excepted, raised the curtain I then dropped, thank God."[26]

Dickens's father had ultimately said he should not go back to the blacking-warehouse, and instead be sent to school. "I do not write resentfully or angrily; for I know how all these things have worked together to make me what I am; but I never afterwards forgot, I never shall forget, I never can forget, that my mother was warm for my being sent back."[27] Dickens knew that his future biographer should get access to this story of his childhood trauma, even as Dickens felt that it had all fed into his creativity as an artist. But he did not yet anticipate how it would specifically play a role in *David Copperfield*, the book he later considered his "best", and "favorite child". We can well believe Dickens's words in the Preface to the original edition of *David Copperfield*:

> It would concern the reader little, perhaps, to know, how sorrowfully the pen is laid down at the close of a two-years' imaginative task; or how an Author feels as if he were dismissing some portion of himself into the shadowy world, when a crowd of the creatures of his brain are going from him for ever. Yet, I have nothing

else to tell; unless, indeed, I were to confess (which might be of less moment still) that no one can ever believe this Narrative, in the reading, more than I have believed it in the writing.[28]

The triumph of *David Copperfield*, I think, consists in how he did not sink to sentimentalizing David's early experiences. Through falling in love with Dora, David falls, in a fresh way, "into captivity." Despite his Aunt Betsy's gentle warnings, David goes ahead and marries a woman who is really a child-bride. However humorous the details of their housekeeping incompetence, Dora proves a poor choice of a wife; only her death rescues David from a lingering addiction to childish ways (the "mistaken impulse of an undisciplined heart"), and the book ends with his being finally happily married to Agnes Wickfield.

For all that Dickens has to teach about childhood, there is something more than a bit rationalistically old-fashioned about what he had to say. In the early twentieth century James Joyce's *A Portrait of the Artist As a Young Man* (1916) would begin with a short paragraph which stands at the beginning of a more contemporary understanding of childhood: "Once upon a time and a very good time it was there was a moocow coming down along the road and this moocow that was down along the road met a nicens little boy named baby tuckoo...."[29] In a not dissimilar way, Freud's postulation of the Oedipus complex is likely to seem on the Victorian side today; it is after all rationalistic to suppose that a small boy sexually craves for its mother. And it can seem simple-minded to think that rational enlightenment of the child can succeed in changing much in the way children suffer. We now know much more than either Dickens or Freud about the underside to apparent maternal affection, and how frightening it can be to be threatened by absorption into any primordial being.

One has to wonder how much Ferenczi's concept of the "confusion of tongues" applies not just to the contrast between adults and children, but to the gulfs that exist between people in general. But let us stick only to the problem of childhood, so strikingly approached in *David Copperfield* as well as in psychoanalytic thinking. Have we really gotten very far in exploring what goes on in the minds of children? To recur to a problem touched on at the outset, modern divorce is something that even Freud knew little about. Children are natural reactionaries, and they want things to hang together, as in the example of the child Erikson cited on the future life; although we have had at least a few studies that purport to examine the long-term effects of divorce, I feel the need for more understanding of just what it can be like experientially for the child to undergo the anguish of his parents coming apart. One of the unexpected effects of the Freudian impact on ideas is that it seemed to sanction adult individualistic selfishness. So people can divorce for the sake of their self-fulfillment, without feeling more duty-bound to respect the needs of family life as a whole. It will take a wholesale collapse of the Chinese Confucian family system for them to be able to appreciate the kinds of psychological dynamics that modern psychoanalysis has been concerned with. (The Japanese, and the Chinese in Hong Kong, are further along in being Westernized.)

Dickens himself could not safely escape from his own traumatic background. His *Oliver Twist* may have "practically reinvented childhood from the child's point of view....;" but, as one of his most recent biographers has commented, Dickens's work continued to be haunted by "the spectre of lost childhood."[30] Not only did he separate from his wife and the mother of his ten children, but he did so publicly, publishing his side of their difficulties; in 1858 his piece called "Personal" came out in his *Household Words*.[31] (Forster had been against Dickens's going public on the subject.) Dickens settled on his wife Catherine a rather niggardly sum of money, as he proceeded to take up with a young actress the same age as one of his own daughters. Dickens broke with friends who did not take his side in the marital disunion, and he tried to forbid some of his children to see their mother. It seems as if his real children were his books, while his biological offspring suffered relative neglect and abandonment. This recent biographer cites the children's "partial absence of self-worth" as an explanation for why they were "made...so curiously estranged from each other after their father's death."[32] He was dead by the age of fifty-eight; he had mercilessly driven himself making money with his immensely successful dramatic readings from his own works (he could successfully hold audiences of close to 4,000 people), which doubtless hastened the undermining of his health.

The poet William Butler Yeats was to be most explicit about the tragedy of the greatest artistic achievements. Yeats was so wound up in his poetic dreams that even as a young man he found what a biographer of Yeats refers to as the "intensity of feeling for life...eluding him." Yeats had written in a letter:

> I have woven about me a web of thoughts. I wish to break through it, to see the world again.
>
> Yesterday I went to see, in a city hotel, an acquaintance who has had sudden and great misfortunes, come in the last few days to a crisis...I saw his hands and eyes moving restlessly and that his face was more shrunken than when I saw him some months before. Of course all this pained me at the time but I know (now that he is out of my sight) that if I heard he was dead I would not think twice about it. So thick has the web got.

A mature poem of Yeats's, *The Winding Stair*, summed up what also seemed to be Dickens's dilemma:

> The intellect of man is forced to choose
> Perfection of the life, or of the work,
> And if it take the second must refuse
> A heavenly mansion, raging in the dark.[33]

The greatness of Dickens's books seemed to make it more likely that his real-life children would prove disappointments, as they became in effect orphans; David Copperfield becomes a successful novelist. In recreating the world, it was possible for Dickens to recreate his self; that was to be the "perfection" of Dickens's work. So he collected the proofs of his various novels and "bound them together with his working notes. These were his memorials for posterity."[34] I have more than a suspicion that Freud would have understood Dickens's choice in his real life, which may have been close to Freud's own; other great analysts have been failures with their own children. Thanks to the impact of psychoanalysis it is illegal today in Buenos Aires to spank a child. Ferenczi might be entitled to feel confirmed in his essential thinking by the existence of even more multiple possibilities of childhood abuse and deprivation than he wrote about. Hopefully everyday historians concerned with such ordinary subjects as historiographical orphans do not have to face as stark a choice as a great poet like Yeats proclaimed in his *The Winding Stair*.

NOTES

1 Paul Roazen, *Freud and His Followers* (New York, Knopf, 1975; New York, Da Capo, 1992), Part VII, Chs. 6-7, pp. 355-71.

2 Sandor Ferenczi, "Confusion of Tongues between Adults and the Child," in *Final Contributions to the Problems & Methods of Psycho-Analysis*, ed. Michael Balint, translated by Eric Mosbacher & others (London, The Hogarth Press, 1955), pp. 156-67.

3 "Dostoevsky and Parricide," *Standard Edition*, Vol. 21, p. 177. See Paul Roazen, "Dostoevsky: The Politics of Suffering," in *Political Theory and the Psychology of the Unconscious* (London, Open Gate Press, 2000), pp. 49-71.

4 Paul Roazen, "Interviews on Freud and Jung with Henry A. Murray in 1965," *Journal of Analytical Psychology*, Vol. 48 (2003). pp. 1-27.

5 *The Letters of Sigmund Freud to Eduard Silberstein 1871-1881*, ed. Walter Boehlich, translated by Arnold J. Pomerans (Cambridge, Harvard University Press, 1990), p. 57; Ernest Jones, *The Life and Work of Sigmund Freud*, Vol. I *The Young Freud*, 2nd edition (London, The Hogarth Press, 1956), p. 116, 177, 190. See also Leonard Shengold, *Soul Murder: The Effects of Childhood Abuse and Deprivation* (New Haven, Yale University Press, 1989), Ch. 10.

6 See Lawrence J. Friedman, *Identity's Architect: A Biography of Erik H. Erikson* (New York, Scribner's, 1999), p. 316.

7 Paul Roazen, *Encountering Freud: The Politics and Histories of Psychoanalysis*

(New Brunswick, N.J., Transaction, 1990), p. 148.
8 Joseph Goldstein, Anna Freud, Albert Solnit, *Beyond the Best Interests of the Child* (New York, Free Press, 1973). See also Joseph Goldstein, Anna Freud, Albert Solnit, *The Best Interests of the Child: The Least Detrimental Alternative* (New York, the Free Press, 1996).
9 Charles Dickens, *Dombey and Son*, ed. Edgar Johnson (N.Y., Dell, 1963), Ch. 16 "What The Waves Were Always Saying."
10 Peter Ackroyd, *Dickens* (N.Y., Harper Collins, 1990), pp. 521, 527.
11 Charles Dickens, *David Copperfield*, ed. Jerome Buckley (New York, Norton, 1990), p. 766.
12 *Ibid.*, p. 10.
13 *Ibid.*, p. 13.
14 *Ibid.*, p. 18
15 *Ibid.*, p. 19.
16 "The Future of An Illusion," *Standard Edition*, Vol. 21, p. 47.
17 *David Copperfield, op. cit.*, pp. 19-21.
18 *Ibid.*, pp. 23-26.
19 *Ibid.*, pp. 35, 39, 43.
20 *Ibid.*, p. 53, 57.
21 See James A. Davies, *John Forster: A Literary Life* (Totowa, New Jersey, Barnes & Noble, 1983).
22 John Forster, *The Life of Charles Dickens*, Vol. 1 (Phil., Lippincott, 1872), p. 48-49.
23 *Ibid.*, p. 51.
24 *Ibid.*, p. 53.
25 *Ibid.*, pp. 57-58.
26 *Ibid.*, p. 69.
27 *Ibid.*, pp. 68-69.
28 *David Copperfield, op. cit.*, p. 6.
29 James Joyce, *A Portrait of the Artist as a Young Man* (New York, Signet Books, 1948), p. 1.
30 Ackroyd, *Dickens, op. cit.*, pp. 453, 873.
31 Charles Dickens, "Personal," in *Selected Journalism* (New York, Penguin, 1997), pp. 51-52.
32 Ackroyd, *op. cit.*, p. 880.
33 A. G. Stock, *W. B. Yeats: His Poetry and Thought* (Cambridge, Cambridge University Press, 1961), pp. 158-59.
34 Ackroyd, *Dickens, op. cit.*, p. 566.

7

EUGENE O'NEILL'S *LONG DAY'S JOURNEY INTO NIGHT*

The whole subject of the impact of depth psychological thinking on Eugene O'Neill's *Long Day's Journey Into Night* has stimulated me finally to weigh the respective themes inherent in the contrasting outlooks of both Freud and Jung that get echoed in O'Neill's great drama. It has long been established that Jung had in particular an influence on O'Neill (1888-1953), to the extent that in the life of the mind it is ever possible to establish intellectual lineage.[1] Freud and Jung espoused enduringly different views on the positive as opposed to the negative aspects of illusion and truth. Abhorrence of sectarianism does not entail that we ignore legitimate past differences of opinion, even great controversies.[2] The key value of toleration in the history of psychoanalysis does not mean we have to settle all past disagreements by the subterfuge of watering-down everybody in order to make a universally drinkable soup. Rather, I think that it is desirable to hold simultaneously in our minds even polar opposites, in this instance both Freud and Jung at their most outspoken, in order to see what their respective perspectives can teach.

Ann-Louise Silver's recent article has highlighted the role in O'Neill's life of Dr. Smith Ely Jelliffe (1866-1945).[3] O'Neill's most recent biographer[4] brings in Jelliffe's name at a few points, but a psychoanalytically interesting essay[5] on *Long Day's Journey Into Night* ignores Jelliffe entirely. Jelliffe matters because, as Silver knows, he was such an eclectic as an analyst. The main source about Jelliffe remains the book by John C. Burnham, containing Jelliffe's surviving correspondence with Freud and Jung as edited by William McGuire.[6] Within the context of rival ideologies Jelliffe was "unorthodox." Jelliffe's last letter to Freud, in 1939, had a passage in which

Jelliffe tried to counter the founder of psychoanalysis's grim view of how his work had deteriorated into being "the handmaiden of psychiatry in America." To Jelliffe the general charge of the "superficiality" of American thought meant that the values of catholicity and tolerance were being underrated. In the history of the reception of psychoanalysis in America, Jelliffe was a major source by which European developments in neurology and psychiatry came to the United States through the printed word. Jelliffe was a prominent editor, journalist, teacher, and publicist; he appeared in court, treated distinguished patients, knew celebrities (like John Barrymore), and coauthored an influential textbook.

The Freud who wrote to Jelliffe was an aging and distant old man, although I suspect that Freud despised Jelliffe for his receptivity to Jung.[7] The Jung correspondence with Jelliffe is the more interesting. Jelliffe was not a great writer, yet he stands in the great American tradition of the generous spirit of Ralph Waldo Emerson and William James. Jelliffe's judgment about people was unusually sound. He was open-minded, if sometimes credulous and naïve about the possible uses of psychoanalysis.

O'Neill's *Long Day's Journey Into Night*[8], so autobiographical that it only appeared after his death, seems to me almost unreadably harrowing, full of raw emotion. Although it is supposed to be set in an American east-coast summer house in 1912, I think it is so barbaric in its themes that it also has to be related to the great tragedies of ancient Greece in the 4th century B.C. Freud had thought that the manners of the New World were intolerable, lacking in the subtle capacities that were so common-place in the Central Europe of old Vienna. Freud was said to have been particularly offended in 1909 at a trip to Niagara Falls, when someone said of him something like "let the old gentleman go first." For Freud, then 53, such a comment, if it went beyond the level of a thought and passed into verbal speech, was a sign of cultural incivility and lack of proper respect for age. Jean-Jacques Rousseau once wrote powerfully about the subject of lies,[9] but Freud was legitimately objecting to American straight-shooting which omitted the kind of white lying that is apt to appear as duplicity to we who have been raised in the States. Different cultures define what is inhumane, and *Long' Day's Journey Into Night* is a representatively tough aspect of American life and at the same time reaches universal levels of understanding.

Long Day's Journey Into Night takes place on one day, and has four main characters, Mary Tyrone (a mother who is a recovering morphine addict), James Tyrone (her husband, an actor), and two sons, Jamie (also an actor) and Edmund (who is ill and about to be diagnosed as consumptive). Edmund is ten years younger than his brother. The family is Irish and takes heavy alcohol-consumption for granted.

At the outset Mary wants to think that Edmund just has "a cold," while Tyrone is uneasily protective about the possibility that she will understand the truth. Mary also talks about her need for "new glasses." The issue immediately arises about whether Tyrone can stop his older son Jamie son from "saying anything that would get" the mother "more upset over Edmund." Jamie shrugs off his father's protectiveness, saying "I think it's the wrong idea to let mama go on kidding herself." To him she was "deliberately fooling herself," and knew better. Both sons berate their father, cruelly, for being too cheap in the doctoring he has ever been willing to pay for. Tyrone allows this insolence from his sons, and calls Jamie's accusation that Tyrone forced him onto also going on the stage "a lie." Tyrone goes on to blame Jamie for having set a bad example for Edmund, and Tyrone and Jamie spar over what is the truth. What Jamie calls "a rotten accusation" of his own is typical of how these family members interact with one another. Jamie is "shamefaced" at his own "sneering jealousy" of Edmund.

It turns out that it has only been two months since Mary's return from a sanatorium. Tyrone maintains about Edmund's illness: "I wish to God we could keep the truth from her." Jamie maintains that she "seems perfectly all right this morning," but Tyrone picks up on Jamie's cautious use of "seems." Jamie hesitantly points to some signs of her backsliding about drug-use. Tyrone struggles to brush off the threat, and resentfully claims that Jamie has " a mind that sees nothing but the worst motives behind everything." Freudian truth-telling, both its merits and limitations, is front-and-center as a problem in *Long Day's Journey*. Mary picks up on Jamie's having been "evil-minded", and "vaguely knows" Jamie is also apt to be protectively lying about Edmund. Tyrone for his part "avoids looking at her".

Mary is "evading" Edmund's eyes, and contrasts other families who have "homes they don't have to be ashamed of." She tries to absolve Jamie and Edmund of "blame," at the same time she indicates how she feels "so lonely." Edmund maintains to her the Freudian maxim that "it's bad for you to forget. The right way is to remember." Mary insists that she be told "the truth"; why, she asks Edmund, is he "so suspicious all of a sudden?" She yearns to "forget for awhile," while Edmund also tries to soothe her by pointing out "a fib." Soon she is maintaining: "It would serve all of you right if it was true!" Later, after she acknowledges to Cathleen, a houseservant, having taken "some of the medicine", she "dreamily" maintains that "It kills the pain. You go back until at last you are beyond its reach. Only the past when you were happy is real."

Jamie and Edmund struggle with the same sorts of issues, Jamie telling his younger brother about the illness that "it would be wrong dope to kid yourself." Both brothers try to avoid looking at each other in connection with their mother's possible relapse. Mary has accused the others of "spying on her," and Jamie reports that Edmund "never knew what was really wrong" until he was in prep school; Tyrone and Jamie had "kept it" from Edmund. Now "for the moment" Edmund "believes what he wants to believe" about Mary. Mary objects that Jamie was "always sneering at someone else, always looking for the worst weakness in everyone." At the same time she avoids Edmund's apprehensive searching eyes, while she keeps "averting" her gaze from him. Her rambling makes Edmund suspicious, as she avoids "the cynically appraising glance" Jamie gives her face and hands. Edmund pleads with his mother that Jamie is a liar, while she maintains that "the past" is omnipotent. Tyrone "knows now," and Edmund "sees that he knows." Tyrone pours himself "a big drink" as he tells Mary that he has "been a God-damned fool to believe in you!"

After Jamie maintains of his mother "what we all know, and have to live with now, again," Edmund brings up the "unpronounceable name" of what Jamie calls Edmund's "pet," Nietzsche. The play continues to revolve around truth as opposed to lies. At one point Tyrone says: "Mary! For God's sake, forget the past!" She replies: "The past is the present, isn't it? It's the future, too. We all try to lie out of that but life won't let us." Now one of Freud's analysands, Philipp Sarasin, did tell me that Freud had privately maintained that "with a good analysis one forgets everything. The goal of analysis is to forget!"[10] But this was in the 1920s, and at odds with Freud's critique of his own early use of hypnosis; Freud was evidently capable of wryly playing on the early psychoanalytic recommendation of patients becoming better by remembering the past. In the play Mary is acutely aware of the danger of self-deception, what she calls "lying to yourself again."

Early on Mary had complained about the fog-horn having disturbed her sleep; but later she maintains that the fog "hides you from the world and the world from you." In what I found to be the single most lyrical passage in the play Edmund describes the fog in a way that sounds to me more consonant with Jung's approach to illusion than Freud's own characteristic dissection of myth and religious superstition, exemplified by his rationalistic reasoning in *The Future of An Illusion*. Edmund said:

> The fog was where I wanted to be. Halfway down the path you can't see this house. You'd never know it was here. Or any of the other places down the avenue. I couldn't see but a few feet ahead. I didn't meet a soul. Everything looked and sounded unreal. Nothing was what it is. That's what I wanted – to be alone with myself in another world where truth is untrue and life can hide from itself. Out beyond the harbor, where the road runs along the beach, I even lost the feeling of being on land. The fog and the sea seemed part of each other. It was like walking on the bottom of the sea. As if I had drowned long ago. As if I was a ghost belonging to the fog, and the fog was the ghost of the sea. It felt damned peaceful to be nothing more than a ghost within a ghost.

In retorting to what Edmund sees as his father's "mingled worry and irritated disapproval" Edmund mocks: "Don't look at me as if I'd gone nutty. I'm talking sense. Who wants to see life as it is, if they can help it? It's the three Gorgons in one. You look in their faces and turn to stone. Or it's Pan. You see him and you die – that is, inside you – and have to go on living as a ghost."

Tyrone in talking to Mary brings up the concept of her "real self." Mary reminds him of the time when he had been brought home intoxicated; Edmund becomes accusingly full of hate for his father, while Tyrone pleads "Mary can't you forget—?" Mary turns on Edmund whose birth she claims gave rise to her own rheumatism. She also strikes out at her husband's close-fistedness about his whiskey in the house. Edmund doggedly is bitter and stubborn in his persistence that he has to go into a sanatorium himself. She "sadly" tells him that "after I knew you knew – about me – I had to be glad whenever you were where you couldn't see me." One of the more shocking parts of the play is when Edmund lets slip that he has had "a dope fiend for a mother!"

The fourth and final act has the three men in various states of drunkenness. One of the funny lines in the play is when Edmund derides his father's loyalty to Catholicism by saying: "Shakespeare was an Irish Catholic. . . ." (Tyrone loyally agrees.) Edmund "aggressively" says to his father: "Let's not kid each other, papa. Not tonight. We know what we're trying to forget." Tyrone pleads for resignation, to which Edmund replies with a prose poem from Baudelaire:

> "Be always drunken. Nothing else matters: that is the only question. If you would not feel the horrible burden of Time weighing on your shoulders and crushing you to the earth, be drunken continually.
>
> Drunken with what? With wine, with poetry, or with virtue, as you will. But be drunken.
>
> And if sometimes, on the stairs of a palace, or on the green side of a ditch, or in the dreary solitude of your own room, you should awaken and the drunkenness be half or wholly slipped away from you, ask of the wind, or of the wave, or of the bird. Or of the clock, of whatever flies, or sighs. Or rocks, or sings, or speaks, ask what hour it is; and the wind, wave, star, bird, clock, will answer you: 'It is the hour to be drunken! Be drunken, if you would not be martyred slaves of Time; be drunken continually! With wine, with poetry, or with virtue, as you will.'"

I do not know enough to be able to say how Jung might have reacted to such a passage from Baudelaire, but I feel certain that Freud, with his known views against alcohol, could not have been sympathetic. (Oddly enough one of Freud's fainting episodes with Jung concerned Freud's trying to wean Jung from Bleuler's teetotalism.) Freud's "deviating" pupils were apt at various points to make a point against Freud's characteristic intolerances of the non-rational and the irrational. Freud brought up about music being alien to him, while Jung was supposedly the prime example of a mystic in psychoanalysis, and even intuition could be denounced by Freud in his old age as a species of hocus-pocus. Science, of which psychoanalysis was supposedly a part,

> asserts that there are no sources of knowledge of the universe other than the intellectual working-over of carefully scrutinized observations – in other words, what we call research – and alongside of it no knowledge derived from revelation, intuition, or divination. . . Intuition and divination. . .may safely be reckoned as illusions, the fulfillments of wishful impulses.[11]

Now O'Neill's *Long Day's Journey* explores even more complicated themes. Tyrone tells Edmund: "When you deny God, you deny sanity." Edmund, despite his earlier defense of the fog, says of his mother: "She'll be nothing but a ghost haunting the past by this time." Tyrone replies that "you must take her memories with a grain of salt." Edmund answers himself in describing the motives behind his mother's behavior:

> The hardest thing to take is the blank wall she builds around her. Or it's more like a bank of fog in which she hides and loses herself. Deliberately, that's the hell of it! You know something in her does it deliberately – to get beyond our reach, to be rid of us, to forget we're alive! It's as if, in spite of loving us, she hated us!

Tyrone "remonstrates gently": "Now, now, lad. It's not her. It's the damned poison." As a professional actor Tyrone appeals for tolerance about Mary's "pretending." Tyrone calls upon his love for Mary, and one does wonder if *folie a deux* is not a central part of loving family situations or the human condition in general. Edmund insists on challenging his father's version of the past, as if the historical truth could be emancipating. It turns out that a suicide attempt of Edmund's had been when he "was cold sober. That was the trouble. I'd stopped to think too long." At the same time Tyrone's account of his own early life proved comforting to Edmund.

Long Day's Journey contains so much savagery that the reader can be left to find his own particular set of horrors. Future students should do the necessary legwork of developing the full details of how Jelliffe might have been an avenue by which Freud and Jung reached O'Neill. Scholarship on Jung is really only starting to get underway on a satisfactorily professional basis. Jelliffe did not take offense at Jung's pre-World War I lectures at Fordham, which were to be so decisive in turning Freud against Jung. In fact, Jelliffe had published three large articles by Jung, "The Theory of Psychoanalysis," in the first issues of Jelliffe's journal, *Psychoanalytic*

Review; this work by Jung constituted a critique of Freudian psychoanalysis. It would not be hard to develop the theme of Freud's own contempt for Jelliffe, although Freud did not want entirely to lose an important American backer and stayed in touch with Jelliffe right up until his death in 1939. Ann-Louise Silver's article should be a beginning to a reconsideration of not just O'Neill as a playwright, but of the whole tortured similarities and differences between Freud and Jung.

NOTES

1 Paul Roazen, "Interviews on Freud and Jung with Henry A. Murray in 1965," *op. cit.*
2 Paul Roazen, *The Trauma of Freud: Controversies in Psychoanalysis* (New Brunswick, N.J., Transaction Publishers, 2002).
3 Anne-Louise Silver, "American Psychoanalysts Who Influenced Eugene O'Neill's Long Day's Journey Into Night," *The Journal of the American Academy of Psychoanalysis*, Vol. 29 (2001), pp. 305-18.
4 Stephen Black, *Eugene O'Neill: Beyond Mourning and Tragedy* (New Haven, Yale University Press, 1999).
5 Bennett Simon, *Tragic Drama and the Family: Psychoanalytic Studies from Aeschylus to Beckett* (New Haven, Yale University Press, 1988), Ch. 6: "A Mistake My Being Born a Man," pp. 177-211.
6 John C. Burnham, *Jelliffe: American Psychoanalyst and Physician, and His Correspondence with Sigmund Freud and C. G. Jung*, ed. William McGuire (Chicago, University of Chicago Press, 1983). See also Paul Roazen, *Encountering Freud: The Politics and Histories of Psychoanalysis, op. cit.*, pp. 195-95; and Paul Roazen, *The Historiography of Psychoanalysis* (New Brunswick, N.J., Transaction Publishers, 2001), pp. 136, 358.
7 See Paul Roazen, *Oedipus in Britain: Edward Glover and the Struggle Over Klein* (New York, Other Press, 2000), p. 31.
8 I have used Eugene O'Neill, *Long Day's Journey Into Night* (New Haven, Yale University Press, 1956).
9 Jean-Jacques Rousseau, *Reveries of the Solitary Walker*, translated by Peter France (New York, Penguin Books, 1979), "Fourth Walk," pp. 63-80, and also see Helene Deutsch, *The Therapeutic Process, The Self, and Female Psychology: Collected Psychoanalytic Papers*, ed. by Paul Roazen (New Brunswick, N.J., Transaction Publishers, 1992), Ch. 9 "On the Pathological Lie (*Pseudologia Phantastica*)," pp. 109-121.
10 Roazen, *The Historiography of Psychoanalysis, op. cit.*, p. 169.
11 "New Introductory lectures on Psychoanalysis," *Standard Edition*, Vol. 22, p. 159.

8

A LIFE IN CONTROVERSY: LETTERS

Writing a letter to the editor requires an intense form of concentration, and conviction, since it is always possible to have opened the door to the possibility of an intemperate or otherwise damaging reply. Any such communications can be surprisingly emotionally draining, and that expense of spirit is why I am reproducing these twenty-six of my own letters. The specific circumstances of each individual occasion need to be remembered if it is to make sense why any writer takes the risk of engaging in such troublesome controversy. I continue to hope that my having felt obliged to participate in such letter-writing has in the long run helped promote fairness and even-handedness, and does not get confused with the various unfortunate intolerances which have so often marked the history of psychoanalysis.

1. In 1967 I was a junior faculty member (Instructor) in the Department of Government at Harvard College, and had before that been a Teaching Fellow there for several years while a graduate student. Dr. Thomas Szasz published a critique in *Trans-action* on the violations of confidentiality inherent in the philosophy and practice of college psychiatry, with specific reference to the Harvard University Health Service. After I wrote congratulating him for his prescience and courage in publishing the piece, he asked for my public support. I felt I could not decline to go into print on his behalf without being cowardly. Szasz has taken many bold positions, not all of which I agree with, but he has been a noticeable force for shaking up complacent thinking. And, most importantly, I thought he had been right in his general point as well as his criticisms of what then were

Harvard's policies on the use of psychiatrists. It remains still true today that not enough attention has been given to how a college psychiatrist should balance the pre-eminent obligation toward the student patient as against the expectations of the institutional authorities for whom he also works. I think a similar dilemma would arise in a business or governmental setting; and Szasz has been consistently outspoken about the possible abuses inherent in a psychiatrist working for someone besides suffering patients.

The letter that follows was not popular with those few social science academics in Cambridge then who were favorably inclined towards psychiatry. (Herbert Marcuse had been as struck by the passionate hatred Szasz aroused among psychoanalysts as by Szasz's unusual intelligence.) I ducked out of an invitation from the Harvard Health Services to present my own views, although not long thereafter I made a presentation there on Freud and Social Science.

College Psychiatrists
Trans-action, Dec. 4, 1967

I read Dr. Szasz's article with the greatest pleasure and approval. He has put into print what so many people here have been worried about, the lowbrow moralism behind so many of the psychiatric pronouncements of the Harvard Health Services. For some time now I have felt discontent with their clinical work with students.

2. My second book, *Brother Animal: The Story of Freud and Tausk*, was miraculously lucky in how it got reviewed in both the daily *New York Times*, as well as in the Sunday *New York Times* where a non-sectarian British analyst (Dr. Peter Lomas) gave the book a good reception. The book also got prominently advertised in the Sunday *New York Times*. I knew that Eissler was already on the warpath against me, and among other efforts he had written a private letter of protest addressed to the home of my publisher, Alfred Knopf. Also it turned out that an author, whose own manuscript on Lou Andreas-Salomé had been rejected as a book at Knopf's publishing company, wrote in accusing me of what sounded like a serious scholarly offense.

Brother Animal (Continued)
Sunday *New York Times Book Review*, Nov. 23, 1969

Rudolf Binion's charge in this space (Nov. 9) that I have appropriated portions of his *Frau Lou* in my *Brother Animal: The Story of Freud and Tausk* is sufficiently serious to require an answer.

In 1964, I started to meet and interview everyone living who had ever known Freud. Very soon thereafter I heard from members of Freud's circle the first outlines of the Tausk story, and began, in cooperation with Tausk's family, to assemble the pieces that eventually made up the narrative of my book. In 1966 – not 1965, as he has it – Mr. Binion graciously allowed me to read a manuscript of *Frau Lou*. . .His book contained documentation that was of some help to me in supplementing Lou's *Freud Journal* and the work of her previous biographer. My debt to him is quite adequately covered by my five footnotes to his book in *Brother Animal*.

Mr. Binion, however, foists on *Brother Animal* a "central thesis," which he claims as his own – that "Freud rejected his disciple Tausk because he was unconsciously jealous of Tausk's mistress, Lou Andreas-Salomé, and because he wanted 'corroborators rather than collaborators.'" If Mr. Binion wants such a "central thesis" for his own book, he is more than welcome to it. I would certainly never commit myself to any such garbled half-truth.

Being indebted, as I am, to the 100 or so pupils of Freud who helped me with *Brother Animal*, and having been aided by a wide variety of published and unpublished material, it seems odd for Mr. Binion to so exaggerate his share in my book. The reader can judge for himself how much our books have in common, and whether *Brother Animal* contains a new story or not.

3. When *Brother Animal* first came out in England, in addition to good reviews it also got a bad one in the *Times Literary Supplement*; in those days *TLS* reviews appeared anonymously. I was new to the politics of reviewing, and wrote a letter of protest that was too lengthy to get accepted. Erich Fromm was brave enough to agree to write them in my behalf, and the *TLS* published his letter. A Chicago analyst (Dr. Samuel Lipton) wrote in unflatteringly about my book. The *TLS* did agree to publish my brief reply to Lipton. I had, in trying to decipher who had written the original anonymous negative review of *Brother Animal*, erroneously assumed that another orthodox analyst was responsible; thirty years later I discovered that the author was, surprisingly to me, Sir Aubrey Lewis, a famous psychiatrist not usually friendly to psychoanalysis. Months before my book came out in England there had been a series of letters (one written by the *New York Times* correspondent Anthony Lewis) about Tausk which came out in the *New Statesman*; on that occasion I declined a specific invitation to participate in a controversy.

Brother Animal
Times Literary Supplement, September 11, 1970

In reply to Dr. Lipton's objection (August 21) to my use of previously unpublished material in *Brother Animal*, I confess I do believe that some of the best points in my book derive from my interviews. It is surprising that a psychoanalyst, whose case histories rest after all on unwritten data, should so complain of the difficulties of validating my work. The back of my book contains 216 notes, of which twenty-seven refer to oral remarks, the rest to articles and books already in print. Of course written history contains many lies of its own, and it is the job of the historian to try to come up with as trustworthy an account as he can manage. As for the documents the Tausk family generously put at my disposal, I hope that eventually they will be deposited in an accessible library.

4. An analyst (Dr. Martin Grotjahn) who was well-disposed toward me had favorably reviewed *Brother Animal*, but in it erroneously stated that I had been analyzed by Helene Deutsch; since another reviewer, in a psychiatric journal, had also put the identical mistake into print, I thought it worthwhile to correct the misunderstanding.

Who analyzed Whom?
Contemporary Psychology, Feb. 1971

Dr. Martin Grotjahn's review of my *Brother Animal: The Story of Freud and Tausk* contains an error in need of correction. Although he states as a fact that Dr. Helene Deutsch was my analyst, this is simply not true; I have never been in any therapeutic relationship with her. It would, of course, hardly be a disgrace to have been analyzed by Dr. Deutsch; but because of the substance of my book and the nature of Dr. Grotjahn's review, the reader is left with an impression casting doubt on the objectivity of my research.

5. Eissler was marshalling his troops against me because of my *Brother Animal*. For a time even Helene Deutsch was responsive to his cry that her cooperating with me had been mistaken. Behind Eissler, I later found out, was Anna Freud, as well as other influential analysts in New York City. Ernst Federn had been among those who had once helped me. In print Eissler said of a key letter of Paul Federn, Ernst's father, concerning Tausk's suicide, that it should never have appeared while Federn's sons were alive. Eissler could never bring himself to quote Paul's Federn's letter, not because of Federn's sons, but for the reason that once one knew Paul Federn's reverence for Freud it became telling how far he went in criticizing Freud's behavior toward Tausk. Paul Federn's letter was an essential confirmation for what Helene Deutsch had told me before, even though I thought both Paul Federn and she went too far in blaming Freud for Tausk's death.

The Human Context, 1973

I very much regret Ernst Federn's expressed annoyance at my going beyond the permission he had given me to publish in 1969 only "the major part" of his father's letter. Some four years ago Ernst Federn had sent me what he called his forgiveness for failing to omit certain passages, and for reporting other material he would have preferred not in print; he credited me with good intentions in the aim of serving historical truth, and therefore I considered the matter long settled. In my *Brother Animal: The Story of Freud and Tausk* I had made known and objected to the tendentious editing of Freud's letters, and I felt I could not cooperate in similar censorship in my own writing. It is my conviction that Paul Federn's full sentiments at Victor Tausk's suicide, whatever their merits, were shared by others in

Freud's inner circle, and the way in which Freud was regarded by his early followers was an essential part of the story I was telling.

6. As a matter of course, while writing my biography of Helene Deutsch, I sent the following letter to the *New York Times Book Review*. Like others who have done likewise in connection with their own biographical efforts, I got virtually no response at all. But the publication of this letter by itself would have alerted Eissler, to his intense annoyance, that Helene Deutsch had authorized me to do her biography.

> Sunday *New York Times* Book Review, 1978
>
> For a biography of Helene Deutsch, the psychoanalyst, written with her cooperation, I would like to hear from anyone who knew her, and would appreciate copies of her letters. Eventually her papers will go to the Schlesinger Library on the History of Women in America at Radcliffe College. Confidentiality is assured if requested.

7. Eissler was bent on pursuing me in multiple forums and different publications. The *International Journal of Psychoanalysis* was a traditional IPA publication, and therefore readily open to him. Although other people, when earlier attacked by Eissler's multiple polemics, chose to ignore his charges, I again thought it worthwhile to defend myself by putting my side of things in print.

> *International Journal of Psychoanalysis*, Spring 1982
> (also translated into French, *Le Coq-Heron*, 1982)
> Paul Roazen on Errors Regarding Freud
>
> The occasion for the letter of K. R. Eissler about "errors" in my work is baffling.[1] He selected four points from an unpublished paper [of his], before it got "buried in the vaults" of the Library of Congress.
>
> Your readers may be less mystified by knowing some facts about the vast collection which the Freud Archives, of which Eissler is the leading figure, has deposited in Washington, D.C. After the year 2000 the bulk of the important material will start to be open for inspection, and then scholars of every persuasion will be free to examine the original Freud. But what is one to make of a system of classification which restricts one of Freud's letters to his deceased eldest son until 2013, and another until 2032? It is remarkable with what precision it is possible to calculate the preservation of privacy (or maintain idealizations about Freud). Josef Breuer must have had something interesting to say for a letter to be sealed until 2102.
>
> The fate of Freud's papers, and how secrecy lends support to myth-making about him, are more important than the four points Eissler makes against me; but they are inter-connected.
>
> 1. The issue of Tausk's height illustrates Eissler's carelessness. He erroneously quotes me as having written that Tausk was "extremely tall"; but

Eissler has confused Tausk with Jung.

Eissler turns to Freud's sensitivity about his height. He calls it a "bizarre" claim that when the group photograph at the Weimar Congress was taken, Freud stood on a box. Earlier, Eissler wrote that he could not "imagine anyone in his right mind" suggesting Freud use a box.[2] Since Eissler thought Jung "miraculously" failed to mention this episode, I offered evidence[3]; yet Eissler now undermines his own point, documenting a source about the "low box" or "stool." But he has so isolated this incident from its larger context that it is difficult to appreciate its significance.

2. Eissler objects to Jones having literally translated Freud's term for Adler as "Jew boy."[4] Taken by itself, that phrase may sound unduly contemptuous; but the reader may judge for himself whether Eissler's preferred expression, "Jewish chap," is the real issue. Adler had died suddenly on a trip to Aberdeen in 1937, and [Arnold] Zweig mentioned in a letter to Freud that he was very much moved by the news. Freud replied: "I don't understand your sympathy for Adler. For a Jew boy out of a Viennese suburb a death in Aberdeen is an unheard-of career in itself and a proof of how far he had got on. The world really rewarded him richly for his service in having contradicted psychoanalysis." The editor of the Freud-Zweig correspondence suppressed this entire passage about Adler, as initially did one editor connected with Freud's reaction to Tausk's death.

3. Eissler attempts to sort-out a matter of priorities between Edoardo Weiss (a friend of Tausk's) and Freud. Eissler cites Weiss, and then puts words in his mouth, saying: "I am sure that in his discussion of this matter with Roazen, Weiss added the words 'without quoting me.'" The issue is a complicated one, not to be settled by Eissler's imputation of words to Weiss. Freud made some remarks to Weiss before he presented a paper at a private gathering in Freud's apartment. The story needs to be told in a fuller context; Eissler could begin by releasing his interviews with Weiss (which Weiss gave me full access to) but are locked up in the Library of Congress until 2057.

4. As to the question of Tausk's suicide, Eissler's peculiar policy about access to material his Archives controls becomes critical. On a selective basis, Eissler has himself used and allowed others to see documentation that is barred to scholars at large. A passage from Ludwig Jekels's reminiscences, found in the Bernfeld papers in the Library of Congress (and simultaneously listed in the catalogue of Eissler's collection to be released in 2010) has only recently come to light: "Freud thought very highly of Tausk's analytical talents yet refused firmly to analyze him. Tausk had asked him repeatedly to do it; I, too, asked Freud to do that, but he replied: 'He is going to kill me!'" My work on Tausk has been limited by the material available; one can now better evaluate the subtitle of Eissler's book against me, "the fictitious case of Tausk contra Freud."

It is difficult to correct either mythmaking about Freud, or the work of debunkers, until the Freud collection at the Library of Congress is open to the scrutiny of independent historians.

8. Janet Malcolm had been rough on me in her *In the Freud Archives*, which originally appeared in the *New Yorker*, at the same time that she took Eissler's side of things in his dealings with Jeffrey M. Masson. In those days the *New Yorker*, unlike today, had no letters to the editor. So when she came after me again, this second time in the *New York Review of Books*, I thought it worth protesting.

New York Review of Books, May 9, 1985

Janet Malcolm's review of Ann Thwaite's *Edmund Gosse* raises the issue of scholarly fact, and the possible motives for error. Therefore I wonder why she has chosen to write, on a second occasion, that K. R. Eissler has written "a whole book" to challenge my *Brother Animal: The Story of Freud and Tausk*, when she knows that he has in truth written two such books against that one of mine.

9. Since the *New York Review of Books* is such a noteworthy publication, I thought it made sense to answer a letter sent in by Eissler's successor as head of the Freud Archives. My writing this letter was one way of alerting the intellectual community to what was going on behind-the-scenes. The audience at the *New York Review* was clearly different from that of the *International Journal of Psychoanalysis*, which explains any repetition of examples. (The reader will remember that I already discussed some of these same points at the beginning of Ch. 5.) Although I have since found Eissler's successor to be personally amiable, I am reprinting this letter as a matter of historical record.

The Freud Archives
The New York Review of Books, Nov. 20, 1986

Dr. Harold Blum's letter, which heralds a "new current policy of The Sigmund Freud Archives," is likely to mislead the unwary.[5]

We are told that everything under the control of the Archives which is being published, or has already appeared in print, will be "open to all scholars on the basis of equal access." It is hard to believe that researchers need much help of the Archives, even on the exalted basis of equal access, for material which is soon to be old hat.

According to a letter to me from the Chief of the Manuscript Division of the Library of Congress, this supposed new policy has solely amounted to Dr. Blum's making unrestricted Freud's adolescent letters to Eduard Silberstein. These letters formed the basis for a 1971 article, and have also been extensively perused by at least one historian who has discussed them at length in print.

If anyone takes up Dr. Blum's suggestion and writes now to The Library of Congress, they will find that access to The Sigmund Freud Collection remains, with the exception of the Silberstein letters, unchanged. The Library of Congress is still subject to the whims of its principal donor, The Sigmund Freud Archives.

Whatever the wishes of those who gave or sold material to the Archives, the Archives's own policy has been that the bulk of the material will only start to be available after the year 2000. It is therefore sophistry for Dr. Blum, now Executive Director of the Archives, to tell "interested persons" to apply to The Library of Congress "for permission to view the material in The Sigmund Freud Collection, subject to the usual rules and regulations of The Library of Congress governing such scholarly use," when in fact The Library of Congress seems helpless in the face of arbitrary actions of the Archives.

A laughable system of classification, imposed by the Archives, means that one of Freud's letters to his deceased eldest son is restricted until 2013, and another until 2032, while a letter of Josef Breuer's is sealed until 2102.

Dr. Blum's announcement contains one sentence which invites conjecture from Kremlinologists: "It is the intention of The Archives to release all letters and documents from restriction, as soon as possible, consistent with legal and ethical standards and obligations." Since it will be Dr. Blum and his Archives which will be implementing this intention, and constructing its own rules, it does not sound to me that this supposed "new current policy" amounts to a hill of beans. We have no way of knowing, for example, whether there will ever be any change in the long-standing policy of the Archives in allowing certain ideologically acceptable individuals to use documentation which is in the meantime barred to scholars at large.

Readers may be interested in knowing that Dr. K. R. Eissler remains, according to The Library of Congress, in charge "as Anna Freud's representative" of allowing researchers to inspect the restricted Series A of the Sigmund Freud Collection.

10. When my biography of Helene Deutsch got attacked in the *Partisan Review*, I felt that some specific points in it deserved answering.

The Partisan Review, 1986

Elaine Hoffman Baruch's review of my book *Helene Deutsch* is an example of how psychoanalytic sectarianism has its Stalinist side.[6] Her attack was inspired by Kurt Eissler, whom she calls "the revered psychoanalyst."

Eissler has been pursuing me for ideological crimes since my book *Brother Animal* was published in 1969. My excellent personal rapport with Helene Deutsch was severely strained as Eissler took up the cause of defending Freud against the imaginary idea (which Baruch repeats) that I had "blamed" Freud for Tausk's suicide. Eissler pressed his attack against *Brother Animal* with two books, two articles, one unpublished essay, and letters to professional journals.

In 1977 I renewed my friendship with Helene, which had first begun in 1964. Whether Helene picked me as a biographer, or I initiated the idea, is impossible for me to disentangle. The decision we reached in 1978 was attractive to us both. I had a lawyer draw up five contracts covering the publication of the biography, her letters, her psychoanalytic papers, her first book on female sexuality, and her diary as a young girl. I believe that casts light on Baruch's contention that "Roazen passes off" the diary "as Deutsch's."

When my book appeared I received a telephone call from a Boston analyst. Eissler had called him with the news that the diary was not Helene's but Christine Olden's. I knew her to have been a patient of Helene's. Baruch does not credit Eissler for this information about the diary. And she is wrong in writing: "Helene Deutsch's cupboard, I'm told, was full of unpublished material by analysands, patients, and colleagues, as well as by her." There was in fact no such quaint-sounding cupboard. With Helene's approval I went through all the papers that she had, and found none of the unpublished works by others that Baruch alleges.

Eissler's own informant about the diary was Edward Kronold. There was no way that I on my own could have come up with the idea that the Madi Fournier of the diary was Christine Olden. Oddly enough Baruch treats Helene's *Confrontations with Myself* as thoroughly reliable, when there is abundant evidence of the quasi-fictional quality of autobiographies. As far as the diary goes, I colluded in a mistake about which I feel very bad.

I would have thought that the next step would be to wonder why this solitary diary was so important to Helene that she had proceeded to make it her own. The diary did I think become a double for Helene, which was the interpretive line I had taken in my biography; both Helene and Olden were infatuated with the identical Viennese actor, involved with married men, hostile to their mothers, etcetera.

Ever since I heard of Eissler's knowing about the issue of the diary, I have been waiting for the other shoe to drop publicly. I expected to hear it from an orthodox analyst in a professional journal. But I had underestimated the eagerness of some to publicize the psychoanalytic Kremlin's latest campaign.

As for the issue of Felix Deutsch's sexuality, my book contains evidence which appears in his correspondence. The two words that Baruch objects to ("another case") in connection with a passage in one of Helene's writings were spoken to me directly by her as I read over to her the whole paper. It is therefore not quite the "nonsense" that Baruch claims. Nor would the account I reconstructed of Felix's sexual history be at odds with his later becoming a beloved analyst.

One sentence in Baruch's review is outrageous: Roazen's "questions, I'm told, eventually had to be stopped by the family because Roazen's insistence upset Deutsch so much." The evasive "I'm told" speaks for itself. At no time did the family ever have to interfere with my interviewing Helene on any such grounds. They subsequently agreed with the *American Journal of Psychiatry* that I write the obituary of Helene.

In Baruch's last paragraph she alleges that in my book I ignore Eissler's contesting *Brother Animal*. On the contrary, I included in *Helene Deutsch*, among other recent new material, an eyewitness account of why Freud refused to analyze Tausk.

I think that knowledge of psychoanalysis is ill-served by blind defenses of an entrenched power center.

11. Ronald Steel had published a biography of Walter Lippmann which I and some others too had thought undermined Lippmann's genuine intellectual stature. Then in a review of a biography of William C. Bullitt, Steel cited a review by Erik H. Erikson which had originally appeared in the *New York Review of Books* but which was at odds with Erikson's final considered opinion. I was trying to call attention to the significance of Erikson's shift in position.

Erikson's Second Thoughts
New York Review of Books, March 16, 1989

Ronald Steel's otherwise excellent review of *So Close to Greatness: A Biography of William C. Bullitt* by Will Brownell and Richard N. Billings [NYR, Sept. 29] quotes two sentences from Erik H. Erikson's review of the Freud-Bullitt book on Woodrow Wilson that was widely influential at the time it first appeared in *The New York Review of Books* in 1967.

I would, however, like to call the interested reader's attention to the fact that the first of those sentences, which said that Freud could have written "almost nothing of what is now presented in print," was completely dropped by Erikson when in 1975 he reprinted the review in his *Life History and the Historical Moment*. Although in his book Erikson did not alert the reader to his changing ground, he did introduce major alterations to his *NYR* account of the collaboration between Freud and Bullitt. Although Erikson still thought the Freud-Bullitt book a bad one, he was now willing to see more of Freud's hand in it. A detailed discussion of all Erikson's alterations in his original *NYR* review can be found in my *Erik H. Erikson: The Power and Limits of a Vision*.[7]

12. Peter Gay, as I spokesman I think for psychoanalytic orthodoxy, had published an account of Freud's relations with his sister-in-law Minna for the Sunday *New York Times* Book Review. I thought it a good occasion for raising several issues connected with Gay's historywriting.

Of Sigmund and Minna
New York Times Sunday Book Review, April 9, 1989

Peter Gay's recent journalism, both in *Harper's* magazine and now in *The*

New York Times Book Review, seems to me too lighthearted.[8] He addresses himself to serious issues in a popular forum, and then when his mistakes are found out he retreats to the line that scholars should have known that the place of publication supposedly discounts the standards by which his arguments are to be evaluated.

A 1981 article of his in *Harper's* purported to be a discovery by Mr. Gay of a previously unknown 1900 book review of Freud's *Interpretation of Dreams.* Then we found out, in a Dec. 21, 1988 letter of Mr. Gay's that has been widely circulated among authorities on early psychoanalysis and created a furor, that he has written: "I must confess... although there is nothing to confess, that the whole thing is a hoax."

I do not know what to make of the errors that appear in his essay for *The Book Review.* He tells the reader in his second paragraph that he "expected no passionate passages" in the letters that Freud and his sister-in-law, Minna Bernays, exchanged. Yet in Mr. Gay's book *Freud* (1988) he told us that the creator of psychoanalysis "wrote some passionate letters to Minna Bernays." Does Mr. Gay not remember what he has just published?

In the course of his article Mr. Gay refers unflatteringly to Carl Jung, supposedly "too unreliable a witness." Historians, as opposed to religious believers, weigh evidence impartially. Mr. Gay is such a devotee of psychoanalytic orthodoxy that he does not seem to realize the implications of critical missing portions of the Freud-Minna correspondence. Although I have over the years been skeptical of stories of a liaison between Freud and Minna, Mr. Gay has now presented reason, in the disappearance of those letters, for me to reconsider the matter.

The main problem in his piece is the lack of explicitness about the possible culprit for the missing letters. If he is accusing Anna Freud or her brother Ernst, then Mr. Gay ought to say so. Twenty years ago I disclosed the tendentious editing of Freud's correspondence; the Freud family stopped it in 1974. But this new "tampering" is altogether on a fresh scale, and if unique would be telling. Anna Freud is no longer alive to defend herself. It would be proper to investigate the living before implicitly accusing the dead.

It is not true, as Mr. Gay maintains, that the letters "remained" at 20 Maresfield Gardens in Hampstead until the Freud Archives took possession of them; nor is Mr. Gay's account of how the letters got to the Library of Congress adequate. According to two former officials of the Freud Museum in London, neither of whom Mr. Gay took the time to question on the specific issue of the missing Freud-Minna letters, the correspondence went to the vault of the Freud solicitor during the renovations on the house; confidants of Anna Freud also had access to the letters after her death.

It is a sign of Mr. Gay's haste that although he maintains that there is a gap in the letters between 1893 and 1910, records at the Freud Museum indicate correspondence for the year 1898 was sent to the Library of Congress. The numbers on the letters, key evidence for the disappearance of documents, would not have been made by museum officials. I would myself have thought that Anna Freud was emotionally incapable of destroying such precious materials.

I can understand why Peter Gay "hurried" to Washington to read these letters; incest is a central theme in Freud's writings, and for that reason students of Freud have been preoccupied with his emotional involvement with Minna Bernays. But it seems to me peculiar for a historian to be so in quest of a scoop as to present the public with a superficial and inherently unsatisfactory account of the story.

13. The issue of the translations of Freud into English seemed to me to merit being addressed in the *Times Literary Supplement*.

Retranslating Freud
Times Literary Supplement, August 4-10, 1989

Freud's own knowledge of different languages was considerable, and he had some experience himself as a translator. Historians should be interested in the sophisticated latitude he accorded to those whom he approved as translators of his own works. The example of James Strachey in England could be fleshed out by different figures in other countries, and in languages besides English.

Meira Likierman repeats the idea that Freud "chose to describe the working of the mind in a deliberately simple German vocabulary," but erroneously includes the term "cathexis" among the "Greek and Latin words" which Freud himself did not employ.[9] I would like to point out that Strachey told me in an interview that although Freud had at first in the 1920s been somewhat doubtful about the choice of "cathexis," Strachey was justifiably proud that by the end of Freud's life he had himself incorporated that term within one of his German texts. In "Psychoanalysis"[10] Freud used the word "cathexis" in English in his original manuscript.

Strachey was scholarly enough to record that although from 1908 on Freud preserved his manuscripts, in the case of works that came out in Freud's lifetime Strachey worked on his translations almost entirely from published texts, and did not consult the original manuscripts. The excellent notes Strachey provided for each of Freud's papers have been translated into German for new editions of Freud.

It would be unfortunate, however, if the consequent limitations of Strachey's splendid edition, and the inevitably interpretive nature of any translation, were to lead to a fundamentalist quest for the so-called true Freud, instead of concentrating on a mature evaluation of the substance and validity of Freud's ideas themselves.

14. Freud's analysis of his daughter Anna has attracted enough attention for me to think that my own role in revealing this story deserves to be kept

straight. When the issue earlier had arisen in letters to the editor in the *TLS* about who had in print first revealed the existence of this analysis, I chose not to participate in the debate.

Anna's Analysis
London Review of Books, Oct. 26, 1989

Adam Phillips's review of Elisabeth Young-Bruehl's *Anna Freud: A Biography* seemed to me splendid and it occasions some thoughts on my part.[11] Twenty years ago, in my *Brother Animal*, I first publicly raised the matter of Freud having analysed his own daughter Anna (the analysis began in 1918, and not in 1920, as Phillips has it). Then again, in my *Freud and His Followers* (1975), I discussed the whole matter at greater length. In 1969 I knew that I was violating a taboo by opening up this issue, but I never realized, either in 1969 or 1975, that the silence over what Freud had done could nonetheless continue.

Until Young-Bruehl's biography there had never been any further extended discussion of the matter; no psychoanalytic journal, as far as I know, ever allowed the subject to get interpreted or explored further. It is typical of what I regard as the shockingly partisan nature of Young-Bruehl's new book that not only does she not credit me for having first revealed this historical incident (instead, she insults my work), but she also ignores everything else I wrote on the subject. As Anna Freud's official biographer, Young-Bruehl handles the analysis of Anna by her father with kid-gloves.

In this connection I would like to repeat a point I made in 1975. (Reviewers of books in this field sometimes claim to object to repetition, but in actuality there is no other way of getting across one's ideas since ideological considerations seem to drown out originality.) Among the many other reasons for Freud's doing what he did, which I have discussed in print already, I would like to single out one now; he was afraid of the damage that any other analyst would do to Anna. I do not know whether it violates any current popular taboo to suggest that analysis can do harm, but I daresay any experienced psychoanalyst would agree. I am not trying to defend what Freud did, but seeing how long it appears to take to get a scholarly dialogue going in this area I think it worthwhile bringing up this matter once again.

15. Since both Jeffrey M. Masson and Malcolm have publicly disapproved of my work, when I have criticized them too it has seemed to me defensive.

Hindsight on Review
The Toronto Globe and Mail, Dec. 28, 1990

A book reviewer's central ethical obligation is to provide readers with both the context and content of the book under scrutiny. Paula Caplan charges me with "something deeply unethical" in my failing to mention Jeffrey Mousaieff Masson's paragraph taking a poke at me in the course of my review of his book *Final Analysis: The Making and Unmaking of a Psychoanalyst*.[12]

Without, I hope, sounding hopelessly arrogant, after my publishing in this area for more than 20 years I consider it virtually impossible for any competent work to be undertaken on this subject without referring in some way to my own research. Dr. Masson did send me a personally inscribed copy of his unfortunate previous book ("in spite of all our differences, with respect for what you've done"), which incidentally came with a blurb on the jacket endorsing it from Dr. Caplan. Readers may be amused to learn that Dr. Caplan is, out of alphabetical order, the first person listed in the acknowledgements to Dr. Masson's *Final Analysis*.

Networking is not necessarily confined to any one gender; not only did Kate Millet applaud Dr. Masson's *Final Analysis*, but he did the same for her last book. Although mentioning Dr. Masson's muddled reference to me would have been beside the point in recapitulating his general argument, in hindsight I do now regret not having succeeded in working the issue into my review.

16. The following two letters effectively took up two weeks of my writing life. A prominent journalist, Michelle Lansberg, married to a former Premier of Ontario, had been caught by me red-handed in tendentious errors. I had been living in Toronto since 1971, and she probably never anticipated that any of her readers would simply dial Duluth, Minnesota to check on her figures. However, she was able to exert enough clout at her newspaper, the *Toronto Star*, to succeed initially in getting my letter cut in half. After I vehemently protested over the phone to various editors at the paper, they brought out the second half of my original letter as a separate publication. This division of my original letter, and the mid-week day when the latter part finally appeared, weakened the effective force of my argument. It is worth recording, I also believe, that civil liberties in Canada are considerably weaker than in the States.

A Good Cause Hardly Justified Any Means
Toronto Star, July 13, 1991

In "Community Mobilizes Against Wife Abusers" Michele Landsberg refers to how Duluth, Minnesota, handles wife battering.[13]

The lesson she draws for us to imitate in Ontario is disturbing.

"When Duluth police are summoned to a 'domestic dispute,' and they have reason to believe the man used or threatened violence, they're under orders to handcuff him at once and take him to jail overnight. No victim-blaming is allowed. Officers may not ask the woman what she did to 'provoke' the beating; they are not allowed to coax, mediate or act as referees."

From what I have been able to learn, the system in Duluth appears to be more humane than what Ms. Landsberg recommends.

The kind of mandatory arrest she writes approvingly of seems to me a form of dictatorship. I thought people are supposed to be presumed innocent until proven guilty.

"Every day," Landsberg tells us, "the papers are filled with ghastly stories of women injured or dying at the hands of brutal partners." All the more reason to be conscientious about facts. Landsberg's irresponsibility will lead to questioning whether these accounts get written by journalists with her own standards of accuracy.

True figures about domestic abuse are appalling in themselves. But a good cause hardly justifies any means. Landsberg is entitled to authoritarian political views, but owes an apology for misleading the public with false numbers.

Duluth Wife-Abuse Conviction Rate Disputed
Toronto Star, July 23, 1991

In her "Community Mobilizes Against Wife Abusers" Michele Landsberg had started off by claiming that "one out of every 23 men in Duluth, Minn. has been arrested and convicted of wife battering." After telephoning Duluth, I had found out that during the year 1990, there were 211 arrests for domestic violations in a city of 89,000; not all the cases have yet come to trial, but the figure for convictions would have to be lower.

Then Landsberg in her piece "Foundation Helps Groups Gain Better Life for Females"[14] has scattered fresh figures, some equally precise-sounding. Until she clears up the Duluth matter, why should anyone not suspect further sleights-of-hand? In her piece about Duluth, for example, she had maintained that in circumstances of spousal abuse "when the cases come to court, more than 80 per cent of the men are found guilty. . . ." But when I looked into the matter, I found out that there were two types of cases that wound up in court: misdemeanors and felonies.

While the first and more frequent type of offence had a conviction rate as high as Lansberg reported, she had neglected to mention the other kind, where the rate of conviction is so far less than half as much.

17. Whatever else people choose to write about Freud, the moving circumstances of Freud's final illness seem to me to deserve the utmost of decent respect.

Freud's Final Weeks Filled With Torment
Toronto Star, May 23, 1992

Phyllis Grosskurth's review of *The Diary of Sigmund Freud* maintains that he continued "to see patients until the very end."[15]

It has been well-established ever since 1957 that Freud, having borne up under cancer of the jaw since 1923, went on with his psychoanalytic treatment of patients until the end of July, 1939. He finally died on Sept. 23, 1939.

Those final several weeks of his life were full of immense torment, such that the founder of psychoanalysis could no longer maintain his profession. Toward the end, his cheek, when the jaw was otherwise inoperable, had to be cut from the outside, and he smelled so badly that his favorite dog would not go near him.

A mosquito-netting had to be put around his sick-bay so that the flies would not be attracted to the wound. When he could no longer read, he called it quits, and asked his personal physician for an easy death.

Yet Grosskurth also falsely maintains that Freud "continued to write... until the very end." She even says that Freud "died quietly." Did Othello die quietly? Or King Lear? I recommend that Grosskurth use her capacities for scholarly research, which are genuine, in some other area than that of Freud's life and heroic character.

18. Even though one particular legend connected to Freud and the Gestapo has long since been exploded, it still keeps reappearing in the literature. This story has such "legs" that it has gone on being repeated.

No Such Words
London Review of Books, July 23, 1993

D. J. Enright's interesting review of J. P. Stern's *The Heart of Europe* (*LRB*, 11 June) states how "an anecdote that catches Stern's fancy has to do with Freud, who when he left Vienna in 1938 was asked to sign a statement declaring that he had not been ill-treated; like a parting guest writing in a hotel visitors' book, he added the comment: "I can recommend the Gestapo most highly to everyone.""[15] This tale has been in print at least since the Fifties, yet it is now established that the story is a myth. Perhaps Freud commented, in conversation or in letters, something to the same effect. But the Gestapo piece of paper contains no such words.

19. Here I was to be partially corrected, since an expert on such matters (Natalie Robbins) was able to send me information from Lippmann's FBI file that she had just used in her *Alien Ink: The FBI's War on Freedom of Expression.*[17]

J. Edgar Hoover's Files
Sunday *New York Times* Book Review, Sept. 13, 1992

Alfred Kazin, in reviewing Scott Donaldson's biography of Archibald MacLeish, is right to be cautious in this statement: "The 600-page F. B. I. file on [MacLeish], Mr. Donaldson tells us, is the longest on any American writer."[18]

There is a much larger F. B. I. file on Wilhelm Reich, which has been referred to in the literature. There is an equally huge file on Herbert Marcuse, which to my knowledge has not yet been utilized. A file of approximately 600 pages is available about Erich Fromm, which remains unexplored. And it will come as no surprise that Lillian Hellman and Dashiell Hammett have considerable dossiers.

If Mr. Donaldson were to take a narrow, biological view of what constitutes an American writer, I think it worth pointing out for the sake of readers and scholars that several hundred F. B. I. pages are extant about Walter Lippmann. No one has explored in print the information about Lippmann that J. Edgar Hoover collected.

20. Under most circumstances authors are better off not replying to critical reviews – that is at least the standard and most widely accepted view of the matter. Here is a response of mine to an author pained by a critical review of my own about a biography of Henry A. Murray, which I think substantiates the position that writers do best by ignoring critiques. But I have myself, as the reader can tell, not always been able to live up to this high principle.

Paul Roazen Replies
The American Scholar, Autumn 1993

I regret how thin-skinned Forrest G. Robinson has been about my review of his biography of Henry ("Harry") A. Murray.

Five blurbs, all written by distinguished people, appear on the jacket copy of *Love's Story Told*. Robinson now chooses to quote from two of these pre-publication comments. I will leave it to others to determine if this praise deserves to qualify as among the book's "earliest reviewers," and whether there is something unnecessary (or unseemly) about such self-promotion now. I had indicated in my review that "perhaps those who knew Harry better than I" will find this biography "more successful."

Robinson's preface tells us that when he "first broached the topic of the biography with Murray in the spring of 1970, he allowed – with a gentle irony of his own – that there was little to tell. Nothing much to it, he said, except for a secret love affair of more than forty years. We never looked back." I think this was a mistake, although I detect a subtle difference in Robinson's new quotation from Murray. Robinson's own account of the love affair between Harry and Christiana Morgan makes him sound selfish and destructive, and I did "not think that this book has done for Harry what he deserves." To repeat the gist of my complaint, *Love's StoryTold* underplays Harry's most creative sides, and especially the ideas he and his co-workers developed.

No words in Robinson's preface concern the dates of his composition of the book. The reader is told that Robinson completed "nearly a hundred interviews, more than half of them in the early1970s." After I looked at the notes to *Love's Story Told*, it did seem to me "as if a great deal of the primary research was done in the early 1970s." Since the almost twenty years of Harry's second marriage got so little attention in *Love's Story Told*,

I mistakenly thought the book read "as if Robinson had written his book in the early 1970s and then put it aside pending Harry's death."

Such a hypothesis seemed to me a generous way of making sense of a striking incongruity in the text itself. We are told on page 294 that Murray's colleague Clyde Kluckhohn had "his own carefully guarded secret life." The only explanation to that mystery can be found in a citation at the back of the book attached to the earlier page 230: "Kluckhohn's homosexuality was no secret to many in the Harvard community." The evidence for this proposition about Kluckhohn, at odds with the other mention of his "secret life," came from a 1985 interview, which made me wonder when the main text got constructed. It seemed to me that Robinson's thinking, if not his writing, was chronologically peculiar. But the news that he started composing the book in 1990 does not absolve him from the responsibility for failing to avoid a contradiction, nor for having neglected to tell why Kluckhohn's anthropological work mattered.

In my review I suspected that Harry himself might find me too puritanical, or "fussy," as Robinson now says. If *Love's Story Told* is to be the beginning of a literature on Murray and the circles he moved in, well and good. But I fear that a future generation will be so titillated by the details about sadomasochism between Harry and Morgan as to downplay, as in my opinion *Love's Story Told* unfortunately does, why Harry's accomplishments, as well as his tragic frustrations, matter to the life of the mind.

Love's Story Told has many remarkable merits, which perhaps I insufficiently alluded to in my review. I hope my comments now are not more one-dimensional as I try to cope with the author's defensiveness.

21. Here I confess to a bit of literary naughtiness. Nobody self-preservative would normally try tangling with Janet Malcolm in print. But in the midst of her legal troubles with Jeffrey Masson I felt pretty sure that her lawyers would insist on her staying silent in the face of any letter from me. At any rate she did not respond to this letter, which I think sets forth what I see as the central flaws in her outlook. Malcolm's account of Sylvia Plath and Ted Hughes in Malcolm's *Silent Woman* provided a distillation of her journalistic credo. Joe McGinnis, who also had once been attacked by Malcolm, independently of me also wrote in.

Crossing Swords
Sunday *New York Times* Book Review, April 17, 1994

In Caryn James's excellent review of Janet Malcolm's *Silent Woman*, Ms. Malcolm is quoted in favor of biographical bias: "The pose of fair-mindedness, the charade of evenhandedness, the striking of an attitude of detachment can never be more than rhetorical ruses."

At the risk of sounding wild or old-fashioned, I have to insist that such words are devastating, and constitute a betrayal of the struggle toward the ideal of objectivity, however elusive truthfulness must inevitably remain. The alternative to opposing Ms. Malcolm seems to me to endorse propagandizing, an art in which I can testify that Ms. Malcolm has become a specialist.

It seems only fair to admit that I am writing now having twice been the butt of Ms. Malcolm's glossy sensationalism. One of my books, for example, comes up arbitrarily within the early pages of the artifice of molding Ms. Malcolm's *In the Freud Archives*. Since Ms. Malcolm has such a complicated ideological agenda, despite her apparent candor, I think she rarely puts her cards on the table. So I am not surprised to find now that she is romanticizing Ted Hughes. He had the good sense (which I belatedly came to myself) not to risk a meeting with Ms. Malcolm. When she was writing so much about psychoanalysis, her devilish sparkle was always directed not only toward a defense of the powers that be in control of archival material, but in behalf of the big battalions in general.

I do now fail to understand how your reviewer does not link more directly Ms. Malcolm's attack on Joe McGinniss, for supposedly betraying Jeffrey MacDonald, to the theme of self-destructiveness. Ms. Malcolm's legal troubles with Jeffrey Masson, and her early allegation that he was his own worst enemy, have attracted journalistic attention, which ought not to be ignored in evaluating her purposes in *The Silent Woman*.

Mr. Masson's lawyers will presumably have to restrain what he might otherwise be buoyantly eager to say in his reaction to Ms. James's review. (To be fair, he and I have been crossing swords for some years.) But for the sake of humdrum academics like me who daily strive to overcome their natural biases, Ms. Malcolm's proposition that the appeal of biography is based on "voyeurism and busybodyism" is an insult, based on pop psychoanalysis, to the reading public as well as scholars. In truth, biography remains a chief means by which history gets communicated from one generation to the next.

Ms. James would seem to be correct that Ms. Malcolm has made the reporter into an "antihero," which then makes relevant the immortal words of Hegel: "No man is a hero to his valet; not, however, because the man is not a hero, but because the valet is a valet."

22. Sylvia Fraser is a major literary figure in Canada, where I lived for over twenty years. In keeping with how I took issue with Malcolm, and I hope in line with everything that I have written, I thought it worth-while trying to correct the record in contrast to the licenses that Fraser had allowed herself to take.

Freud and Incest
Saturday Night, May 1994

Although I have spent thirty years researching the founder of psychoanalysis, I do not recognize Sylvia Fraser's Freud.

It is not true, as Fraser alleges, that in the early period of his work Freud was "using free association." It is also false that "Freud's humble about-face" on the subject of incest "was lauded by his peers as an act of great courage...." The truth is that Freud publicly disguised his reversal for years, so that it passed virtually unnoticed when he finally admitted to having too readily accepted the hypothesis of incest. The most credible modern scholars now believe Freud was guilty of suggesting the possibility of incest to credulous people in trouble.

There is no scholarly evidence whatever to support the idea that Freud ever had "a breakdown" involving anything like "hysterical paralysis of his writing hand" or other symptoms Fraser has cooked up for him. It was not the case that, during the fifteen years he suffered from cancer of the jaw and continued to practice his profession, the illness succeeded in "almost robbing him of the power of speech...." The decision to abandon the seduction theory was not one that "haunted" Freud "all his life." Nor did Freud ever "beg" his physician to end his suffering.

No-one would contest that incest is a serious issue, but Fraser has done the subject a disservice by wholly distorting the history of Freud and his interest in the matter.

23. I suppose I should have let this review of a book I edited slide by, but it appeared in a professional monthly that I have written for fairly steadily. Since I have staked out the historical territory connected with Tausk, I thought it worth-while defending the value of his work. Oddly enough, the reviewer I was criticizing, Richard Chessick, came from the ranks of the psychoanalytic Left, which made his acceptance of orthodox platitudes about Tausk all the more galling.

Returning to the Work of Tausk
The American Journal of Psychiatry, September 1995

I belatedly saw the book review by Richard Chessick, M.D., Ph.D., of Tausk's work *Sexuality, War, and Schizophrenia: Collected Psychoanalytic Papers*[19], of which I was the editor.

This review seems to me to express, alas, a bias that is characteristic of too much psychoanalytic orthodoxy. The five references to the review give a specious display of erudition. The first reference appropriately lists my work, *Brother Animal: The Story of Freud and Tausk*. The problem here is that Dr. Chessick does not seem aware that a second edition of the book came out in 1990, with a new introduction that brings the reader up to date.[20] The story of the reception my work first received in 1969, and how powerful figures in psychoanalysis sought to discredit my book, is a tale important in its own right.

Instead of pursuing the task of evaluating evidence, as is characteristic of serious scholarship, Dr. Chessick falls back on the work of Peter Gay[21], without mentioning any of the literature that has been critical of Gay's orthodoxy.

Had Dr. Chessick carefully read the notes to my introduction to Tausk's papers, he would have known of the second edition of *Brother Animal*. That new introduction is significant enough for it to have already appeared in French.

Academics with a devotion to the subject of the history of psychoanalysis are unlikely to share Dr. Chessick's belief that Gay's book "appears to be more objective and less acrimonious." Gay achieves the appearance of calm, for instance, by completely failing to mention the name of someone like Wilhelm Reich. Gay's text contains a bibliographical essay that trashes virtually everyone in the field, save for those who are devout defenders of orthodoxy.

Dr. Chessick's conclusion that "Tausk's creative talents were largely wasted because of his inability to study any subject in depth" merely echoes part of Freud's lengthy obituary of Tausk, without including any of the glowing points that Freud also had to make about Tausk's achievements.

Psychiatrists should know that it was on the occasion of Tausk's presentation of his work on the "so-called war psychoses" that Freud first presented his ideas about mourning and melancholia. This is significant because when Freud came to publish "Mourning and Melancholia" he chose to cite a different paper of Tausk's that was interesting in its own right but one that Dr. Chessick does not allude to in his review.

Dr. Chessick's conception of what will, or will not, be of interest to clinicians betrays a pessimistic view of how ignorant of academic matters practitioners can afford to be.

24. For reasons that continue to escape me, even many scholars on the Holocaust prefer to think that Hitler failed to come to power democratically. As a political scientist I know that viewpoint to be false, and I consider it in principle bad for democrats to under-estimate the public's potential — almost anywhere — for voting fascism into office. I had made the reference to the legal Nazi accession to power in the course of reviewing a book about Hannah Arendt's relation to Martin Heidegger. The reader who wrote in to protest provided the statistic about the German electorate having been 45% pro-Hitler.

Soft-Hearted Hannah
The American Scholar, Winter 1997

Liberal democrats have had a hard time accepting the fact that by comparative political standards Germany in 1933 wanted Hitler. Of course in any parliamentary system no one votes directly for the future chancellor or prime minister. But 45 percent is an immense proportion of the electorate, more than many American presidents have received, and a larger mandate than most parliamentary winners elsewhere have earned. It might seem comforting to think of Hitler as having been "appointed," but in the long run it is more dangerous for friends of popular government to dodge the enthusiasm for Nazism.

25. Through a bureaucratic mix-up at the offices of the *New York Review of Books* this letter, although originally accepted for publication, failed ever to appear. I was in touch privately with the historian Carl Schorske, and I gathered that he had no objection to my letter coming out. His response to me struck me as a model of scholarly modesty. Since I have been for years concerned with John Stuart Mill as a key figure in modern political liberalism, especially in connection with Freud, that accounts for my reprinting my letter here. The late Professor John Robson, a great Mill expert, helped me draft my letter, and he wanted it in print.

Carl Schorske, "Freud's Egyptian Dig"
Unpublished, 1993

Carl E. Schorske's interesting "Freud's Egyptian Dig" maintains: "On Brentano's recommendation, Gomperz enlisted Freud to translate some of John Stuart Mill's most radical essays, including 'The Subjection of Women' and 'Socialism'."[22]

There is a mistake here, since Freud translated not "The Subjection of Women" (1869) but the earlier "Enfranchisement of Women" (1851), written by Harriet Taylor.

A history of confusion about Freud's translation of Mill's volume got started in a published letter of Freud's to his future wife, and was compounded by Ernest Jones's biography of Freud. Jones says: "Three of Mill's essays were concerned with social problems: the labour question, the enfranchisement of women, and socialism. In the preface Mill said that the greatest part of these was the work of his wife. The fourth, by Mill himself, was on Grote's Plato."[23] Jones is unreliable here, since only the piece on enfranchisement of women should be attributed to Harriet Taylor; all the rest are by Mill, and were written after her death.

The relationship between Freud and English thought is important enough, as Schorske himself argues, not to have further mix-ups in the literature.

26. This final letter of mine was designed to deal as non-combatively as possible with a Boston psychoanalyst who, almost twenty years after my biography of Helene Deutsch appeared, returned to criticize a matter that I had thought long settled. I hope that the mildness of my response to how I evidently had continued to be stalked by orthodoxy, combined with the generosity with which Schorske reacted to my correcting him in my letter #25, serves to make a suitably unpolemical conclusion to this chapter.

A Correction
Journal of Clinical Psychoanalysis (Vol. 12, in press)
In response to Sanford Gifford's "Authorship of An Adolescent Diary, 1900-04: Helene Deutsch or Christine Olden?", I am baffled.[24] Starting in 1986 I have, in reconsidering my 1985 biography of Helene Deutsch[25], publicly acknowledged the mistake in attributing the diary's authorship to Helene Deutsch. I cut out the 10 pages about the diary for the French and German editions of my biography, but when the 2nd edition of the biography in English appeared in 1992 it would have cost me some $10,000 to omit the chapter about the diary and reset the whole book. Along with other new information and biographical reflections prompted by hindsight I discussed in the new Introduction for the 2nd edition the problem of the diary, and how I had gone wrong.[26]

I would have thought it unnecessary further to flog a historical dead horse. In 1978, besides the legal contracts Helene Deutsch signed with me authorizing me to publish her biography, her collected psychoanalytic papers, her first book on female sexuality, as well as her letters, she also signed a formal agreement that I publish her diary as a young girl. (Once I had had the diary manuscript professionally translated, and we discussed it, I decided it was not publishable; the contract, besides dealing with the question of royalties, had said "Deutsch releases Roazen from and waives any and all claim, demand or liability whatsoever in connection with the writing, publication and sale of the Book.") Despite the unfortunate mix-up about the authorship of that diary, I did eventually bring out a book of her papers[27] and a fresh edition of that early text on female psychology[28], both of which have also appeared in translation abroad. Readers should be able to judge for themselves whether I have, long ago, adequately dealt with the issue of the diary.

Real work entails, in my view, a willingness to engage in controversy. Although acrimony in itself should seem undesirable, it is often necessary actively to combat what one genuinely regards as mischievous. As long as the occasions for sometimes rather barbed comments do not get out of hand, the life of the mind can be enhanced by such efforts to achieve enlightenment. When I read book reviews, I often turn first to the letters to the editor section, since one is likely to find there legitimate differences of opinion without the false courtesies so often associated with the civilized manners of most book reviewing.

NOTES

1 Kurt R. Eissler, "Letter to the Editor," *International Journal of Psychoanalysis*, Vol. 62 (1981), pp. 371-72.

2 Eissler, *Talent and Genius, op. cit.*, p. 12.
3 Paul Roazen, "Reading, Writing, and Memory: Dr. K. R. Eissler's Thinking," *Contemporary Psychoanalysis*, Vol. 14 (1978), pp. 345-53.
4 Ernest Jones, *The Life and Work of Sigmund Freud*, Vol. 3 (New York, Basic Books, 1957), p. 208.
5 Harold Blum, *New York Review of Books*, July 17, 1986.
6 Elaine Hoffman Baruch, "Truth and Fiction," *Partisan Review* (1986).
7 Paul Roazen, *Erik H. Erikson: The Power and Limits of a Vision* (New York, Free Press, 1976, Northvale, New Jersey, Jason Aronson, 1997), pp. 13, 201-203.
8 Peter Gay, "Sigmund and Minna? The Biographer as Voyeur," *New York Times* Sunday Book Review, Jan. 29, 1989.
9 Meira Likierman, "NB," *Times Literary Supplement*, July 7-13, 1989.
10 "Psychoanalysis," *Standard Edition*, Vol. 20, p. 266.
11 Adam Phillips, "Review of Young-Bruehl's Anna Freud," *London Review of Books*, Sept. 14, 1989.
12 Paula Caplan, "Letter to the Toronto *Globe and Mail*," Dec. 8, 1990.
13 Michele Landsberg, "Community Moblizes Against Wife Abusers," *Toronto Star*, July 6, 1991.
14 Michele Landsberg, "Foundation Helps Groups Gain Better Life For Females," *Toronto Star*, July 13, 1991.
15 Phyllis Grosskurth, "Review of Molnar, ed., *The Diary of Sigmund Freud*," *Toronto Star*, May 16, 1992.
16 D. J. Enright, "Review of J. P. Stern's *The Heart of Europe*, *London Review of Books*, June 11, 1993.
17 Natalie Robbins, *Alien Ink: The FBI's War on Freedom of Expression* (New York, Morrow, 1992).
18 Alfred Kazin, "Review of Scott Donaldson's *Archibald MacLeish: An American Life*," *New York Times* Sunday Book Review, July 12, 1992.
19 Victor Tausk, *Sexuality, War, and Schizophrenia: Collected Psychoanalytic Papers*, ed. Paul Roazen (New Brunswick, N.J., Transaction Publishers, 1991).
20 Paul Roazen, *Brother Animal: The Story of Freud and Tausk*, op. cit.
21 Peter Gay, *Freud: A Life for Our Time* (New York, W. W. Norton, 1988).
22 Carl E. Schorske, "Freud's Egyptian Dig," *New York Review of Books*, May 27, 1993.
23 Jones, *The Life and Work of Sigmund Freud*, Vol. 1, 2nd revised edition (London, Hogarth Press, 1954).
24 Sanford Gifford, "Authorship of an Adolescent Diary, 1900-1904: Helene Deutsch or Christine Olden?", *Journal of Clinical Psychoanalysis*, Vol. 10 (2001), pp. 293-98.
25 Paul Roazen, *Helene Deutsch: A Psychoanalyst's Life* (New York, Doubleday, 1985).
26 Paul Roazen, new Introduction, 2nd edition, *Helene Deutsch: A Psychoanalyst's Life* (New Brunswick, N.J., Transaction Publishers, 1992).
27 Paul Roazen, ed., Helene Deutsch, *The Therapeutic Process, the Self, and Female Psychology: Collected Psychoanalytic Papers*, with an Introduction (New Brunswick, N.J., Transaction Publishers, 1991).
28 Paul Roazen, ed., Helene Deutsch, *Psychoanalysis of the Sexual Functions of Women*, with an Introduction (London, Karnac, 1991).

9

FREUD'S CORRESPONDENCES WITH FERENCZI AND ABRAHAM

Although the third and final volume of the Freud-Ferenczi letters appeared only in 2000, we are still at an early stage of understanding Freud as a correspondent. Even though so far there are over a dozen books of Freud's letters in English, there is still much more to come in the future: for example, the long-awaited correspondence with Freud's future wife Martha has still not been published. And other fresh books of Freud letters can be expected to be steadily appearing over the next couple of decades. Further, new editions of Freud's already published letters to Lou Andreas-Salomé, Oscar Pfister, and Arnold Zweig are required since unfortunately the original editions of these three correspondences were expurgated on no consistent principles. Although a future generation will able to be more secure in its assessment of Freud's letter-writing, I think that the Freud-Ferenczi correspondence, and in particular this last volume, will continue to be of outstanding interest. (I have found it more absorbing than either the Freud letters to Fliess or the Freud-Jung correspondence, but that could be a distortion of interest due to my own subjective response or a consequence of my own particular expertise.)

It is already the case that the work of Sandor Ferenczi (1873-1933), who was Freud's chief disciple in Hungary and someone for many years (starting in 1908) dear to his heart, has given rise to a whole separate literature. Judith Dupont's excellent Introduction here makes the point that Ferenczi's approach was that "of a therapist who sought above all to treat. Freud's own approach was something else entirely. He wished to understand; it was fundamentally knowledge, science, that interested him."[1] And so Ferenczi has recently succeeded in giving rise to a whole branch of psychotherapeutic teachings. Dupont also pertinently remarks that "of course the debate between analysts for whom a cure is an extra benefit and those for whom therapy is what matters (theory being the extra benefit) is still unresolved."[2] Several books have already come out about Ferenczi, and some texts have even appeared abroad about the history of psychoanalysis in Hungary; I would expect the full publication of the Freud-Ferenczi letters will do something to encourage further work on the whole Hungarian tradition in psychotherapeutic matters, about which altogether too little remains known today.

One of the central objectives to the initial project of publishing the Freud-Ferenczi letters has been definitively to rehabilitate Ferenczi's reputation against the legend that has seen him as someone whose final so-called mental illness interfered with his relationship with Freud. Freud's biographer Ernest Jones, himself analyzed by Ferenczi, had in 1957 made public charges against Ferenczi's emotional stability that have taken almost half a century to correct. Freud had been generally inclined to invoke analytic diagnoses to account for the most serious disagreements that his students had with him. But what might have been a private judgment on Freud's part became, in the instance of Jones on Ferenczi, blown up into an *ad hominem* accusation that Ferenczi's innovations were to be ignored. Even today we find literature written under orthodox analytic inspiration too ready to invoke Ferenczi's pernicious anemia, which ultimately killed him, instead of trying to absorb the merits of his alternatives to the way Freud had himself proceeded. The evidence in this third volume of the Freud-Ferenczi letters should provide the grounds for once and for all settling as a despicable canard Jones's contention that Ferenczi's supposedly scandalous ideas deserved to be put aside. To disagree with Freud was terribly painful for Ferenczi, but the final difficulties between Freud and Ferenczi cannot be written-off only as a product of the madness that Jones once claimed for Ferenczi. Fairness in intellectual history is a more laborious process than one might imagine, but the re-establishment of Ferenczi's legitimate standing has been the one great success story in the historiography of psychoanalysis with which I have over the years been proud to be associated.

But what interests me most now is what can be learned that is new in Vol. 3 of the Freud-Ferenczi letters. I confess that I was almost stopped cold by an early paragraph in a 1920 letter of Freud's about Eugenia Sokolnicka. (She was Polish, from Warsaw, and had been analyzed by Freud in 1913-14; she briefly was Andre Gide's analyst and helped establish psychoanalysis in France before finally killing herself in 1934.) By 1920 she was being treated by Ferenczi. Freud indicated that he could not stand her; although it was common practice in those days for analysts to continue their analyses while on summer holidays, Freud wrote to Ferenczi:

> Don't let yourself resolve to take Sokolnicka along on vacation. She has always been repugnant to me, despite undeniable talent.

Her...analysis seems quite excellent to me; the therapeutic prospects should be good. For you know she always held onto her men, not out of love but rather out of unsatisfied anger, and you gave her the possibility of finally getting this affect out. But she also won't let go of you so soon. I don't consider her a paranoia but a basically disgusting person; she doesn't want to see now that she has already become an old woman. In that there is little to be done, and the development of quite crazy [*meschuggener*] traits can hardly be impeded.[3]

It is true that Freud's outburst had been preceded by a letter containing Ferenczi's various complaints about problems in analyzing her. Nonetheless Ferenczi continued to treat her (she had started practicing in Paris), and also reported to Freud later in 1924 that Ferenczi was taking her along on holiday as a patient. Ferenczi's immense clinical tolerance, and his disagreements with Freud on this score, found its most systematic expression in Ferenczi's important *Clinical Diary*[4], which only appeared in print decades after his death. I cannot forget interviewing someone in the mid-1960s, at the time Ferenczi's reputation was still at low ebb, who reported of Ferenczi that he was memorable as "the milk of human kindness."

Aside from the issue of Freud's capacity for clinical intolerances, I was struck in this volume of letters by Freud's unrelieved hostility toward all things American. When Ferenczi toyed with the idea of moving to the States, Freud was apt to interpret it as a sign of Ferenczi's continuing emotional attachment to his stepdaughter Elma, who had married an American. Freud came down hard against Ferenczi going there, on the grounds, among other points, that "you would feel bad in America without pupils and friends, in an extremely unfree society which really knows only the hunt for the dollar."[5] (Ferenczi did, for example, come over for some lectures and the training of candidates.) In the past it has seemed to me that there was evidence that Freud used America, the source of his best-paying patients, for purposes of his personal projections. But in addition I think there are grounds for thinking, amidst all the myriad list of Freud's various objections to America, that Freud's racial prejudices also played a key role. In 1925 we find Freud writing Ferenczi: "It would be interesting to know where the American newspapers get their wealth of fabricated news. I recently offended an American with the suggestion that the Statue of Liberty in New York harbor should be replaced by a monkey holding up a Bible. I.e., I tried; he didn't seem to understand me at all."[6]

Now Freud did not like acknowledging his dependencies, and American wealth had already seemed to be seducing away students like Otto Rank; also, Freud was irritated by the American opposition to the practice of lay analysis. But in addition to all the rational (as well as irrational) grounds for Freud's anti-Americanism, I think the issue of race has to be accorded its proper place. Rank had pointed out in a 1941 book that Freud had expressed his conviction about the futility of individual psychotherapy in terms of "the white-washing of a negro."[7] When Freud objected to Franz Alexander's moving to the States in the 1930s, it is clear from recently released interviews of Kurt Eissler's with Alexander that Freud considered America as Indian territory that would soon be overwhelmed numerically by blacks. It is in the context of various remarks of Freud's, reflecting racial convictions, that I think that passage of Freud's about replacing the statue of liberty with a "monkey" holding a Bible needs to be understood. (Freud's hostility to Christianity and religion also took multiple forms, including his cooperation with William C. Bullitt in their critique of President Woodrow Wilson.)

Alongside with what these Freud-Ferenczi letters have to teach about Freud's clinical approach, as well as his attitude toward America, I think that we find most strikingly here his torment about the difficulties associated with the loss of Rank. Now Jones's version had it that Rank was merely another traitor in the history of psychoanalysis, someone supposedly Freud had over-estimated. (Jones also publicly accused Rank of having been mentally ill, and Jones did this on more than one occasion.) Those I met who knew Freud and Rank, though, testified to how terribly painful it was for Freud to have to give up someone whose creativity Freud had done so much to encourage. Freud's genuine agony about Rank comes through in writing to Ferenczi:

> I don't understand Rank at all anymore...For fifteen years I have known him, tenderly concerned, obliging, discreet, absolutely dependable, just as prepared to accept suggestions as he was uninhibited in working up his own ideas, on my side in all contentious matters, without inner compulsion, so I thought...Now, who is the real Rank, the one I have known for fifteen years, or the one whom Jones has wanted to show me for years?[8]

Although the sequence of events is still not widely acknowledged, the emotional crisis over Rank had been set off by Freud's first getting his jaw cancer in 1923; up until then Freud had considered Rank his successor, but Rank's reliance on Freud was threatened by the upheaval associated with Freud's illness. At the same time that Rank had to adjust himself to the prospect that Freud might die, Freud was forced to face newspaper reports that he was dying and that Rank was considered his psychoanalytic heir. And then Freud did not die, but went on to live with that cancer; in the meantime, however, Rank had emotionally already separated himself off because of the threatened loss of his leader. In all this subtle tangle of tragic emotions, we find Freud in these letters also blaming Rank's young wife "Tola" for what had happened: "Something is happening with him under the influence of the ambitious little woman."[9]

That 1923 first cancer of Freud's also was associated with Freud's dismissal of his personal physician then, Felix Deutsch, who was although still only an internist also married to the analyst Helene Deutsch. Freud consulted with Felix Deutsch when Freud first spotted the growth in his mouth; one of the grounds for Freud's choosing to turn to Felix Deutsch then was that he had recently accepted Freud's recommendation of Siegfried Bernfeld as Felix Deutsch's analyst. Freud subsequently felt his trust had been misplaced, in that Felix Deutsch had not only proceeded to deceive Freud about the nature of his illness, but not unnaturally under the circumstances also chattered to his analyst Bernfeld, who in turn, Freud felt, had also been indiscreet about the illness. Freud's fury about Felix Deutsch comes through clearly in Freud's writing to Ferenczi in the summer of 1924:

> I gave up Felix Deutsch as my physician, told him so, and since then have received two long letters from him. The surprising impression from his behavior and utterances is that he has to be counted among the constitutionally *stupid*, a diagnosis to which one does not resort often enough. I have encountered unseemly indiscretions with him; in addition to that, he constantly brags about his intention to deceive me as to the nature of my illness.[10]

On this issue connected with Felix Deutsch I think the notes are hopeless although I fear their length may give the illusionary impression of being authoritative. We are told:

> Dr. Felix Deutsch (1884-1964), husband of Helene (née Rosenbach). *Privatdozent* for internal medicine at the University of Vienna and director of a clinic for organ neuroses; one of the pioneers of psychosomatic medicine. He was a member of the Vienna [Psychoanalytic] Society (1922-1938), in analysis with Siegfried Bernfeld and under supervision with Otto Rank. Deutsch was Freud's personal physician, who concealed the diagnosis of Freud's cancer from him out of the fear that he would commit suicide, whereupon Freud, enraged, replaced him with Max Schur. In 1935 he immigrated to Boston, where he served as a training analyst (from 1951 to 1954 he was president of the Society there), and he taught at Harvard University, among other things.[11]

Now this editorial note reduces what was a terribly complicated human dilemma down to what sounds to me like soap opera. Freud did not, "enraged," in any way replace Felix Deutsch with Max Schur. This very volume of letters to Ferenczi records that by 1926 Freud was relying on Ludwig Braun as his personal physician. Schur did not come into the situation as a doctor until 1929, and he was chosen then not by Freud himself so much as by the "camarilla" of significant women analysts in Freud's world, mainly the Princess Marie Bonaparte and Ruth Mack Brunswick. I believe that the proper check on the editing of letters should come from biography and history, not only further letters; for when the editorial note refers to Felix Deutsch having been "under supervision with Otto Rank," that is pure fiction, inspired by Deutsch's attempt to defend himself in unpublished letters to Freud.

Reality is not exhausted by what appears in letters, published or not. It is a mystery to me how anybody could agree with the editors that "Rank was Deutsch's control analyst." Deutsch was just starting his analysis with Bernfeld, and how could Rank, although by then an old friend of Felix's, be considered capable of being a real supervisor of Deutsch? It was not an active suicide in any event that Felix Deutsch was afraid of, but rather a much more elusive and hard to pinpoint lack of self-preservativeness. Rank was already, in any event, in an acute emotional turmoil of his own with Freud, which must have made Deutsch's dragging him in here as a so-called control all the more offensive to Freud. It is relatively minor for the editors who have so jumbled key things up to add the demonstrably false information that Deutsch afterwards taught at Harvard University, when his central university teaching position in the States was in reality at the Smith College School of Social Work.

The reader gets editorially, I think, a seriously botched account of this important medical crisis in Freud's life. (It complicates things further that Felix Deutsch's wife Helene, already established as an analyst, was in the meantime angry at both her husband – and Freud – for this incident over the cancer having threatened her relationship with the creator of psychoanalysis.) Nor does the Steinach operation, which was rejuvenatory surgery on Freud's testicles as a way of mobilizing the life instincts in order to overcome the death drive, get adequately explained. (The Index accordingly does not even refer to the name Steinach.)

To continue on more positively with an evaluation of what I think can be especially learned from Vol. 3 of the Freud-Ferenczi letters, I think the reader gets some fresh information connected with the troubles Freud had with Karl Abraham before his death in 1925. (Freud turned to Ferenczi for support in Freud's dealings with Abraham.) And it is notable what a central role Ferenczi played, along with Rank, in revising Freud's approach not only to the issue of motherhood, but to the whole larger problem of the nature of femininity itself. Ferenczi knew Freud well enough to make (in private) some sound-seeming conjectures about the unconscious roots of Freud's various blocks connected with female psychology, and how this interfered with Freud's general clinical practices.

But the central tragedy recounted in Vol. 3 of the Freud-Ferenczi letters concerns the final falling-out between Freud and Ferenczi in mid-1932. In this one episode we can detect the interplay of a variety of different theories and contrasting personalities. For some years Freud had been encouraging Ferenczi, who had first proposed the creation of the International Psychoanalytic Association in the first place, to assume the role of being IPA President. Ferenczi, however, like Jung before him, was hesitant to get himself involved in squandering his energies in the politics that would inevitably be involved in holding such a formal position within the psychoanalytic movement. To Freud, Ferenczi's various long-standing illnesses were signs of hypochondria, whereas by the summer of 1932 Ferenczi was genuinely ill. Freud had felt that any sign of Ferenczi's being less than an enthusiastic letter-writer meant Ferenczi was "isolating" himself from Freud. (Essentially Freud had interpreted Jung's earlier estrangement on the same basis of someone's diminishing commitments as a correspondent.) And as with Jung, Freud (who had once been Ferenczi's analyst) could stoop to interpreting psychoanalytically one of Ferenczi's slips of the pen; Freud did not seem to realize, as in the instance of Jung, how such a maneuver would reinforce the very infantilism in Ferenczi that Freud was apt to feel entitled to complain of.

In a famous late 1931 letter to Ferenczi Freud criticized in a cruel way Ferenczi's innocuous experiments of allowing himself to exchange (nonerotic) kisses with patients. Freud let himself go as he went on at length about the dangers here for newcomers to analysis:

> There is no revolutionary who is not knocked out of the field by a still more radical one. So-and-so many independent thinkers in technique will say to themselves: Why stop with a kiss? Certainly, one will achieve still more if one adds "pawing," which, after all, doesn't make any babies. And then bolder ones will come along who will take the further step of peeping and showing, and soon we will have accepted into the technique of psychoanalysis the whole repertoire of demiviergerie and petting parties, with the result being a great increase in interest in analysis on the part of analysts and those who are being analyzed. The new ally will, however, lay too much claim to this interest for himself, the younger of our colleagues will be hard put, in the relational connections that they have made, to stop at the point where they had originally intended, and Godfather Ferenczi, looking at the busy scenery that he has created, will possibly say to himself: Perhaps I should have stopped in my technique of maternal tenderness *before* the kiss.[12]

Freud, when aroused, could rise to the heights of his polemical writing capacities. Freud seemed to have now put aside everything he had once written to Ferenczi about the merits of Ferenczi's concentration on the significance of "tact" within the technique of psychoanalysis. Ferenczi might have countered — if he had been more of a polemicist — that because a physician recommends a particular patient eat less food does not thereby make the doctor a promoter of human starvation. But Ferenczi, altogether the milder of the two men, expressed himself in words which remain far less well known than Freud's own torrential accusations about the slippery slope Ferenczi had supposedly embarked upon. Ferenczi merely replied to Freud's indictment:

> You will probably recall that it was I who declared it to be necessary also to communicate matters of technique, so long as one applies them methodically; you were more in favor of being sparing with communications about technique. Now *you* think it would be dishonorable to keep silent, and I must counter that by saying that the *pace* of publications should be relegated to the tact and insight of the author.[13]

At the end of August 1932, when Ferenczi read to Freud the draft of a paper to be presented before an impending psychoanalytic Congress, Freud felt it was potentially scandalous, and wanted Ferenczi to postpone his presentation. According to Ferenczi's heart-broken-sounding report afterwards, Freud had finally turned his back on Ferenczi and walked out of the room. The paper itself, "The Confusion of Tongues Between Adults and the Child,"[14] seemed to me when I first read it in the 1960s an excellent one; on re-reading it now it seems to me even more a classic critique of much that was for too long accepted unquestioningly as a model of how the psychoanalyst should proceed by the standards of "neutrality" and distance. Any clinician can, I think, still expect to learn from Ferenczi's whole approach, even though it once sounded so heretical to Freud.

In this whole account of the falling-out between Freud and Ferenczi, it is to me Freud, and not Ferenczi, who is more the tragic figure. Of course it is to Freud's credit that he had been so taken with Ferenczi over those many years. Ferenczi died in 1933, and that was terribly premature to be sure. But the tragedy I am impressed with is how Freud could have gone on to be so curiously blind to what he had been doing with Ferenczi. It seems to me strikingly sad that Freud went on living in such a dream-land of his own innocence, with so little self-reproach or self-understanding despite all his own propagandistic philosophizing about the significance of self knowledge.

I would like to single out only one other point in these letters, although others will doubtless find different ideas that they find equally fascinating. Many of the earliest generations of analysts, who often were themselves unanalyzed, considered it a tragedy that Freud himself had had to rely only on a self-analysis. In this spirit Ferenczi had written (1926) to Freud:

> I find it actually tragic that you, who endowed the world with psychoanalysis, find it so difficult to be – indeed, are not at all – in a

position to entrust yourself to anyone. – If your heart ailments continue, and if the medications and diet don't help, then I will come to you for a few months and place myself at your disposal as an analyst – naturally: if you don't throw me out.[15]

It is a testimony to the unusually good relationship Freud and Ferenczi then had that Freud took no offense whenever Ferenczi repeated any such proposal. (Freud had stopped exchanging dreams with Jung on the 1909 trip to America, on which Ferenczi went along too, because of the excuse that it risked endangering Freud's "authority", which in itself, according to Jung, lost Freud authority in Jung's eyes.)

These letters in Vol. 3 make for wonderfully interesting reading. I am glad to have reprinted here also examples of the circular letters exchanged by Freud and Ferenczi as members of the so-called secret Committee, designed to protect Freud's "cause", but these letters, not just addressed to one recipient but to a small group of insiders, are all far less poignant and interesting than the real Freud-Ferenczi letters themselves. In the recent volume of the Freud-Jones correspondence[16], no such examples from the circular letters were allowed to appear, which in that case made possible a single-volume collection of texts. In Germany there is already a four-volume edition of all the circular letters (*Rundbriefe*), written by each Committee member, underway. Although it is uncertain whether continuing interest in the history of psychoanalysis will commercially justify the translation of such books, they are at least if not more important than the hard-to-follow four-volume edition of the *Minutes* of the Vienna Psychoanalytic Society which came out a long time ago. Better editing of Freud's correspondences might make it more likely that future generations will take fully seriously the significance of all these documents in the history of psychoanalysis.

The absolutely splendidly edited *The Complete Correspondence of Sigmund Freud and Karl Abraham*[17] replaces the earlier 1965 abridged edition of the Freud-Abraham letters[18], one that had many defects associated with the period in which it appeared. The experienced translator Eric Mosbacher was so offended by the role Abraham's daughter Hilda played in that 1965 book that he refused to have his real name attached, and therefore the pseudonym "Bernard Marsh" appears along with Hilda Abraham as the co-translators. As already indicated, three more major examples of Freud's published correspondences will also need redoing: for the ones to Lou Andreas-Salomé, Oskar Pfister, and Arnold Zweig remain now incomplete. In the meantime, it looks like the letters between Freud and Max Eitingon may be the next volume to appear, although commercial considerations could make translations of that huge amount of text into English questionable. It might be that the Freud-Rank correspondence will be out not long thereafter. Since the ultimate extent of all Freud's letters may well exceed in size the *Standard Edition,* future generations should have the benefit of what many of us may not live long enough to savor. Intellectual historians are going to have plenty of work cut out for them, since for example the Jung children never even read the approximately 1,000 letters between their parents, on the grounds of not wanting to trespass privacy. Approximately the same amount of letters exist between Freud and his wife Martha, some of which Ernest Jones selected for use in his official biography; but a full edition will be an event in the history of ideas.

Although Abraham was not as personally close to Freud as Sandor Ferenczi, and therefore these letters lack the fuller intimacy that can be found in the recent wonderful Freud-Ferenczi volumes[19], Abraham did succeed in creating the Institute in Berlin, left a significant body of writings as well as trained important analysands; therefore Freud's correspondence with him seems to me a truly engrossing reading experience. The wonderful notes by Falzeder, a great expert on Freud's manuscripts and handwriting, leaves the field permanently indebted to him. Falzeder played a key part in the Freud-Ferenczi letters too, but that project was such an extensive one as to have involved many others as well, under the leadership of André Haynal in Geneva.

Unlike Ferenczi, the originality of whose final ideas about therapy are still being absorbed, Abraham never posed a comparable threat to Freud's recommended ways of proceeding. Freud instead seemed readily to welcome how Abraham almost immediately became a convert and adherent, and thereby eager to become an instrument in behalf of the psychoanalytic "cause" that appeared at the time indistinguishable from personal loyalty to Freud himself. But simultaneously the founder of psychoanalysis could be irritated by Abraham's self-righteous tone. For example, even by Abraham's first contact with Freud in 1907 Abraham had not gotten on well with Jung at the Burghölzli in Zurich, and rather took a lead in encouraging that famous split in the history of psychoanalysis. Although Freud had later to acknowledge Abraham's prescience about Jung (Abraham proved wrong about Pfister), I suspect that Freud in 1923-24 also never forgave Abraham for having helped come between Freud and his special favorite Otto Rank. Just before Abraham's premature death, at the age of forty-eight in 1925, Freud and he had been arguing over the merits of a Berlin motion picture about psychoanalysis. In rare editorial oversights, the notes to the revised Freud-Abraham letters underplay Sandor Rado's observations about the rival Viennese movie proposal by Siegfried Bernfeld and Adolf Storfer, as well as ignore Rado's conjecture that Abraham's medical treatment was so unusual as to conclude that his death was accelerated by the wish to evade a conflict with Freud.

Falzeder's excellent "Preface" sets the stage by rehearsing the history of the various publications of Freud's correspondences. Although even as a teenager Freud was confident enough of his literary prowess as to recommend that his friend Emil Fluss start saving his letters, later on he surely knew that his correspondents were collecting what he sent out; yet in 1927 he wrote to Pfister: "I have the intention to prevent a literary utilization of my correspondence...."[20] Jones too said he thought that by publishing extracts from Freud's letters he could help block the eventual full-scale appearance of the various correspondences. Falzeder's editing, like the earlier notable William McGuire edition of the Freud-Jung letters (1974), sets a high standard for future editors.

Falzeder's "Preface" is notably outspoken on the issue of using patients' names: "psychoanalytic theory does not enter into analysts' heads like a demon from nowhere – it springs precisely from their personal and intimate experiences. In cutting these out, the missing links between the theoreticians and their theories – psychoanalytic epistemology and the 'context of discovery' – are obscured....[O]ne has to decide to publish the correspondence as it is, or not at all."[21] The "Introduction" by André Haynal and Falzeder also repays the closest sort of attention, as it is discerning and fair-minded about the sources of some of the most well-known conflicts in the history of psychoanalysis. Although it has taken all these years since that first 1965 edition of the Freud-Abraham letters, I think that intellectual historians can be proud of the work that has most recently been going on.

It may be impossible adequately to summarize the fascinating content of these unabridged letters between Freud and Abraham. A natural imbalance occurs, since Freud's literary capacities are so outstanding, while Abraham, on the plodding side anyway, is eager to be obliging in fulfilling what he takes to be Freud's mission. At the outset of their contact Abraham, who unlike Freud had had a psychiatric background, sent Freud a paper on dementia praecox (later known as schizophrenia) and hysteria. It should be noted that Freud considered that he found a "complete analogy in the pre-history of these neuroses" to be "really very peculiar."[22] In those days Freud was still relying on his concept of what he had called "narcissistic neurosis," and it would not be until the 1920s that he publicly differentiated, long after the falling-out with Jung, a psychiatrist, between neurosis and psychosis. Within a few months of being in contact with Freud, Abraham announced his intention to leave Zurich for Berlin instead. Freud replied by hoping that if he could "forthrightly refer to you as my pupil and follower...I shall be able to back you energetically."[23]

When Freud, early in 1908, observed of a hallucinating patient that an "attack" represented "a coitus or, rather, his rage at such an act of coitus observed by him," and that the patient's spitting was "sperm-ejaculation,"[24] one can perhaps appreciate the grounds of skepticism about Freud by old-line psychiatrists. Abraham responded by a case illustration that he felt "stuck" about after "two sessions." Freud replied to Abraham: "Take your time...Mental changes are never quick, except in revolutions (psychoses). Dissatisfied after only two sessions. At not knowing everything!"[25]

Any such pioneers could allow themselves exaggerations that are bound in hindsight to stand out in a way that can sound embarrassing, and the wonder may be that they succeeded in keeping their footing.

One aspect of Freud's communications deserves to be high-lighted, since Falzeder's editorial sleuthing has unearthed new evidence about the founder of psychoanalysis's implicit approach to the problem of race, unfortunately not unusual for someone of that time and social class. In 1908 Freud had concluded a letter to Abraham "hoping that 'white-washing' the nervous will soon be as disagreeable to you as it has become to me...."[26] In the 1965 edition the expression "white-washing" was toned down in the translation to "cleaning up neurotics." Falzeder's editorial note points toward Jeremiah 13:23, which asks whether the Ethiopian can change his skin, or the leopard his spots. Falzeder tells us that the "white-washing" expression was already used by Freud in *Studies on Hysteria*, but was omitted from the *Standard Edition*. In 1924 Freud could write Abraham that he was going on holiday "taking with me a well-capitalized negro who will certainly not bother me more than one hour in the day."[27] Jones had reported that at the outset of Freud's medical practice in the late 1880s his "consultation hour was at noon, and for some time patients were referred to as 'Negroes.' This strange appellation came from a cartoon...depicting a yawning lion muttering 'Twelve o'clock and no Negro.'"[28] It is high time that we give up the anti-historical bias that for too long has insisted that we look at Freud only as a reflection of ourselves today.

As early as 1942 Max Graf, the father of "Little Hans," reminisced of the pre-World War I Wednesday-evenings in Vienna that he had absorbed "the atmosphere of the foundation of a religion....Freud's pupils were his apostles...."[29] Abraham wrote Freud once about living *in partibus infidelium*, Latin for "in the land of the unbelievers"[30]; the notes explain the reference to where ordained bishops were not permitted to act as such in places they were ordained for. In those days patients could become converts, "scientifically interested in the cause."[31] Abraham once wrote to Freud that he had spoken at a psychiatric meeting not "*propagandae fidei causa*" (Latin "for the sake of propagating belief.")[32] And, following up on Latin usage in these letters, Freud could use the expression *consilium abeundi*[33] about Jung, as he had earlier about Adler; the notes tell us that those two Latin words refer to advice given to a student to leave an institution of learning before they are expelled.

These Freud-Abraham letters also record the exact steps by which Berlin became the great center for psychoanalytic education, as well as Freud's perhaps exaggerated disdain for his Viennese following that came up in his enthusiasm for Berlin. His intense distaste for America, going beyond that of other cultured people of that era, does sound authentic. Freud's 1909 trip to America for the sake of the honorary degree from Clark University seems to have soured him for good.

The volume is full of rich concrete examples of clinical situations that deserve exploration in the future. Of course everything needs to be put in the context of a cultural world that has long since ceased to exist. And readers will find here sharp reminders of how Freud was willing, with the help of Abraham as well as others, to fight for "the cause." One of the remaining jobs of intellectual historians is to try to put all Freud's books and essays in the context of the various and shifting contestants he had in mind.

It is hard to give a summary of how dazzling a writer Freud was. Rado happened to be with Freud in Vienna when news came of Abraham's death. Freud "immediately sat down and wrote a statement which was hurriedly put into an almost fully printed copy of the *Zeitschrift.* . . ."[34] How Freud could write off the top of his head is illustrated not just by these letters but by that obituary too.[35] One non-professional letter by Freud to Abraham's wife Hedwig stands out for me; in late 1920, after the Hague Congress, Freud had given Abraham 100 guilders for presents to his two children. With the help of a patient Abraham got them both bicycles.

> Dear Mrs. Abraham,
> Your children's letters were too charming – I hope they did not cost them too much trouble or even tears, were not rewritten several times, etc. I should have answered the little ones directly, but I was afraid of undermining their morals, because I should certainly have thought of confessing that the finest gifts are spoilt by having to say thank you for them. It would also have embarrassed me either to go on playing the part of the great patron or having to admit that I had made them happy by means of the resources of others. When the opportunity arises, please tell them the true state of affairs, to which the moral can be attached that also by work like the practice of psychoanalysis it is possible to acquire a few Dutch guilders sometime late in life.
>
> From your news I pick out the one that your husband is now at last well enough. We were already quite annoyed by his illness. Here too we are haunted by more illness than is actually indispensable.
>
> Wishing you all a Happy New Year, richer in fulfillment and entirely devoid of anything disagreeable,
> Your faithfully devoted
> Freud[36]

I believe that everything written by Freud belongs not just to psychoanalysis but to the literature of world thought as well.

NOTES

1 *The Correspondence of Sigmund Freud and Sandor Ferenczi*, Vol. 3, 1920-1933, edited by Ernst Falzeder and Eva Brabant, with the collaboration of Patrizia Giampieri-Deutsch, translated by Peter T. Hoffer, with an Introduction by Judith Dupont (Cambridge, Harvard Univ. Press, 2000), p. xxxix.
2 *Ibid.*, p. xix.
3 *Ibid.*, p. 29.
4 *The Clinical Diary of Sandor Ferenczi*, edited by Judith Dupont, translated by Michael Balint and Nicola Zarday Jackson (Cambridge, Harvard Univ. Press, 1988).
5 *The Correspondence of Sigmund Freud and Sandor Ferenczi*, Vol. 3, *op. cit.*, p. 47.
6 *Ibid.*, p. 227.
7 Otto Rank, *Beyond Psychology* (New York, Dover Publications, 1941), p. 272. I am indebted to Robert Kramer for this citation.
8 *The Correspondence of Sigmund Freud and Sandor Ferenczi*, Vol. 3, *op. cit.*, p. 166-67.
9 *Ibid.*, p. 160.
10 *Ibid.*
11 *Ibid.*, p. 63.
12 *Ibid.*, p. 422.
13 *Ibid.*, p. 424.
14 Sandor Ferenczi, *Final Contributions to the Problems and Methods of Psychoanalysis*, edited by Michael Balint, translated by Eric Mosbacher (London, The Hogarth Press, 1955), pp. 156-57.
15 *The Correspondence of Sigmund Freud and Sandor Ferenczi*, Vol. 3, *op. cit.*, p. 250.
16 *The Complete Correspondence of Sigmund Freud and Ernest Jones 1908-1939*, edited by R. Andrew Paskauskas (Cambridge, Harvard Univ. Press, 1993).
17 *The Complete Correspondence of Sigmund Freud and Karl Abraham 1907-1925*, edited by Ernst Falzeder, translated by Caroline Schwarzacher with the collaboration of Christine Trollope and Klara Majthényi King, Introduction by André Haynal and Ernst Falzeder (London & New York, Karnac, 2002).
18 *A Psychoanalytic Dialogue: The letters of Sigmund Freud and Karl Abraham 1907-1926*, edited by Hilda C. Abraham and Ernst L. Freud, translated by Bernard Marsh and Hilda C. Abraham (New York, Basic Books, 1965).
19 *The Correspondence of Sigmund Freud and Sandor Ferenczi*, Vol. 1, 1908-1914, ed. by Eva Brabant, Ernst Falzeder, & Patrizia Giampieri-Deutsch, translated by Peter T. Hoffer (Cambridge, Harvard Univ. Press, 1993); *The Correspondence of Sigmund Freud and Sandor Ferenczi*, Vol. 2, 1914-1919, ed. Ernst Falzeder and Eva Brabant, with the collaboration of Patrizia Giampieri-Deutsch, translated by Peter T. Hoffer (Cambridge, Harvard Univ. Press, 1996).
20 *The Complete Correspondence of Sigmund Freud and Karl Abraham 1907-1925*, *op. cit.*, p. xiv.
21 *Ibid.*, pp. xvi-xvii.
22 *Ibid.*, p. 1.
23 *Ibid.*, p. 9.
24 *Ibid.*, p. 16.
25 *Ibid.*, pp. 17, 21.
26 *Ibid.*, p. 45.

27 *Ibid.*, p. 507.
28 Ernest Jones, *The Life and Work of Sigmund Freud*, Vol. 1 (New York, Basic Books, 1953), p. 151.
29 Max Graf, "Reminiscences of Professor Sigmund Freud," *Psychoanalytic Quarterly*, Vol. 11 (1942), pp. 471-72.
30 *The Complete Correspondence of Sigmund Freud and Karl Abraham 1907-1925, op. cit.*, p. 46.
31 *Ibid.*, p. 48.
32 *Ibid.*, p. 153.
33 *Ibid.*, p. 245.
34 Paul Roazen and Bluma Swerdloff, *Heresy: Sandor Rado and the Psychoanalytic Movement* (Northvale, N.J., Jason Aronson, 1995), p. 89.
35 "Karl Abraham," *Standard Edition*, Vol. 20, pp. 277-78.
36 *The Complete Correspondence of Sigmund Freud and Karl Abraham 1907-1925, op. cit.*, p. 437.

10

FREUD AND HIS FOLLOWERS

In the late 1890s Freud, who had been trained as a Viennese neurologist, created a new field, psychoanalysis, which was designed to understand and treat neurotic afflictions. An essential key to Freud's thinking about psychopathology lies in the character of the last days of the Hapsburg Empire. A yawning gulf then between reality and official ideology stimulated a general intellectual revolt, a search for the actualities beneath the pious formulas of public truth. This uprising was led by those ideally placed to see the discrepancy because they had nothing to gain from accepting the official view, the educated Jews. Mordant irony was their weapon for piercing the veil of the structure of formal beliefs. The cultural conflict between East and West that had its vortex in Vienna's cosmopolitan intellectual life, and the sense that liberal culture was on the verge of being undermined, would be reflected throughout Freud's mature thought.[1]

Freud's starting point as a therapist was the existence of inner conflicts that interfered with the lives of suffering patients. He proposed that symptoms be looked upon as substitute satisfactions, the result of failure adequately to deal with early childhood patterns. Freud highlighted persistent infantilism as the ultimate source of adult neurotic problems. Freud held that neuroses are psychologically meaningful, and he interpreted them as compromise formations between repressed impulses and censoring parts of the mind. One portion of every symptom was understood as the expression of wish fulfillment, and another side represented the mental structure that reacted against the primal drive. Initially Freud thought that neurotic anxiety arose from sexual sources; specifically, Freud indicted dammed-up sexuality as the physical basis for neurosis.

Freud conceived sexuality so broadly as to include virtually all aspects of childish pleasure seeking. Fantasies of sexual gratification stemming from early childhood were allegedly the source of adult neurotic dilemmas. Freud proposed that a person's emotional attitude toward parents encapsulated the core problems of neurosis, and he coined the term Oedipus complex to describe a boy's first childish desires for his mother and a girl's earliest affection for her father. Freud understood that someone's emotional attitude toward a family consisted of conflicting emotions involving rivalry as well as guilt, not just desire. And Freud believed that the most troublesome feelings stemmed from emotional problems about which the individual remains unconscious.

Freud was proposing that people have motives that can be operative without their knowing anything about them. His special viewpoint was that of a psychologist, and he sought to pierce the mysteries of memory and false recollections. Freud thought that the compromise formations in constructing our image of the past were just like those in dreaming, as well as the ones underlying neurotic symptomatology, and everyday slips of the tongue or pen. He thought that the past lives on in the present, and psychoanalytic treatment consisted in the exploration of each patient's early history.

Freud was ambitious as a theorist, and his notion of neurosis became part of a full-fledged system of thought. A central implication of his approach amounted to an assault on confidence in our ability to think rationally. For Freud was insisting that people are fundamentally self-deceptive. Neurosis was a form of ignorance, and Freud saw it as his task to utilize the power that could come from enlightenment.

As much as Freud's work can be understood as a critique of the capacity for self-understanding, he was superlatively rationalistic about psychoanalysis itself. He thought he had discovered a science of the mind, and that he had uncovered a realm of meaning that could be objectively verified. The technique of free associations, which he relied on during treatment, was one that others could be trained to use. Once patients submitted to the analytic situation, involving daily meetings each lasting fifty minutes, such commitment could be used by the analyst to promote personal autonomy. Freud was relying on a structured situation in order, like Rousseau's proposal, to "force" people to be "free".

One of the chief defects in Freud's approach was his unwillingness to concede the full philosophical underpinnings to his approach. He was convinced that psychoanalysis was capable of transforming thought and undermining previous moral positions, yet he fancied that he had been able to do so without importing any ethical baggage of his own inside his teachings. Yet Freud was clearly expressing a morality of his own; he once explained to a patient that the moral self was the conscious, the evil self being the unconscious. Freud qualified this distinction by maintaining that his approach emphasized not only evil wishes but also the moral censorship that makes them unrecognizable. He was insistent that morality was self-evident, at the same time he himself supposedly held to a higher standard of ethics than humanity as a whole.[2]

Since Freud wrote so much about abnormality, it might seem that he would have been obliged to discuss his picture of mental health. But whatever Freud had in mind has to be teased out of his system of thought, since he remained loath to deal frontally with a concept like normality. It is clear that he did not envisage a utopian version of personal happiness; anxiety and despair were to him inevitable parts of the human condition. Freud sought not to eradicate human conflicts, but to teach how one can come to terms with such anguish.

As much as Freud claimed to be intent on steering away from speculative theorizing, repeatedly he allowed himself to become engaged in social philosophy. In each of the last three decades of his life he wrote a book centering on different aspects of the psychology of religion. He made the analogy between religion and obsessional neurosis, and pointed out how often outer forms have obliterated the inner religious intention, as with any other self-defeating neurotic structure. The one social coercion Freud felt to be humanly unnecessary was religion. In *The Future of An Illusion* he stressed that inner instinctual core that strains beyond culture's reach; he was differing from the classical liberal tradition to the extent that he saw man not as a unit, but as an opposed, divided self. Yet it is also the case that Freud proposed that there was deep within mankind a central portion of the self that had to remain in opposition to society.

It was Freud's Enlightenment heritage that led him to denounce religious belief in so bold a manner. As of 1927, Freud insisted that human helplessness was at the origin of religious conviction; people need religion because of the failure to outgrow the dependency of childhood. Religion is an illusion in the sense that it is the product of wish-fulfillment. Freud skeptically saw religion as a pack of lies, fairy-tales that were a product of emotional insecurities. Because religion was based on irrational fears, its unreality may undermine the civilization it currently supports. Illusions are dangerous, no matter how comfortable. Freud ignored his earlier comments on religion, relating it to fears of death and guilt as he now concluded that superstition is intolerable. He was so intolerant of the infantile and the regressive that he had difficulty understanding their constructive functions.

Freud saw the family as the prototype for authority relationships. As he had argued that God the father was needed to allay the deepest fears, so he thought that the Oedipus complex also illuminated the social cohesion of political groups. He elaborated these ideas in his *Group Psychology and The Analysis of the Ego*. Freud was suspicious of the masses and disdainful of the lower classes; his elitism lay behind a good deal of his social thinking. Religion always seemed to Freud a more intolerable irrationality than political authority. Politically he was impressed by the extent of human inner instability and the craving for authority. Although Freud's whole form of therapy aimed at liberation and independence, politically he was a pessimist.

In *Civilization and Its Discontents* Freud eloquently expressed his full sense of the conflictedness of life. He stressed the inevitable pervasiveness of suffering in civilized society. Although he could, as in *The Future of An Illusion*, write like an eighteenth century libertarian, here his sense of the inevitable cruelties of life was uppermost in the argument. For civilization to be powerful enough to protect people from each other and against nature, it must, according to Freud, have at its disposal an equally intense energy. Throughout Freud's thought there is a sense of the limits of life, the truth behind the maxim that one cannot have one's cake and eat it too. Social unity can only be achieved on the ruins of human desires. People need the security of civilized life so deeply that they renounce the gratification of instincts in exchange for society. Freud concluded that the frustration of sexual and aggressive drives is entailed by their very character. Only if society can successfully internalize human instinctuality can civilization be maintained.

SOCIALISM

A long tradition of left-wing thinkers has dismissed psychoanalysis as a decadent form of soul-searching. At least starting with Lenin, Marxists have been unhappy about what to do with Freud. Yet within socialism there has been a history of theorists eager to unite Marxist concepts with those of Freud. Trotsky, for example, was open-mindedly receptive to the significance of Freud's teachings, and in personal contact in Vienna with Alfred Adler (1870-1937), one of the earliest members of Freud's circle that was first founded in 1902. Adler, although one of Freud's first students, was also a socialist who went on to found a school of "individual psychology" apart from Freud's own.[3] Adler had a special concern with the social and environmental factors in disease, and highlighted the role of compensations for early defects in his study of organ inferiority; he was proposing that under the best circumstances defects in a child could create a disposition toward better performance. Adler was not as exclusively concerned with infantile sexuality as Freud, but was instead preoccupied with ego mechanisms and aggressive drives. In contrast to Freud's own lack of interest in politics, Adler sought to improve the world through education and psychotherapy.

In 1911 Freud decided to bring his differences with Adler to a head, and the result was Adler's resignation, along with half the membership of the Vienna Psychoanalytic Society. Adler was stressing the extent to which emotional problems stemmed from current conflicts and cultural disharmonies rather than from the patient's childhood past. Adler interpreted symptoms as a weapon of self-assertion, often arising from deep-seated feelings of inferiority. But he looked on the patient's wholeness as the key to neurosis; Adler was concerned with what are now known as character problems.

Adler proposed to help patients with their feelings of inferiority, by leading them out of their self-preoccupied isolation into participation in the community. Through the cultivation of social feeling and by means of service to society one could subdue egotism. Adler was pioneering with his interest in the ego as an agency of the mind, and thought he could thereby help to bridge the gap between the pathological and the normal. By 1920 Adler had directed his efforts to setting up consultations with schoolteachers; he had been intrigued all along with the psychology of the family group. He was especially compassionate toward victims of social injustice, and thought it of primary importance to help promote human dignity.[4] Women in particular were suffering from socially patterned oppression. Adler understood how people, out of their own inadequacies and lack of self-esteem, could bolster themselves by degrading others. Once a group or class has been treated as inferior, these feelings can be self-sustaining and lead to compensatory maneuvers to make up for self-doubts. Chronic neurotic suffering stems from psychological over-sensitivity, and feelings of inferiority are often compensated for through protest and fantasies of greatness. Adler understood some of the key social bases for destructiveness, and those concerned with race as a psychological force in the modern world – including Frantz Fanon and Kenneth Clark – have acknowledged themselves in Adler's debt.

Wilhelm Reich (1897-1957) was a Viennese psychiatrist who was also one of Freud's most talented pupils. Freud had conceived of neurosis primarily as a memory problem, while Reich tried to show that the real issue to be studied was not symptomatology but the whole personality. In his work on character analysis in the 1920s, Reich broadened the earlier conception of what was suitable for analytic concern.

While Reich helped to shift the focus of attention to nonverbal means of expression, he failed to convince analysts of the diagnostic significance of orgastic sexual satisfaction. Reich thought that mental health depended on orgastic potency, and he was in favor of full and free sexual expression. (Freud sharply disagreed with these ideas.) As a practical reformer Reich held that many adult problems would never develop if sexual expression were not prematurely stifled. What orthodox analysts called sublimation, the transmutation of instinctual drives into cultural expression, was deemed by Reich to be the rationalized product of bourgeois sexual inhibitions. He started to argue in the late 1920s that Freud was betraying, out of conformist pressures, his original revolutionary stand in behalf of the rights of libido. Freud in turn objected that Reich was trying to limit the concept of sexuality to what it had been before psychoanalysis.[5]

Reich was not only a Marxist but also a Communist, and he became one of the few analysts to start building bridges between psychoanalysis and social thought. He proposed to prevent the rise of oedipal problems rather than simply study and cure them after the fact. The key, he thought, was to ameliorate human suffering through changes in the traditional Western family structure. He believed that only the dissolution of the middle-class family would lead to the disappearance of the Oedipus complex. Freud viewed neurosis as an outgrowth of the biological necessity of the family, and composed his *Civilization and Its Discontents* as an answer to Reich's position.

Reich's *The Mass Psychology of Fascism* first appeared in Germany in 1935, and was written at the high point of Reich's involvement with Freudian and Marxist concepts.[6] The central interpretive thesis was that modern man is torn by contradictory impulses toward conservatism and revolution. He craves authority, fears freedom, but is simultaneously rebellious. The authoritarian patriarchal family, Reich held, distorted some of man's most generous and cooperative instincts. Fascism represents not so much any one political party as the organized expression of the average man's enslaved character. Reich's main sociological point was that society is capable of transforming man's inner nature, producing a character structure that then reproduces society in the form of ideologies. In Reich's time, the distressed German middle class became members of the Nazi radical right, and he chose to explain modern nationalism as an outgrowth of suppressed genital sexuality.

Erich Fromm (1900-1980), another Marxist psychoanalyst, published *Escape From Freedom* in 1941, and it immediately became a notable event in intellectual history. He won the enmity of the orthodox analysts of his day for daring to discuss factors such as the role of the environment in personality development, and the creation of "social character". Societies do tend to produce and reproduce the character types they need to survive and perpetuate themselves; "social character" gets shaped by the economic structure of society through processes of psychological internalization. In turn, the dominant personality traits become forces in their own right in molding the social process itself. As external necessity becomes part of the psyche, human energy gets harnessed for a given economic or social system. In this way, we become what we are expected to be.[7]

Fromm was concerned with the pathology of normality and considered it legitimate to speak of an "insane" society and what happens to people in it. Fromm's earliest papers in the 1930s had focused on the alleged defects of the middle-class liberalism implicit in Freud. As Fromm turned away from the pessimism of Freud's instinct theory, Fromm insisted on the potential significance of changes in the social environment as a means of altering the human condition. (Fromm acknowledged the impact of Reich's general influence on him.) Freud had not been much interested, aside from criticizing sexual mores, in the social sources of suffering and exploitation. Fromm, by contrast, was intrigued with the way our culture fosters conformist tendencies by suppressing spontaneous feelings and thereby crippling the development of genuine individuality.

Instead of seeing the unconscious as something frightening, Fromm held that truth is repressed by an unconscious that is basically socially determined. He also thought that too often we fear our superior potentialities and, in particular, the ability to develop as autonomous and free individuals. He traced destructiveness to unlived life rather than to Freud's mythical death instinct. If cruelty is one of the ways of making sense of existence, it only illustrates Fromm's theory that character-rooted passions should be considered psychosocial phenomena.

For Fromm selfishness was not, as in Freud, the same as self-love. Fromm thought these traits were diametrically opposite, and therefore the possibility of altruism as an aspect of self-expression becomes a real one. Whereas Freud liked to debunk the legitimacy of altruism, Fromm – like Adler – tried to combat egocentricity. Too often we hold our ego as a possession, the basis for identity, a thing.

In addition to assailing egotism, Fromm set out to combat greed and human passivity, bewailing the prevalence in the modern world of competition, antagonism, and fear. He distinguished between subjectively felt needs and objectively valid ones. He had in mind the aim of self-realization; for him self-affirmation was a process of exercising human reason in a productive activity. Fromm believed that reason properly exercised will lead to an ethic of love. Love for Fromm was a process of self-renewing and self-increasing. Society has aimed not, as Freud thought, to repress sex, but to vilify sex for the sake of breaking the human will. Social conformism succeeds to the extent that it breaks independence without our even being aware of it.

In 1955 Herbert Marcuse (1898-1979) published *Eros and Civilization*, an important critique of so-called revisionist Freudian psychology like that promoted by Fromm. With great polemical skill, Marcuse punctured the inspirationalist pretensions of writers who had tried to update psychoanalytic thought in a culturalist direction. Marcuse had first turned to a serious examination of Freud during the late 1930s, when he felt forced to reformulate Marxist premises. Bourgeois society had survived economic crises, the proletariat was susceptible to fascist appeals, and the Soviet Union, both domestically and internationally, had not fulfilled revolutionary hopes. Marcuse disclaimed an interest in the clinical side of psychoanalysis, but selectively picked those concepts from within orthodox Freudian writing that might support his purposes. Relying on what he called a "hidden trend" in psychoanalysis, Marcuse tried to demonstrate the feasibility of a nonrepressive society. He maintained that Freud was the true revolutionary and that his cause had been betrayed by those who had diluted his message for purposes that turned out on inspection to be socially conservative.[8]

Marcuse had launched a fundamentalist Freudian attack on revisionists like Fromm. By drawing on the reasoning in *The Future of An Illusion,* and through building on the Marxist concern with alienation, Marcuse was able to make use of classical psychoanalytic theory for socially utopian purposes. It seemed to Marcuse that to abandon, or minimize, the instinctivistic side of Freud's theories was to give up those concepts that underlined the opposition between man and contemporary society. Marcuse relied on Freud's instinct theory in order to ensure the energy and drive basis within individuals for the hope of challenging the status quo.

It had been Fromm's intention to alter psychoanalytic thinking in the direction of socialism. Fromm and Marcuse, former colleagues in the Frankfurt school of critical sociology, represent (adapting a distinction of William James's) the tender-minded and the tough-minded union of Freud and Marx. But although Marcuse was accurate in pointing out the somewhat Pollyannaish-sounding flavor to much of the psychoanalytic writing since Freud's death, Marcuse did not sufficiently appreciate the pragmatic and moral grounds on which these writers set out to alter their earlier commitments to certain doctrines. They had, for instance, abandoned Freud's instinct theory for the sake of avoiding what they saw as Freud's unnecessary pessimism that could seem to border on therapeutic nihilism.

Marcuse relentlessly pursued what he considered the banalities of the revisionists. In addition to attacking Fromm, Marcuse went after the ideas of Karen Horney and Harry Stack Sullivan; Marcuse indicted their emphases on the relevance of the need people have for growth, and how cultural biases blinded Freud to his biologistic prejudices.[9] Despite the injustices of Marcuse's attacks, it is hard not to admire the conceptual power of his mind as he criticized the way analysts can belabor the obvious. A kind of potential social conformism can be seen as implicit in the sort of mental massage advocated by such revisionist theorists. For Marcuse there was no possibility of free personality development in the context of a fundamentally unfree society, in which basic human impulses have been made aggressive and destructive.

CONSERVATISM

If psychoanalysis has been used by Marcuse and others for radical social purposes, Freud has proven no less useful for conservative aims. Carl Gustav Jung (1875-1961) led the most painful of the "secessions" from psychoanalysis; of all the pupils in Freud's life, Jung played the most substantial intellectual role. His contact in the 1930s with the Nazis only put the final seal of disapproval on a man Freud's pupils had already learned to detest.

Long-standing sources of difference between Freud and Jung existed even during their period of cooperation from 1906 until 1913; but Freud had come to depend on Jung as his "crown prince" destined to lead the psychoanalytic movement in the future, especially in the world of psychiatry which in central Europe was then distinct from neurology. Nevertheless, Jung had hesitated to extend the concept of sexuality as broadly as Freud wished, and Jung came to interpret much so-called infantile clinical phenomena as of secondary rather than primary causal importance; current difficulties, he held, could reactivate past conflicts. Jung insisted that the past can be used defensively to evade the present, a clinical point which would command widespread later agreement; but at the time they split apart Freud saw Jung as merely retreating from the boldness of psychoanalysis's so-called findings.[10]

Less rationalistic and suspicious of the unconscious than Freud, Jung began to formulate his own views on the compensatory functions of symptoms. No better critique of Freud's excessive rationalism can be found than in Jung's collected works. He proposed that symptoms are always justified and serve a purpose. Also, he was interested in other stages of the life cycle than the oedipal one. It is still not widely known how early Jung emphasized the central importance of the personal rapport between patient and analyst if therapy is to be successful, as he warned against the dangers of authoritarianism implicit in neutral-seeming analytic technique. And Jung also, as the son of a pastor, took religion as a far more deep-rooted and legitimate set of human aspirations than Freud would acknowledge.

At the time of their falling out before World War I, Freud publicly accused Jung of anti-Semitism. After Hitler came to power, Jung accepted the leadership of a German psychiatric association, in what he described as an attempt to protect psychotherapy there. Continuing to live in Switzerland during this time, he helped numerous Jewish therapists to escape to England and elsewhere. But Jung had described some of the characteristics of Freud's psychoanalysis as Jewish, and Jung allowed his comments on the differences between Jewish and "Aryan" psychology to appear in a 1934 article published in Nazi Germany. The closeness of Jung's distinction to the Nazi one between "Jewish science" and "German science" has to be chilling. Despite the opportunistic collaboration with the Nazis, which has damaged Jung's historical standing, his genuine psychological contributions deserve to be acknowledged.

Freud's seeing creativity as the result of the denial of other human capacities was, to Jung and Reich too, an expression of Freud's sexual inhibitions. While Freud was consistently suspicious of the human capacity for regression, Jung saw the non-rational as a profound component of human vision. Jung had appreciation for the creative potentials of the unconscious, and saw in the unknown as much of the life forces as of death drives. Jung held that the therapist must be prepared to meet the patient at all levels, including the moral. Jung tried to deal with the philosophical dimensions of depth psychology, and was willing to discuss the implications of these ideas for a modern conception of individualism. Further, Jung used his notion of the collective unconscious to stress that an individual always exists in the context of a social environment.

The issue of the rise of Hitler serves as a reminder of how easily psychology can be miss-used for the worst kinds of conformist purposes. Dr. Matthias Göring, a distant cousin of Hitler's deputy, headed an Institute that claimed to be housing psychotherapists.[11] To a remarkable extent in Nazi Germany, so-called psychotherapists were able to achieve the support of professional institutionalization. The success of the Göring Institute, its links to the notorious S.S. and its part in helping the Luftwaffe promote the war effort, has to besmirch the whole tradition of German "psychotherapy." We should be wary of the implications of any ideas that aim to harmonize the individual and the social order, a point that stands out when the society is Hitlerian. Since the practice of psychoanalysis could only be preserved in Germany by means of the departure of Jewish analysts, and the cover of the Göring name, a fatal flaw had to mar the existence of the psychotherapeutic profession in Hitler's Germany.

Matthias Göring's organization had solid links to pre-Hitlerian practitioners, as well as to those in post-World War II Germany. Göring had joined the Nazi party as a matter of conviction and national loyalty, and he also condemned the Jewish influence in his occupation. As early as 1933-34 Göring made *Mein Kampf* required reading for all his therapists. Göring was sufficiently partisan so that his relationship with his deputy ruptured in early 1945, over Göring's insistence that those in charge of the Institute serve as advisers to the last German units defending Berlin against the Russians. Göring insisted, in the face of the argument that such actions were futile, that it would be defeatist to do otherwise.

For reasons that are worrisome in terms of intellectual history, earlier philosophical ideas, and in particular a Romantic tradition in German psychology, could be made use of by the Nazis. A special irony can be found in the Nazi conviction that in principle mental disorder within the "master race" could not be considered essentially an organic or biological matter, which was why Göring's applied depth psychology had its special role to play under the Third Reich. It might almost go without saying that therapists at the Göring Institute were not permitted to treat Jews. To protest against the Nazi reign would have risked not only personal destruction but also damage the whole profession of "psychotherapy" itself, which amounts to a damning indictment of what Göring's Institute accomplished. No one has ever been able to understand how patient confidentiality can be maintained under totalitarian political circumstances. So the Nazi regime had succeeded in destroying psychotherapy as it should be known. The German practitioners of their craft betrayed an obligation they owed to patients, humanity at large, and to the people in countries that the Nazis assaulted.

Although I hesitate to bring it up after discussing Hitler's Germany, and without exploring the abuses of psychiatry in Soviet Russia and the People's Republic of China, the full-scale development of ego psychology, one of the main currents in psychoanalytic theory since the late 1930s, had its own special conservative implications. And it was Freud himself who set this theoretical change in motion. In the 1920s he maintained that the ego functions as a protective barrier against stimulation, whether coming from the drives in the psyche or from external reality. The ego's main task is to keep an individual on an even keel of psychological excitation. Anxiety is a danger-signal against the threat of helplessness in the face of overwhelming stimulation. The ego was increasingly discussed as a coherent organization of psychic forces.[12]

One does not have to look far within early psychoanalytic theory to find how Freud's negativism had been reflected in his earlier work, and why ego psychology later proved so attractive. His whole system was designed to explain motivation when a person is in conflict, and the ego has relatively failed at its integrative task. As a therapist Freud was preoccupied with pulling problems apart and tearing fixations asunder, on the assumption that the patient's ego would be able to put the pieces back together again. For Freud analysis was automatically synthesis; constructive processes had originally been taken for granted by him, an issue which Jung had challenged him on.

Freud was a master at understanding the means of self-deception, but he ignored many processes of self-healing. Therefore, a main trend after his death was to correct this imbalance, and to focus on the ego as an agency integrating inner needs and outer realities. The ego has a unifying function, ensuring coherent behavior and conduct. The job of the ego is not just the negative one of avoiding anxiety, but also the positive one of maintaining effective performance. The ego's defenses may be adaptive as well as maladaptive. Adaptation is itself bedeviled by anxieties and guilts; but the ego's strength is not measured by the earlier psychoanalytic standard of what in a personality is denied or cut off, but rather by all the extremes than an individual's ego is able to unify.

A defective ego identity can be responsible for pathology that once would have been traced to instinctual drives. Rage, for example, can result from an individual's blocked sense of mastery. Aggression can stem from an inability to tolerate passivity. Because of ego psychology's explicit attention to the interaction of internal and external realities, it opened up possibilities for interdisciplinary cooperation in the social sciences.

At the same time that ego psychology shifted from the more traditional concern with the defensive ego to the problems of growth and adaptation, it looked for the collective sources of ego development. For instance, there can be a need for a sense of identity to be confirmed by social institutions, as Erik H. Erikson (1902-94) pointed out; and here organized religion and ritual can play a positive role.[13] But there are those who have wondered whether the upshot of ego psychology must not be inherently conservative. Society can either stimulate or cripple the development of the individual self, and also offer a pseudo-identity in place of an authentic self.

It is possible for ego psychology to give an undue weight to conformist values. Erikson was correct, in that the role of work was often neglected in earlier Freudian thinking. Yet it would be misleading to look at work just individualistically and not also socially; the spirit in which work gets done may matter little if its social purpose is questionable. It may even turn out to be an advantage not to have a secure sense of self. A peripheral standing can be a source of creativity, and alienation may be meritorious. Ego psychology can fail to distinguish between genuine and artificial continuities, in keeping with its tolerance for myth and legend.

It is striking how Erikson could take one-sided views of his biographical subjects.[14] In studying Martin Luther Erikson concentrated on the young man, isolating the ethical preacher from his career as an active political leader with mixed results for human betterment. And Erikson saw Mahatma Gandhi as only reconciling religious and political propensities. In each case Erikson sanctified a hero, leaving the impression of advocating bold change while ignoring the reactionary implications of the life under scrutiny.

Erikson's concepts always specified respect for the inner dimension of experience. But the "sense" of identity can be different from genuine identity, and illusory feelings do not equal social reality. Ego psychology can communicate too much of what we want to hear, and hopefulness should not be only linked to social conservatism. Ego psychology needs to confront the possibility that there may be few social groups worth being "integrated" with. On the other hand Freud's own kind of hostility to illusions does not guarantee that psychology will not be used complacently to justify the status quo. His own politics in the 1930s led him to justify a reactionary Austrian regime, and he wrote more warmly about Mussolini than one might have liked; Freud's International Psychoanalytic Association cooperated with the Nazi regime, agreeing that the Jewish members in Germany resign "voluntarily" in order to "save" psychoanalysis there.[15]

Walter Lippmann (1889-1974), the foremost American political pundit of the twentieth century, was one of the first in the English-speaking world before World War I to recognize the significance of Freud's contribution to moral thought. When the British Fabian socialist Graham Wallas was teaching at Harvard while Lippmann was still an undergraduate, Lippmann became his course assistant; and Wallas, already the author of a famous text on *Human Nature in Politics*[16], had a lasting influence on Lippmann's orientation. Lippmann seems to have first picked up on the significance of Freud through a friend who was translating Freud's *The Interpretation of Dreams*. World War I had a central impact on Lippmann's political thought; and starting with his *Public Opinion* he grew increasingly critical of liberalism's naïve hopes for public participation in decision-making. This book was centrally concerned with the role of the irrational. Lippmann introduced an unforgettable contrast between the complexities of the outside world and the distortions inherent in our need for simplifications in our heads. This antithesis between the immense social environment in which we live, and our ability to perceive it only indirectly, has continued to haunt democratic thinkers. Not only do our leaders acquire fictitious personalities, but symbols can govern political behavior.[17]

Between each of us and the environment there arises what Lippmann considered a "pseudo-environment". He thought that political behavior is a response not to the real world but to those pseudo-realities that we construct about phenomena that are beyond our direct knowledge. The implications Lippmann drew went beyond the importance of propaganda. Along with other critics of utilitarian psychology, Lippmann held that social life can not be explained in terms of pleasure-pain calculus. Despite all the criticisms of Benthamism that many writers (from Dickens to Dostoevsky) have advanced, self-interest still dominates the motives social science is apt to attribute to people; yet advantage, Lippmann believed, is itself not an irreducible concept.

In the light of the psychological insights he was emphasizing it is no wonder that Lippmann questioned idyllic conceptions of democracy. It is still hard for many people to accept the degree to which democracy, designed for harmony and tranquility, rests on symbols of unity, the manufacture of consent, and the manipulation of the masses. Yet Lippmann offered reasons enough for permanent skepticism about dogmas of popular sovereignty.

Perhaps the peak of Lippmann's conservatism came during the Eisenhower years, when the place of businessmen in high public office helped to evoke his most elitist proclivities. His *The Public Philosophy* was a natural law critique of democratic government, and yet his writing continued to belie his own most reactionary principles; in seeking to be a public educator, he never lost the rationalist faith that clear-headedness on public matters can be communicated to the people effectively.[18] He did not relinquish the democratic ideal that the voters can be rallied in defense of the public interest. Although Lippmann became doubtful about the capacity of democracy to survive under the complicated conditions of modern life, he devoted his journalistic talents to the democratic ideal of purifying the news for the public's consumption. He remained troubled by the inability of the democratic electorate to secure the needed information on which to act rationally.

LIBERALISM

In his respect for the dignity of his patients that made his innovations possible, and by means of his conviction that despite appearances all people are psychologically one, Freud ranks as a great heir of the Enlightenment. He was among those who are ever demanding more freedom. At the same time, however, in the development of psychoanalysis the open-ended quality of liberalism led to a revision of some of its most cherished premises. For Freud represents an aspect of liberalism's self-examination. It was an Enlightenment ideal to relate political impulses with the aim to achieve the best in us.

The trouble with the liberal tradition was its narrowness of understanding. It is frequently maintained for instance that *The Federalist* exhibits a realism about human motives, as well as a lack of utopianism about history, that might well benefit contemporary political thinking.[19] Yet in comparison to Freud *The Federalist* seems as shallow on human nature as much of the rest of liberalism. For while Madison, Jay, and Hamilton had a shrewd eye for human motivation, they lacked a sense of the limitlessness of human lusts and ambitions. Madison tells us that ambition can be made to counter-act ambition; human drives can supposedly be rearranged and engineered until a clocklike mechanism of checks and balances emerges to ensure constitutionalism. This smacks more of a utilitarian gimmick than of modern psychological depth. In Freud's quest for an understanding of human feelings he transcended liberalism and joined hands with thinkers usually associated with traditions alien to it. Along with Edmund Burke he recognized the intensity of destructive urges and the sense in which societal coercions can be psychologically necessary. With Marx he extended our appreciation of the extent of self-deception, self-alienation, and bad faith.

Freud also challenged traditional liberal democratic theory. He demonstrated the degree to which the child lives on within the adult, the way psychological uncertainties prevent people from ruling themselves. Liberalism in the spirit of John Stuart Mill has long sought for an elaboration of what a fully developed person would be like, and psychoanalytic conceptions of normality, including notions like individuation and the life cycle, are at least one such model of humanity.[20]

In some sense Freud does fit into the liberal tradition's quest for a theory of individualism; his whole therapeutic approach did encourage a kind of self-expression that was congenial to the aims of thinkers like Mill. Whatever the excesses to which psychoanalytic ideas were sometimes put, the historical Freud did not advocate self-indulgence; he might romantically posture in defiance of Western traditions, yet he stood for order and civility.

Freud might be appalled how now the public craves personal knowledge about historical figures and all public people. So that privacy today gets used in a manipulative way, and this state of intimacy is a political and social reality of contemporary life. Freud himself used his disguised autobiography, in his *The Interpretation of Dreams* and *The Psychopathology of Everyday Life*, to establish his principles. By daring to treat dreams and symptoms as meaningful, Freud had marked the end of an era that considered such material legitimately personal and outside the bounds of historical inquiry. Although Freud worked in behalf of autonomy, the implications of his ideas may have helped undermine central features of the ideals of privacy and individualism.

Freud was ready to call certain feelings and acts neurotic, yet he was cautious about describing what health might consist in. Normality is one of those ideas that can be discussed endlessly, not because it is an unreal question but precisely on the grounds that psychological health remains such a challenging idea. When one thinks what it might mean to treat patients in the context of a social environment of varying degrees of cruelty or social injustice, the significance of having some broad view of normality – as opposed to proposing a conformist adaptation to whatever the status quo might be – should be apparent.

The humanistically oriented revisionists of Freud's views, like Fromm or Erikson, were trying to inject genuine humanitarianism into a psychoanalytic worldview that appeared to end in therapeutic despair and ethical nihilism. In Fromm's neglected retort to Marcuse's famous dissection of neo-Freudianism Fromm accused Marcuse of ultimately advocating a nihilistic position.[21] There may be less danger in psychoanalysis being a devastating threat to Western culture than its lending undercover support to objectionable conformist practices. As an aspect of the success of Freudian ideas, psychodynamic notions of normality have become part of the prevailing social structure around us. One need only think about how Anna Freud (1895-1982) and her collaborators at Yale Law School came up with defending the idea of "psychological parenthood" and used it to support the notion that continuity in child custody cases should prevail over what these "experts" considered mere biological parenthood.[22] The value of continuity can be as unthinkingly enshrined as a part of middle class morality as the alleged dangers of traumas were once used to frighten people into conformity.

In correspondence and conversation Freud acknowledged that health was only one value among others, and that it could not exhaust morality as a whole. If he was wary about this whole subject of normality it was because he realized what kind of potential quagmire he was in danger of entering. He touched on the subject of normalcy only on the rare occasion. Once, in an essay designed to refute Jung's views on psychological types, Freud said that an ideally normal person would have hysterical, obsessional, and narcissistic layers in harmony; his idea communicated one of his characteristic demands about how high a standard he expected of people, for to be able to bear that much conflict and still function effectively presupposes a considerable degree of self-control and capacity to endure stress. Freud typically took for granted that the people he liked best to work with were creative and self-disciplined.

Freud feared that the more original and disturbing aspects of his ideas would be destroyed by the widespread acceptance of his work in the New World. But I wonder whether he did enough to prevent precisely this outcome. By not providing more hints about normality, and not owning up publicly to the wide variety of psychological solutions he found both therapeutically tolerable and humanly desirable, Freud contributed to what he most sought to prevent. He had set out, in the spirit of Nietzsche, to transform Western values; he was eager to go beyond accepted good and evil. When he assaulted "love thy neighbor as thyself" as both unrealistic and undesirable, he was explicitly trying to overturn Christian ethics.

It is logically impossible to talk about neurosis without at the same time implying a standard of maturity as well, and yet despite how powerful psychology can be in outlining human defects and weaknesses, it has not been nearly as successful in coming to terms with the positive side of human strength and coherence. In the end, the issue of the significance of normality and its relationship to nihilism has to be left an open question. Freud's psychology did contribute to our understanding of what it can mean to be human, and in that sense his ideas will be permanently interesting to political theorists. But it is impossible to attempt to spell out in a definitive way the ideological implications of psychoanalysis. For the wide range of writers who have been influenced by Freud constitute enough people to satisfy his fundamental aim of using his concept of the unconscious to transform how we think about ourselves.

To take one notable example, Freud ended up giving a significant stimulus to modern feminist theory. At the outset of Freud's work many of his most well known patients were women, and although as we saw he rejected Adler's pre-World War I invitation to change psychoanalytic thought to acknowledge the social sources of the plight of women, Freud's movement proved attractive to women who became leading analysts. As early as 1910 the issue of equality arose connected with a proposal for admitting women as full members of the Vienna Psychoanalytic Society. Freud personally insisted that it would be a "gross inconsistency" to "exclude women on principle."[23] Although the members were a generation younger than Freud, a vocal minority was opposed to Freud's open-mindedness, and he claimed at the time that it would therefore require him to proceed with great caution on this point. In fact Freud almost immediately did as he pleased and went on to welcome women analysts to an unusual extent, and in the context of the history of twentieth century professions his field became outstandingly receptive to the contributions of women.

As a matter of fact the novel ideas of two of his followers, Helene Deutsch (1884-1982) and Karen Horney (1885-1952), helped push Freud in the 1920s to composing essays specifically on femininity. Freud was characteristically sensitive on the issue of priorities, and he suspected that these women disciples were in danger of stealing a march on the topic of female psychology. Although it is these particular articles that Freud wrote in response to the innovations of Deutsch and Horney that created the body of his work that in the 1960s and 1970s would be subjected to so much later feminist criticism[24], it has still gone relatively unnoticed how Deutsch in particular was able to succeed in departing from Freud while at the same time remaining loyal to his basic conceptualization. Deutsch's *Psychoanalysis of the Sexual Functions of Women* first appeared in 1925, in a work where she was proud to have brought "the first ray of light on the unappreciated female libido". It was to be the first book by a psychoanalyst on the subject of femininity.[25] (According to Freud's thinking libido had to be necessarily masculine.) In later books Deutsch went further in the direction of developing her own views on women that substantially differed from Freud's theories.[26] Horney though had publicly disagreed with both Deutsch and also Freud, and it was Horney's views on the role of culture[27], in line with those of Fromm, that subsequently became publicly heralded as having pioneered in modern feminism.

Deutsch's more subtle differences with Freud have not gotten enough attention, although she had proceeded on the basis of her own human experience; and it was she who had the most appropriately philosophic attitude toward the perplexing issue of normality. In her earlier years, when she had been one of the most prominent teachers in the history of psychoanalysis (Reich was only one of her protégés), she used to make it a practice to ask prospective analysts in the course of interviewing them for acceptance into training what they thought a normal person would be like. It is of course an ultimately unanswerable conundrum, and yet one that as civilized people we too are obliged to consider repeatedly. Like all genuine questions in political philosophy, the problem of normality can never be solved; it remains a real issue, nonetheless, to the extent we choose to find it intolerable to contemplate a universe lacking in moral values.

NOTES

1. William M. Johnston, *The Austrian Mind: An Intellectual and Social History* (Berkeley, Univ. of California Press, 1972); Carl Schorske, *Fin-de-siecle Vienna: Politics and Culture* (New York, Knopf, 1979); Stefan Zweig, *The World of Yesterday* (London, Cassell, 1953).
2. Philip Rieff, *Freud: The Mind of the Moralist* (London, Victor Gollancz, 1959).
3. Bernhard Handlbauer, *The Freud-Adler Controversy*, translated by Laurie Cohen (Oxford, Oneworld, 1998); Edward Hoffman, *The Drive for Self: Alfred Adler and the Founding of Individual Psychology* (Reading, Mass., Addison-Wesley, 1994).
4. Manès Sperber, *Masks of Loneliness: Alfred Adler in Perspective*, translated by Krishna Winston (New York, Macmillan, 1974).
5. Myron Sharaf, *Fury on Earth: A Biography of Wilhelm Reich* (New York, St. Martin's Press, 1983).
6. Wilhelm Reich, *The Mass Psychology of Fascism*, translated by Vincent R. Carfagno (New York, Farrar, Straus & Giroux, 1970).
7. Daniel Burston, *The Legacy of Erich Fromm* (Cambridge, Harvard Univ. Press, 1991); Erich Fromm, *Escape From Freedom* (New York, Holt, Rinehart & Winston, 1941); Erich Fromm, *Man For Himself: An Inquiry into the Psychology of Ethics* (New York, Holt Rinehart & Winston, 1947); Erich

Fromm, *The Sane Society* (London, Routledge & Kegan Paul, 1956).
8 Herbert Marcuse, *Eros and Civilization: A Philosophical Inquiry into Freud* (Boston, The Beacon Press, 1955). See also Russell Jacoby, *Social Amnesia: A Critique of Conformist Psycholgy from Adler to Laing* (Boston, Beacon Press, 1975) and Martin Jay, *The Dialectical Imagination: A History of the Frankfurt School and the Institute of Social Research1923-50* (Boston, Little Brown, 1973).
9 Karen Horney, *The Neurotic Personality of Our Time* (London, Routledge & Kegan Paul, 1937); Harry Stack Sullivan, *Conceptions of Modern Psychiatry* (New York, Norton, 1953); Clara Thompson, *Psychoanalysis: Evolution and Development*, with an Introduction by Paul Roazen (New Brunswick, N.J., Transaction Publishers, 2002).
10 Henri Ellenberger, *The Discovery of the Unconscious: The History and Evolution of Dynamic Psychiatry* (New York, Basic Books, 1970); Carl G. Jung, *Two Essays on Analytical Psychology*, translated by R. F. C. Hull (New York, Meridian Books, 1953).
11 Geoffrey Cocks, *Psychotherapy in the Third Reich: The Göring Institute*, 2nd edition (New Brunswick, N.J., Transaction Publishers, 1997).
12 Lawrence J. Friedman, *Identity's Architect: A Biography of Erik H. Erikson* (New York, Scribner, 1999).
13 Erik H. Erikson, *Childhood and Society* (New York, Norton, 1950); Erik H. Erikson, *Identity:Youth and Crisis* (New York, Norton, 1968).
14 Erik H. Erikson, *Young Man Luther: A Study in Psychoanalysis and History* (New York, Norton, 1958); Erik H. Erikson, *Gandhi's Truth: On the Origins of Militant Nonviolence* (New York, Norton, 1969).
15 Paul Roazen, *Cultural Foundations of Political Psychology* (New Brunswick, N.J., Transaction Publishers, 2003), Ch. 1.
16 Graham Wallas, *Human Nature in Politics* (London, Constable, 1908).
17 Walter Lippmann, *Public Opinion* (New York, Macmillan, 1922).
18 Walter Lippmann, *The Public Philosophy*, with an Introduction by Paul Roazen (New Brunswick, N.J., Transaction, 1989).
19 Alexander Hamilton, James Madison, and John Jay, *The Federalist*, ed. Benjamin Wright (Cambridge, Harvard Univ. Press, 1961).
20 John Stuart Mill, "On Liberty", in *The Philosophy of John Stuart Mill*, ed. Marshall Cohen (New York, The Modern Library, 1961).
21 Erich Fromm, "The Human Implications of Instinctivistic 'Radicalism': A Reply to Herbert Marcuse," in *Voices of Dissent*, ed. Irving Howe (New York, Grove Press, 1958), pp. 313-320.
22 Joseph Goldstein, Albert Solnit, Sonja Goldstein, and Anna Freud, *The Best Interests of the Child: The Least Detrimental Alternative* (New York, The Free Press, 1996).
23 *Minutes of the Vienna Psychoanalytic Society*, Vol. 2: 1908-1910, ed. Herman Nunberg and Ernst Federn, translated by M. Nunberg (New York, International Universities Press, 1967), p. 477.
24 Susan Brownmiller, *Against Our Will: Men, Women and Rape* (New York, Simon and Schuster, 1975).
25 Helene Deutsch, *Psychoanalysis of the Sexual Functions of Women*, ed. by Paul Roazen, translated by Eric Mosbacher (London, Karnac, 1991); Paul Roazen, *Helene Deutsch: A Psychoanalyst's Life*, 2nd edition (New Brunswick, N.J., Transaction Publishers, 1992).
26 Helene Deutsch, *The Psychology of Women*, Vols. 1 & 2 (New York, Grune & Stratton, 1944-1945).
27 Karen Horney, *Feminine Psychology* (New York, Norton, 1967).

11
CANADA: POLITICAL PSYCHOLOGY

Although it is a source of perpetual frustration to Canadians that outsiders, especially in the States, take so little notice of events taking place north of the long border with America, it is not easy for outsiders to follow events in Canada. I did happen to live and teach at York University in Toronto for almost twenty-five years; inevitably I tried to get acquainted with not only what might be most characteristic of psychoanalysis in Canada, but more specifically with how one might understand leading psychological issues in Canadian political and social life. I happened to be only in the country for a few short months when a leading Canadian historian, once he became acquainted with my special interests, alerted me to the "problem" associated with the life and career of William Lyon Mackenzie King (1874-1950). Although psychoanalysts like to think of themselves today as attentive to the external world, and politics in particular, in reality the extravagances of the phenomena of tyrants like Hitler or Stalin seem more relevant than the more commonplace appearing issue of democratic leadership.

Professional students of Canadian politics are generally agreed that King was the most successful politician in Canada's history. King became leader of the Liberal Party in 1919, and before his retirement in 1948 he had served as Prime Minister a total of 22 years (1921-1930 and 1935-1948). King had succeeded in leading the country through the trying days of the Great Depression and World War II. What is more, King was intellectually serious: he enjoyed listening to classical music; as a young man he had been a student of the economist and social theorist Thorstein Veblen; and he was an avid reader who wrote books of his own.

Once Mackenzie King's spiritualism, however, became public shortly after his death, the standard evaluations of his reputation began to shift.

The man renowned in his lifetime for political caution and moderation, with the acute antennae able to balance the complex shifting forces of Canadian life, was also capable of having consulted mediums for the sake of contact with "the other world," and he regularly used to relax with a "rapping table" at the end of the day's work. Any leader who reads the Bible daily, as did Woodrow Wilson too, and like King makes marginal comments of his own, seems odd enough to our secular ears. It had long been known that King also had a special devotion not only to the memory of his deceased mother – a prominent feature in King's study was a portrait of her, lighted at all times by a special lamp despite his being a cheapskate – but also to a succession of terrier dogs. But Mackenzie King became a national joke after it became public that he thought he could communicate with dead political leaders, on at least one occasion claiming to have called a national election based on such a conversation, and thought of himself as having extrasensory means of communicating with living politicians.

The gradual release of King's monumentally extensive diaries provided abundant evidence of the scope of his obsessions and superstitions; in particular, the high-sounding moralism of this dull, lonely old bachelor looked hypocritical in the light of what would appear to be his youthful frequenting of prostitutes. Evidently he was saving his diaries for use in future memoirs; more than once he left instructions for them to be destroyed after his death. According to his will, only the parts he had marked were to be preserved, but since he never got around to going through them, the literary executors decided that everything was to be kept. The privacy he had taken pains to safeguard was now impossible, and the conceit of this failed program of partial literary suppression ruinously hurt his reputation. Not unlike Richard Nixon with his tapes, King's diaries discredited him, at least initially, in the eyes of history.

One 1916 incident in King's life, curiously overlooked by historians, highlights what evidence about psychopathology might teach on the subject of King's political successes. In the midst of some key personal losses in life, while temporarily out of power and working in the United States for John D. Rockefeller, Jr. and the Rockefeller Foundation, King at the age of 41 consulted an eminent Canadian neurologist in Baltimore, Maryland, Lewellys F. Barker (1867-1943), with whom King stayed in contact for medical consultations until Barker's death. At the same time King also saw the distinguished psychiatrist Adolf Meyer (1866-1950). Due to the successful publicity that Freud's students have attained, combined with the impoverished state of psychiatric history in general, Meyer's name is almost forgotten. Meyer was born and educated in Switzerland; in 1892, at the age of 26, he came to the United States. By 1910 he was the founding head of the Phipps Clinic at Johns Hopkins, a university that already had notably benefited from Rockefeller philanthropy and would do so again. Overall, Meyer became arguably the most important single figure ever to teach psychiatry in twentieth-century North America. Meyer's informal clinical notes to himself about King have survived, and so have the hospital records at Johns Hopkins where King briefly stayed from October 30 to November 11, 1916, having teeth extracted and adenoids removed. (In 1930 Harold Lasswell made a prediction about the future significance of such hospital records for political leaders.)

King's diaries report his own version of his 1916 troubles and his clinical encounters. For example, King's curious conviction about the power of "electrical" influences in his life does add a special dimension to his later spiritualist beliefs and practices, that otherwise might seem to be accounted for by how widespread such notions were around the turn of the century. (Freud himself wrote about his own involvement with the occult.) In King's case, however, he was troubled enough then to seek medical help. A specific instance of what he called "the phenomena of regarding people as near at times and of their exerting an influence upon me" is that while King was coming out of the anesthesia for an operation at Johns Hopkins, he saw the letters "Hughes" before him; it was presidential election day in 1916, and King took this vision to be a sign of the electoral success of Charles Evans Hughes. Once it was instead clear that Woodrow Wilson had in fact been re-elected, thanks to the Western returns, King concluded that he had only been accessible to the influence of Hughes's Eastern support, and that that accounted for the misleading visual communication.

The world of 1916 is so far away from us now as to require that we guard against any hasty retrospective diagnoses. This period in King's life does involve clear signs of psychopathology: in Barker's words, "ideas of reference (electrical influences), sensitiveness, obesity, pathological emotivity, hallucinations of perineal sense...[and] insomnia." The hospital records record the diagnoses "Psychoneurosis" and "Psychasthenia," the former term Freud's and the latter one coined by the Parisian Pierre Janet. However, it is essential to recall not only that King recovered quickly in 1916, but to keep in mind the almost supernormal way in which King later bested his opponents and so successfully governed Canada for all those years. Even though psychoanalytic ideas have so often been misused for reductionistic purposes, belittling human accomplishments, Freud himself used to like to quote Prince Hamlet: "There are more things in Heaven and Earth, Horatio, than are dreamt of in your philosophy."

By the time King went to work for Rockefeller in 1914, he was unsure about his future. King had already acquired a considerable reputation as a labor mediator; he had helped organize a new Department of Labour, and won election to the House of Commons at the age of 33. When the Liberal Government was defeated in 1911 King had lost his seat. Although he was re-nominated in 1913, parliament extended its life because of the war and King had no chance to contest the seat until the next election in 1917. After Canada entered World War I in 1914 King had not taken part in the war effort, as his energies went to helping the Rockefellers, especially with their mining problems in Colorado. But in 1916 the urgency of the original call from the Rockefellers was over; Colorado was quiet and the mines were becoming profitable again. By the summer of 1916 Canadian troops in Europe had already suffered badly. Canada's casualties in that war were proportionately to exceed by far the American dead and wounded. King's absences from Canada were politically awkward enough that later, by April 1920, he had to defend himself in the House of Commons against the charge of cowardice.

In 1916 King was also being buffeted by the specter of familial losses. King's father, who finally died on August 30, had been ill and blind for some time; one of King's sisters, a year older, had died in the spring of 1915; and his mother was in poor health – she was to die on December 18, 1917. Before the death of his older sister, King already knew that his only brother, a physician who was four years younger, had contracted tuberculosis (although he would live until 1922). We do know that as a young man doing graduate work in Chicago King was "nervous and worried...fearing a breakdown he consulted a doctor...."[1]

Exactly what transpired medically in the summer of 1916 remains obscure. King had discontinued his diary, then started it up again (perhaps a sign of personal distress) from June 22 to July 2, and finally resumed it on October 13 after which the record for the rest of the year is pretty complete. On June 22 he wrote that he had "literally fled" to Kingsmere, his country house outside Ottawa, Canada's capital, "away from the world of humans." His suspended political career and family conditions "added to my unsettled state and caused me to fret and worry, acting impulsively...." Writing that he was "depressed and disheartened," King found himself "in an encounter with my own nature such as I have never known before. It has been at times as though a fire would devour me, and I have been unable to get rest by night or day." The entry for June 23-26 includes his belief that "the mind itself [is] the instrument of a higher something which is the real spiritual self....Experiences I have had have shewn me wherein one's self may pass almost completely as it were from the body, and that the invisible and intangible is more real than the visible." For June 27-29 he wrote:

> I continue to worry over the nervous condition I find myself suffering from at times. I fear that there maybe some injury to my spine, that the pressure in the nerves of it is the cause....The tendency to worry is something I must guard against. I...become unduly suspicious that things are against me, when there is no reason for it....

King's general hypochondriacal predilections and paranoia were observed by many, and seem consistent with his vanity and self-involvement. Paranoid thinking may have given King a special edge in politics, though on occasion it also proved an interference. At this time King (a lifelong bachelor) also wrote: "What I should like most of all to settle is the settlement for life with one I could love."

Soon after resuming keeping his diary, on October 16 he reported that a "sculptor in Italy" had "written suggesting a bust of mother in marble. I fear I cannot resist it. After all she and father are more to me than all else, why should I not preserve as far as I may be [able] all the inspiration of their lives." King would soon mention the matter in his interview with Meyer.

On October 24 King had been summoned to New York by wire the preceding day. King said that when John D. Rockefeller, Jr. had asked him "how I was, I told him that I had suffered a great deal from nervousness and was going to consult a specialist." Rockefeller recommended Dr. Simon Flexner who promptly spoke to King, learned the nature of his trouble, and then advised King to consult at Johns Hopkins. On October 25th Flexner wrote to Barker, "He has consulted already a number of Canadian doctors... and what he now needs is to be set up by an authoritative person whom he will trust implicitly and whose directions he will carry out without feeling that he must still get other advice." On October 26th Barker examined King and wrote Meyer, "The principal subjective disturbance is that of being influenced electrically by others and of influencing others in this way." On October 27 King had an x-ray of the head and he claimed that "I could feel the electric sparks on the back of my head as the rays were shot through the skull onto a plate beneath."

Barker also commented on King's "hallucinations of perineal sense." No medical historians I have consulted have been confident on the issue of what could have been meant by this, other than to suggest that either hallucinations of smell or tingling sensations at the anus might have been implied. King was more than a little concerned about the state of the base of his spine and insisted that he be x-rayed there in order to rule out trouble.

King recorded about his

> Long interview with Dr. Adolph Meyer, Specialist in Mental Hygiene at Johns Hopkins. I outlined the conflict in my thoughts between spiritual aspirations and material struggles and conflicts, the fight with myself. This he explained was unnecessary and wrong, that all the phenomena I had described to him were natural enough...and that what was health, I was mistaking for an evil passion....Told me at all costs to maintain my independence of thought....To become calm as respects the internal conflict I had described, and then proceed 'like a sun on its course' regardless of other men, or their views. To be myself. He was very strong on this, also on my preserving my idealism.

King was clearly pleased with Meyer:

> I felt this man had a soul which could understand mine. That he too was a man with ideals and understood the ideal....As I left him he shook hands with me twice. Spoke of the pleasure it was to meet me, said he hoped we might meet again and that he could expect great things of me. This was one of the really important interviews of my life....All day I have been comparatively free of the feelings I had entertained before....My mind is greatly relieved tonight....I had come to a point where I thought my work for the future would be undermined by this nervous dread. Now I believe it will be greater than ever.

Adolf Meyer was knowledgeable about Freud, a founder of the American Psychoanalytic Association (1911) although clearly no adherent or disciple; Meyer had met Freud when he came from Vienna to receive an honorary degree from Clark University at Worcester, Massachusetts in 1909. By then Meyer was a celebrity in his own right: he, along with Carl G. Jung from Zurich, was one of the three to be honored with a doctor of laws degree. Meyer picked up immediately on the sexual material in King's clinical material. Meyer wrote a letter to Barker about King: "The problem of our patient [is]...first, a perfectly obvious elimination of natural sex life from the intensely religious and spiritual trend of affection, which only once became focused away from his mother on a nurse, unfortunately without response on her part...."

It had been Freud who had maintained at his now famous Clark lectures how "pathological symptoms constitute a portion of the subject's sexual life or even the whole of his sexual life...."[2] (Few psychoanalysts would speak that way nowadays.) It has to be striking that while in Baltimore in 1916 King made a little trip to visit the woman he had once been seriously interested in marrying, the nurse – now herself married – who had in 1897 helped him through a strictly medical crisis, but whom King's family had objections to his marrying.

However, the text of King's diaries itself has to be considered a subject for interpretation because he had a notoriously convenient memory, and, without actually directly lying, left out inconvenient conversations. For example, on the critical issue of marriage, which King would allude to throughout the remainder of his life, he chose to cite Barker's advice that if he found the right woman he ought not to put off getting married. King never mentioned in the diary, however, Meyer's opinion that was decidedly against King's marrying. So, while King did not see Meyer after 1916 (there are a few brief letters between them) and King continued to consult Barker right up into World War II, King followed Meyer's advice even though what Barker told him fit in better with King's conception of himself. The unreliability of King's diary, in leaving out Meyer's emphatic opposition to King's taking a wife, has considerable importance for King's diary as a whole. Because King's version of things is often the only one available, historians have been too apt to accept King's accounts as unquestionably the truth.

The example of King's life can do something in itself for our understanding of psychological theory. I do not think we have been adequately prepared for the idea that someone so privately odd could nonetheless function in a political democracy in such a successful manner. If his 1916 problems did not turn out to function as a political deficit, it was because his genuine assets were so large. I believe that King's lack of "normalcy," which was so extreme as to lead clinicians (whom I have asked for advice) to think in terms of a so-called latent psychosis or even schizophrenia, must have lent a special edge to his political capacities. It is not possible to sustain the early hope of Lasswell that democratic character can be identified with psychological health, not to mention the suggestion once forwarded by Freud's biographer Ernest Jones that cabinet ministers, like foreign secretaries, ought to submit themselves to psychoanalytic inspection before being appointed to their posts.

I leave the reader with a quandary. We know that every historical explanation has to imply certain psychological assumptions about human behavior. We also think that Freud's conceptualization makes possible a critically important understanding of human motives. But even when we have psychiatric evidence, as in the case of Mackenzie King, that does not by itself settle everything. I was first drawn to Freud because of a central concern with how we ought to live, and the moral implications of psychology. King's life does successfully challenge certain naïve stereotypes. King played such an immense role in Canadian public affairs that it is a nonsensical question to ask whether what he did was good or bad for the country. It would be like questioning whether an immensely long-standing marriage was successful or not. Canada and King are now unthinkable without each other.

Nowadays, thanks partly to the impact of the Freudian revolution in ideas, a North American political candidate's private life is so much a public matter that privacy gets used manipulatively. So, to the extent that King becomes more interesting because of his psychological peculiarities, it may be that someday it will seem that the release of his diaries turns out to be, instead of a self-inflicted wound, another bit of canniness on the part of this political magician.

Heather Roberston's *Lily: A Rhapsody in Red*[3] is a zany, rollicking novel that has insights about Mackenzie King that are important for social scientists. It is the sequel to *Willie: A Romance*, which had begun by describing King as "a passionate man unable to love." That premise puts the issue of his emotional life in a nutshell, making more sense to me than elaborate conjectures based on psychoanalytic theories of neurosis. Although many of the incidents in *Willie* about King's sexuality may appear far-fetched,

Robertson has an intuitive understanding of King's character that ought to be added to the more standard outlooks on his personality and career.

Robertson is more ambitious than just aiming to understand King's personality, for in *Willie* she sought to link King and the First World War in "the birth pangs of our nationality." Volume I of *The King Years* was based on an imaginative reworking of King's diary, and Robertson created fictional characters alongside historical ones. She also made partial use of the medical report based on King's stay at Johns Hopkins in the fall of 1916, which makes her the only one to have paid any significant attention to that interesting tale; her quotations from the report of the psychiatrist-in-chief (Meyer), who at the time was the most eminent figure in his profession in North America, appears so late in the novel that it may have been easy for many to think of it as fictionalized. But in her acknowledgments at the outset of *Willie* she did alert the reader to a "medical report" along with other papers from the Public Archives.

Lily is a good deal shorter than the first volume of *The King Years*, and starts from a supposed secret marriage between King and Miss Lily Coolican. The whole Coolican family is entirely fictional. It seems to me that Robertson is right in thinking that King had one of the more convenient memories in political history and, for example, chose to manipulate his relationship with Laurier and his wife into a legend that would promote King's career. King certainly wrote and talked about the need for a wife to share his life, although not enough attention has been devoted to scrutinizing the implications of his desire and the meaning of its frustration.

Much of *Lily* is devoted to Lily's growing involvement in radical politics; during the Depression she joins the Communist party. Robertson has relied on the Edmonton *Bulletin* for the trials of John Brownlee and Owen McPherson. But entirely aside from the picture of Canadian life that Robertson has decided to emphasize, *Lily* presents meaningful aspects of King's characteristic behavior. Lily's mother is both an inmate of an insane asylum as well as later a prominent spiritualist, and King is described as her "most frequent correspondent."

Robertson brings in Freud at a number of points, but I have the suspicion that there is something anachronistic about involving him quite so much in King's way of thinking. I doubt Robertson is right that it is because of Freud, as opposed to the late nineteenth-century spiritualist heritage, that King paid so much attention to his dreams and "visions." She quotes from the diaries so often, and has such a remarkable capacity to recreate the spirit of King's writing, however, that I would not want to challenge her without having gone through every passage of King's diary with care. Robertson has King acknowledging Freud's help in understanding the danger of unguarded moments like slips of the tongue, and she gives Freud a part in Lily Coolican's consciousness that is historically out of place in Canada for that period, however much sense it makes in the present-day climate of opinion.

I think Robertson is intuitively correct, even if the diaries should not bear out the specific interconnections she makes, in bringing together King's discussion of spiritualism, the "need for constant watchfulness," and his longing for a happy marriage. Robertson is absolutely right in highlighting King's psychiatric symptom connected with the influence of electrical currents. Although she does not make the point, one hypothesis would be that a paranoid disposition on King's part could have helped give him an edge on his political opponents. Robertson also, I think, takes the correct attitude towards discounting the issue of manifest homosexuality, and in emphasizing the role of King's egotism in his problems with memory.

The novel is an enormous amount of fun: the valet Nicol (who could in reality be indiscreet), McLeod the butler, secretaries like F. A. McGregor and Edward Pickering, as well as Mrs. Patteson, all have walk-on roles. Bethune, Massey, "young Forsey," Meighen, Lord Byng, and even Houdini play their part. The diaries are sometimes the more humorous since one cannot be certain whether a passage is really the prime minister's own writing, or the product of Robertson's imagination. A visit to Mussolini struck me as hilarious.

For Robertson, King is "the quintessential Canadian." In the combination of idealism and mysticism, craftiness and nuttiness, King does emerge remarkably similar to characters we are familiar with from Robertson Davies's novels. If this subject is to be properly assimilated into our understanding of the Canadian past, however, the full story ought to extend to how this side of King managed to remain known to a few while hidden from most, as well as the circumstances under which it finally became public.

Those who thought the opposition to Prime Minister Brian Mulroney's proposed Meech Lake accord was miss-guided or even unpatriotic are not going to like *Deconfederation: Canada Without Quebec* by David Bercuson and Barry Cooper[4]. So far I have seen it attacked in both *MacLean's* and the *Montreal Gazette*. Yet I found it a splendidly argued, well-written and mostly convincing book.

The title is at best awkward, for I doubt that "deconfederation" is a word authorized by any dictionary. The subtitle is also an unwise one, because the book itself is really an essay on the past and future fate of decent liberal democracy in Canada, a matter that should interest psychoanalysts as citizens. A reader might think by the way the book has been packaged that what can be expected is only a treatise on what lies ahead after the failure of the Meech Lake agreement to get implemented. Mr. Bercuson, who is a historian, and Mr. Cooper, a political theorist, both teach at the University of Calgary, and they have come up with a serious inquiry into how we arrived at where we are now, as well as what we ought to expect in the future.

The short preface to *Deconfederation* is unfortunate in that it sounds too embattled. The authors contend, in a book dedicated to the memory of the separatist Rene Levesque, that he was right: "Canada cannot survive when French-speaking and English-speaking Canadians relate to each other like two scorpions in a bottle. It is time to break the bottle, allow the scorpions to escape, and rebuild what is left." As if that were not enough to raise hackles, one of the authors admits he was never either a supporter or an opponent of official bilingualism, but considered it "beside the point." It seems all right for the proverbial man-in-the-street to say as much, but academics are supposed to bow loyally to the merits of bilingualism.

Both authors begin with the premise, which many other serious observers also share, that Meech Lake was a terrible idea, one that would have meant an acceleration of the process of decentralization of power to the provinces. Bercuson and Cooper do not have much to say about the Free Trade agreement, which may have been mandated by the increasingly international nature of commerce and finance; but I would be hardly alone in thinking that Free Trade weakened the hands of the federal government in a way which, combined with Meech Lake, would have meant the end of the Canadian federal system as we have known it.

The authors openly state, and here is perhaps where they have caused controversy: "the Canadian experiment has failed." They do not like the idea any more than any other responsible citizen, but they have been willing to call a spade a spade. Both French-speaking and English-speaking Canadians have been "in an endless dance with the devil," and the authors are insistent "that the music must end. Someone must shoot the piano player." They claim that they are prepared to have readers choose to shoot them in return, but I doubt any author is adequately prepared for a terrible reception to work that is in fact thoroughly good.

After the preface the book settles down to become an engrossingly good read about an important contemporary democracy. *Deconfederation* is unambiguous in its advocacy of the independence of Quebec. The authors argue that Canadian constitutional and economic crises are bound together, and that one will not get solved without the other. Their thesis ought not to be confused, as it no doubt will be, with a know-nothing attitude of "good riddance!" to Quebec. They are proposing the possibility of an amicable and harmonious separation, not because they expect it to be painless but for the reason that "the demands of Quebec's ethnic and cultural nationalism are simply incompatible with the continued existence of Canada as a liberal democracy."

Deconfederation is a fine inquiry into the nature of modern constitutional government. According to all the classic theorists of liberalism, like John Stuart Mill in England, the state is supposed to be a neutral sphere in which social conflicts can be successfully resolved. The authors not only see contemporary Quebec nationalist aspirations as at odds with the ideal of liberal democracy, but they are also opposed to such trendy concepts as state-supported "multiculturalism." They think that for the state to support ethnic and cultural nationalism, it has to be at odds with the ideal of people being treated equally before the law.

Canada is in a mess, according to Bercuson and Cooper, because economic and political crises have taken a back seat to the Quebec problem; this one central issue has been paralyzing. Granting new special treatment to Quebec means giving fresh areas of power to the other provinces as well. As we saw dramatically in the collapse of the old Yugoslavia, and may yet witness elsewhere in eastern Europe and the former Soviet Union as well, when the authority of the state dissolves it can let loose frightening dogs of historical prejudice. The authors do not mention the possibility of violence, but they do note the logical link between Meech Lake and the claims of the Mohawks to a distinct society, and how explosive the situation at Oka became; and they point out how ironic it was for Bourassa's provincial government to call upon the help of the army of Canada to deal with the native people.

Bercuson and Cooper talk tough about how Ottawa has sacrificed its responsibilities for fear of offending Quebeckers: "And when Quebec proves that it is as incompetent as Ottawa, as it surely did at Oka and Khanesatake, Ottawa steps in without complaint and without criticism to pull the province's chestnuts out of the fire." Canadians have been living in a country that has been lavish in allowing bureaucracy to grow out of all proportion; the kinds of indexed pensions members of parliament are entitled to is only the tip of the iceberg. The authors think that it is time political leaders focused their attention on the real problems of Canada, and put aside a seemingly endless series of constitutional crises which each time get resolved to the detriment of democracy conceived as the equality of all citizens before the law.

In 1960 the interest costs servicing the existing federal deficit totaled about 11 percent of the budget; thirty years later that figure had grown close to 40 percent. One does not have to be a professional economist to realize that something has gone wrong here, and the authors almost gleefully cite polling data to indicate just how disaffected from the political system most Canadians are. Canada's massive overextension is merely illustrated, according to the authors, by the cost of the policy of official bilingualism. Some of the most persuasive portions of the book come in the sections on how Canada came to its later situation, and here as far as I can tell the authors make no miss-steps.

Yet I do have reservations about *Deconfederation*. Why does the book contain no criticism of Pierre Elliott Trudeau? His policies are being implicitly assailed here without his philosophy undergoing any kind of reasonable challenge. One wonders whether he did not try over-centralizing the country, and a later generation was left to pay the price for that approach.

But I would suggest even more subversively than the authors that the root problem may lie in contradictions within democracy itself. The Canadian system worked satisfactorily as long as elites governed without much outside interference. To take an extreme example, if you ask the Croatians and the Serbians what they think of each other, the results are going to be appalling. Compromises have to be made with the glittering ideals of liberal democracy, and that is what most of Canadian history has been about. Bercuson and Cooper, however, are calling for more popular sovereignty: referenda, citizen initiatives and the recall of elected members of parliament. The public may instead be entitled to more genuine leadership.

For those who rightly lament the way the fabric of Canada may seem to have come unstuck, and longingly look south, I would remind them that up to his death in 1826, Thomas Jefferson, when he used the expression "my country," was still referring to his native state of Virginia. Not until the tragedy of the Civil War was America cemented into a nation, and presumably Canada will find a happier resolution to its latest difficulties. Bercuson and Cooper may have violated the taboo of thinking the unthinkable, as they speculate about different alternative terms of divorce between Canada and Quebec. But surely public debate and the democratic process can only be enhanced by fairly weighing the pros and cons of their argument.

Canada was conceived as a country following what was understood as the trauma represented by the American Civil War. And although Canada has therefore had a far weaker federal government than America, with more power reserved to the Canadian provinces than that to the American states, the existence of a tradition of civil liberties in Canada has been far more fragile than that mandated by the American Constitution. In *Uncivil Obedience: The Tactics and Tales of a Democratic Agitator*[5] Alan Borovoy, the general counsel of the small Canadian Civil Liberties Association, draws on his experience as a reformer to distil a splendid account of activist tactics that work while preserving a free democratic community. Borovoy is thought provoking precisely because he has been so centrally committed to the cause of civil liberties. An idealist without being in quest of a utopia, he describes in concrete detail the compromises he has made to maintain the cohesiveness of his own organization.

Aside from tips he offers about how to promote social change, Borovoy takes some stimulating stands. For example, he was opposed to Trudeau's idea of a constitutionally entrenched bill of rights on the grounds that the judiciary is an inherently undemocratic institution that cannot be relied on to protect freedom. Borovoy shares the faith of the founders of liberalism that human reason is capable of assessing social alternatives without the aid of artificial assistance such as laws against the promotion of hate. So Borovoy thought it unwise for the Canadian authorities to have prosecuted Holocaust deniers like James Keegstra and Ernst Zundel.

Borovoy offers a broad menu for human rights activists and illustrates how to go about championing liberty. *Uncivil Obedience* is both passionate and practical in advocating such devices as publication, dislocation, litigation, and coalition. Disadvantaged people, he asserts, have many alternatives to lawbreaking, as he recounts how it has been possible for him to agitate without crossing the border into unlawfulness. He presents an admirable example of someone who has been a hell-raiser without ceasing to be a pragmatist.

In reflecting back on the debate over Mulroney's Meech Lake agreement, many observers were reminded of Shakespeare's suggestion that first we ought to "kill all the lawyers." Trudeau may have over-centralized the country through the Charter of Rights, and Mulroney's efforts to get Quebec to sign on to the constitutional repatriation of 1982 may have been misguided; but among the chief culprits, I think, have to be ranked the experts who draft things for the respective parties, and are still being called upon to speak out as political pundits.

No matter how tempting it may be for the Canadian public to regard constitutional issues as a bore, by June 1990 the country felt that the failure to pass Meech Lake presented a watershed in Canadian history. For some, like Trudeau, the whole Mulroney initiative was a "total bungle," mismanaged from the start. According to Trudeau's view sleeping dogs should have been left alone. For others, however, Quebec had to be "brought back" into the political family.

Patrick J. Monahan is a law professor who was an adviser to both Ian Scott, then Ontario attorney general, and Ontario premier David Peterson; Monahan takes the position that the deal first struck by the premiers in 1987 represented a legitimate compromise that met a crying need. Monahan's *Meech Lake: The Inside Story*[6] is an effort to play catch-up on earlier accounts that cast doubt on the merits of the Mulroney efforts.

Monahan's book is splendid in its blow-by-blow account of the events during the three-year struggle to get Meech Lake passed by all the provinces. And he does a good job of laying out exactly what was missing, from the point of view of Robert Bourassa, premier of Quebec, in the loose strings left by the original repatriation. *Meech Lake: The Inside Story* exemplifies why the deal itself failed. For this is a lawyer talking, and what is missing is more of a philosophic and political perspective.

The opponents of what Mulroney had cobbled together were not just concerned with preserving the equality between all the provinces. They also sought to uphold an ideal of citizenship incompatible with the decentralization that Meech Lake symbolized. Monahan has a strong concluding chapter, which is pessimistic about the way ahead for Canada. He has, though, with all his excellent details, missed how Meech Lake related to the earlier U.S. free-trade agreement. The argument over Mulroney's policy of free trade bore a complicated relationship to the Meech Lake issue itself, and it will not do for Monahan to duck the earlier matter.

Although democratic theory has roots as far back as ancient Greece, it was only in the eighteenth century that thinkers began to propose that democracy was part of the wave of the future. The specific form of parliamentarism as Canadians know it was largely a product of nineteenth century developments, and Canada's political institutions owe their origins to a Western European heritage. British thinkers insisted on the desirability of regular elections, with governments being responsible to a broad electorate, while French theorists worked out a defense of the legitimacy of political parties and of fundamental laws, such as written constitutions.

In *Direct Democracy in Canada: The History and Future of Referendums*[7] Patrick Boyer makes the case for more direct participation by citizens in decision-making; his book documents in conscientious detail Canada's history of reliance on referendums, right up to 1992. He deals with the 1942 national plebiscite releasing Mackenzie King's government from its 1940 promise of no conscription for overseas military service, as well as the 1898 vote on the prohibition of alcohol. The 1898 vote was so close that Laurier's government ignored the results but the 1942 decision does seem to have given King more room to maneuver.

Boyer has performed an important service in placing the Charlottetown Accord of constitutional amendments within historical context. Boyer, who was a Progressive Conservative Member of Parliament starting in 1984, is obviously a genuine expert on Canadian election laws. He believes that Canadians have been burdened with political institutions that are too paternalistic. Deference to authority has alienated voters from the political process, and referendums, he thinks, far from being divisive are a way of helping ensure that governments, once they get into power, do not allow themselves to drift too far from the wishes of the governed.

While it is impossible to challenge Boyer's knowledge of his subject, he does not nail down his argument because he fails adequately to consider the counter arguments. Boyer mentions Joe Clark, after the 1992 referendum, asking: "Do you still believe in referendums?" seeming to expect Boyer, who was pro-accord, to say no. But there are more abstract problems associated with reconciling plebiscites with democratic theory than Boyer might like to think.

Around the same time as Boyer's book was being written, the citizens of Colorado approved a referendum that would bar any law that protects homosexuals from discrimination. Americans have had a history of their own in connection with direct democracy, and populism has at times promoted racism. It would be simplistic to reaffirm Al Smith's 1920s maxim that the cure for democracy is more democracy. Ross Perot had been promoting the use of electronic town meetings, and many progressive people of good will have shuddered at what the results of such an institution might be. In times of great stress an electorate can become fascistic, which is why Sinclair Lewis wrote a novel called *It Can't Happen Here*, warning against complacency.

I wonder why Boyer, in his account of Canada's "long journey towards direct democracy," does not put a reform like that of proportional representation within a comparative national framework. Although the opponents of proportional representation have exaggerated the extent to which it contributed to Hitler's success in becoming head of Germany's elected government, I would have thought that the fact that the most highly educated country in Europe could vote that way would be a chilling restraint on how far Canada should change. To take another unsettling historical case: does post-Tito Yugoslavia support Boyer's general faith that "human nature requires power to be diffused, not concentrated"?

Germany has recently been in the process of banning political parties and taking more strict legal measures against the free expression of opinion than I think it necessary for us to imitate in North America. But the case for democracy is not secure unless we forthrightly examine the problems that lie in its path, even if these potential obstacles have been raised by thinkers far less generous and intellectually attractive than Boyer appears to be himself.

In 1964, when U. S. Senator Barry Goldwater was challenging President Lyndon Johnson in an election, a remarkable number of eminent American psychiatrists responded to an inquiry for their political opinions from a now-defunct magazine, *Fact*. The bulk of the political responses, couched in psychiatric lingo, were so unfair that Goldwater sued and won a substantial settlement.

Such psychiatric guesswork lent support to the view that psychiatrists are prone to make excessive claims about how much they know about human nature. In 1965 the American Psychoanalytic Association formulated an excellent rebuttal to such partisan uses of psychiatric knowledge in politics:

> Although the presence of severe and crippling mental illness is, of course, disqualifying, these conditions do not escape public recognition. Apart from such instances, however, there are no valid, well-established criteria which can be applied in the evaluation of a political leader. It is not the presumed underlying bases of behavior which count, but how these are resolved in final aims and actions.
>
> At the present state of our knowledge, therefore judgments about a political candidate must be based on his views, the political company in which he moves, his past opinions and actions, and those aspects of his character which are open to the scrutiny of all, rather than an assessment of his emotional conflicts and idiosyncrasies.

In Canada, a little more than thirty years later, psychiatry once again got discredited by armchair psychoanalytic reasoning. Quebec's separatist Premier Lucien Bouchard may have been terrible for the future of Canada, and many again feared for the possibility of a break-up of the nation. But Dr. Vivian Rakoff's kind of name-calling, in the course of a written report but based on no personal knowledge of Mr. Bouchard, was objectionable. The idea that Dr. Rakoff could explain Mr. Bouchard by throwing around the supposed diagnosis of "esthetic character disorder," something no psychiatrist I know has ever heard of, could only undermine the public's confidence in psychiatric knowledge.

Governments have a history of turning to psychiatrists to account for their opponents. Toward the end of the Second World War, President Franklin Roosevelt's administration commissioned a now-notorious study of Adolf Hitler. When someone proposed that Josef Stalin also be subjected to scrutiny, the suggestion was quickly shot down on the grounds that Stalin was an ally, not an enemy. But at least the Hitler project was based on extensive interviewing with people who had once known him.

Psychiatrists are, alas, notorious for arrogance; diagnoses without sufficient homework do get privately pinned on colleagues, and sometimes on patients. Perhaps it is well that Dr. Rakoff's work alerts the public to psychiatry's limitations. But social scientists have also been prone to ask for too much from psychiatry. As the author of a book-length study of Prime Minister Mackenzie King, who in 1916 actually consulted a famous psychiatrist for serious-sounding problems, I know how hard it can be for even highly educated people to be open to psychiatric evidence without demanding that it explain too much.

I am concerned that Dr. Rakoff's partisan and sensationalist assessment of Mr. Bouchard will do more damage in the long run to Canadian psychiatry than to Mr. Bouchard's career. Dr. Rakoff cannot have been so naïve not to anticipate that his written assessment would sometime see the light of day. Doctors, like plumbers and the rest of us, have every right to their political views, but legitimate objectives such as Dr. Rakoff's do not justify irresponsible means to accomplish their ends. It does not serve the cause of trying to bring together psychiatry and social studies to continue to have wild uses of "science" in politics.

NOTES

1 R. McGregor Dawson, *William Lyon Mackenzie King: A Political Biography*, Vol. I (Toronto, University of Toronto Press, 1958), p. 59.
2 "Five Lectures on Psychoanalysis," *Standard Edition*, Vol. XI, p. 49.
3 Heather Robertson, *Lily: A Rhapsody in Red* (Toronto, James Lorimer, 1986).
4 David Bercuson and Barry Cooper, *Deconfederation: Canada Without Quebec* (Toronto, Key Porter, 1991).
5 A. Alan Borovoy, *Uncivil Obedience: The Tactics and Tales of a Democratic Agitator* (Toronto, Lester Publishing, 1991).
6 Patrick J. Monahan, *Meech Lake: The Inside Story* (Toronto, University of Toronto Press, 1991).
7 Patrick Boyer, *Direct Democracy in Canada: The History and Future of Referendums* (Toronto, Dundurn Press, 1993).

12
USING ORAL HISTORY ABOUT FREUD: A CASE IN HIS "SECRET ESSAY"

Personal interviews, whatever their inevitable shortcomings, can be a unique historical avenue of knowledge. In the midst of my collecting information from many people who knew Freud, Helene Deutsch – she and I were then living in Cambridge, Mass. – became one of my key sources of information. It was a typical part of my questioning routine to ask any of the early analysts I met about the precise details connected with the patients they may have received as a referral from Freud. Various legends about the most famous quarrels in the history of psychoanalysis could be addressed by attending to what exactly any of my informants knew for certain by their personal acquaintance. And in dealing with Freud's clinical practices I tried to be as concrete as possible.

On May 22, 1965 Helene Deutsch, on what was becoming a then regular Saturday morning interview, happened to mention, in connection with one of Freud's cases, the Swedish millionaire named Ivar Kreuger. (I took notes during the interviews themselves, rewrote them immediately afterwards, and they are all being deposited in a Collection at Boston University.[1] Helene had been born in 1884, and had not yet turned 81 at this time. She was in full possession of her faculties, and went on to live until 1982.) Although I knew nothing then about Kreuger (1880-1932), I later realized that because he had founded a pre-World War I trust for matches he became known as the "match-king"; his international financial agency was later wrecked by fraud, and Kreuger committed suicide. Interestingly, Freud noted " Krueger suicide" in his chronicle that has now appeared as *The Diary of Sigmund Freud, 1929-39*. After Kreuger died Lord Keynes said of him he had been "maybe the greatest financial intelligence of his time." Kreuger himself had maintained: "I've built my enter-

prise on the firmest ground that can be found – the foolishness of people."
John Kenneth Galbraith was harsher than Keynes about Kreuger: "He was, by all odds, the biggest thief in the long history of larceny – a man who could think of embezzlement in terms of hundreds of millions." The editor of Freud's *Diary*, to whom I am indebted for all these citations about Kreuger, also pointed out how intriguing Kreuger was to the public, because of his wealth and unmarried state; a Swedish psychoanalyst wrote a study of him, and Graham Greene modelled a millionaire on Kreuger in his *England Made Me*. But it has remained unknown "what aspect of" Kreuger's suicide "intrigued Freud enough to report it in his diary."[2]

Now it turns out that Freud had in analysis, sometime after World War I, a "partner" of Kreuger's. He, in turn, had a fiancée whom Freud sent to Helene Deutsch as a patient. My notes record: "That's how they all got their first patients," which would have been a rough-and-ready version of what Helene had said to me. During 1918-19 Helene was analyzed by Freud, and she would have been referring to her earliest experiences as an analyst. At the time Freud had told her that if there should be clinical "difficulties," he was willing to see her about patients that he sent her. At this time there was as yet no formal center of psychoanalytic training in Vienna, and Helene thought that Freud's way of proceeding was in a sense the origins of control analysis. (She became the founding Director of the Vienna Psychoanalytic Institute in January 1925.[3])

Helene brought up this example of the fiancée of the Kreuger partner Freud sent her as part of Freud's great interest and concern for his patients' welfare; she considered him "a great clinician." According to my notes, she said she saw Freud about a typical patient perhaps ten times throughout the course of a treatment. In later rereading my notes, as I did again and again in the course of my subsequent interviewing as well as while writing various books, I noted that her account reminded me of Siegfried Bernfeld's (1962) version of his own informal early psychoanalytic training.[4] Every time Freud sent Helene a patient, she later said to me, she took it as a sign of his personal affection. But in connection with this first account of Freud's referral practices, she commented to me that he took a personal interest in those early cases he sent her because of their relation to his own patients.

On April 2, 1966 Helene happened to return to a discussion of that fiancée of Freud's patient; by then I had seen a broad range of other early analysts, including, thanks to Helene's recommendation, Anna Freud. Helene spoke to me "at length" about the case.[5] She had in mind what my notes report that she considered a special kind of "support" Freud gave his patients. When Freud saw an analysis could be helped through changes in the external life of the patient, he would "intervene." He had in analysis that case which "mattered very much to him." The man was engaged to a girl, but she "shrank from every sexual approach that he made to her." Freud sent the girl to Helene for analysis. He told her then that there was "a secret"

175

behind the referral, which he would leave Helene to find out on her own. (To myself I later remarked that there was half-a-joke in the reference to the existence of that secret.) Helene reported that Freud must also have told her that previously his patient had tried to kill himself, but that he had been rescued and recovered from what she remembered as a shot in the head. According to Helene's account, the engagement itself was a self-curative (which would have been my term) attempt that the analysis had set going.

The "secret" was that the man had had an affair with the girl's mother, who was also his sister-in-law. (The square young person that I was then dutifully marked down the explanation that in other words the man had had an affair with his brother's wife; he was the uncle of the young woman, his niece, whom Freud had sent to Helene.) Nowadays – in the light of all the kinds of questions she and I had been discussing — Helene commented she would have asked herself "why" Freud had sent the girl to her – was she, perhaps, intended to serve as a "mother figure" for the girl?

Anyway, Helene subsequently told Freud that she now knew the "secret," but that there was a part of the secret that Freud himself did not know. For Helene had come upon another aspect to the story: the girl had the unconscious fantasy that she was the child of the illicit pair. So of course she drew back from the advances of Kreuger's partner. (I remarked in writing up my notes that that sounded reminiscent of the tangle in Freud's Dora case.) According to Helene, Freud had not known for sure beforehand whether the girl herself was aware or not of the affair between her uncle and her mother. (In "another case," that of "a Swedish millionaire," Freud sent Helene the son. That analysis did not last, since the son was "rebellious and bent on devaluating and proving worthless that which was of such importance for his father." I don't know how many Swedish millionaires Freud had had contact with, but I doubt that Helene would have remembered, nor did I, that earlier example she had alluded to.)

The next time[6] I saw Helene (April 9th) I reminded her of the case of that niece and her uncle; she agreed that the intrigue was in some ways parallel to the Dora case. But Helene also thought it was like the case of a homosexual woman whose husband was of "great importance" to Freud. He was a Zionist leader; Helene was very concerned that after "a good deal of analysis," the woman was neither depressed nor anxious but happy with a female friend. Helene subsequently wrote up this case.[7] Freud relieved Helene when he said such an arrangement could be a good resolution for a woman whose children had grown up: she no longer had sexual relations with her husband, but he needed her as a social representative and was more concerned with dignity than intimacy.

Helene thought that she had learned from Freud that the objective of an analysis was to teach one where to compromise; and the example of the patient who was proposing to marry his niece was part of a pattern that Freud had (perhaps surprisingly) viewed as a normal resolution of analytic treatment. In a 1959 paper on "Psychoanalytic Therapy in the Light of Follow-up", Helene went on to conclude:

> What we conquer are only parts of psycho-genesis: expressions of conflicts, developmental failures. We do not eliminate the original sources of neurosis; we only help to achieve better ability to change neurotic frustrations into valid compensations. The dependency of psychic harmony on certain conditions makes immunity unattainable.[8]

In connection with Freud's treatment of that case involving an uncle and a niece, I had asked Helene whether it was unusual for Freud to have taken a suicidal case. But, she explained, the suicide attempt by Kreuger's partner had been made much earlier, and it was years afterwards (when he was stabilized) that he came to analysis. It had to have been after some time had passed; for the girl's problem of whether her uncle was her father was founded on what Helene called a "preconscious perception" about the affair when the niece was a child. Helene generalized that there were three categories of patients that Freud sent her: (1) patients who mattered very much to him personally, as this uncle did; (2) relatives or friends of patients who meant a lot to him – like the fiancée; and (3) quite anonymous patients, whom he might not even have seen. (It was like Helene to organize material into such categories. But she was implicitly assuming I understood the significance of Freud's own relatives, at least one of whom he also had referred to her.)

Freud "always" gave only one name in such a referral, she thought, on the grounds that neurotics do not want to be given a choice and desire to be sent to someone in particular. (But I can now think of one person, Herman Blumgart, to whom Freud gave the names of three possible analysts, but Freud was not keen on Blumgart, then married to Ruth Mack, who was already involved with Mark Brunswick.[9]) Helene did qualify what she had already told me by saying that she could not quite remember whether this uncle's relationship with his niece was a therapeutic product of the analysis with Freud or was a precipitating condition for it.

By early June I had unexpectedly discovered, in the course of rereading Freud's works, that he had twice in print discussed the case Helene had earlier been telling me about. The first (and I think most revealing) account was in a 1921 paper on "Psychoanalysis and Telepathy" that only appeared in print in 1941, two years after Freud's death. (Helene did not seem to own the *Standard Edition*, and it would have been hard for her to think of anything new by Freud appearing after his death.) I read the following extended passage aloud to Helene:

> A few years ago a young man came to me who made a particularly sympathetic impression on me, so that I gave him preference

over a number of others. It appeared that he was involved with one of the best known *demi-mondaines* and that he wanted to get free from her, because the relationship deprived him of all independence of action but he was unable to do so. I succeeded in setting him free and at the same time I obtained full insight into his compulsion. Not many months ago he contracted a normal and respectable marriage. The analysis showed that the compulsion against which he was struggling was not a tie with the *demi-mondaine* but with a married lady in his own circle with whom he had had a *liaison* from his earliest youth. The *demi-mondaine* served merely as a whipping-boy on whom he could satisfy all the feelings of revenge and jealousy which really applied to the other lady. On a model that is familiar to us, he had made use of displacement on to a fresh object in order to escape the inhibition brought about by his ambivalence.

It was his habit to inflict the most refined torment on the *demi-mondaine*, who had fallen in love with him in an almost unselfish fashion. But when she could no longer conceal her sufferings, he in turn passed over on to her the affection he had felt for the woman he had loved since his youth; he made her presents and propitiated her, and the cycle started on its course once more. When, finally, under the influence of the treatment, he broke with her, it became clear what it was that he was trying to achieve by his behavior to this substitute for his early love: revenge for an attempt at suicide of his own when his love had rejected his advances. After the attempted suicide he had at last succeeded in overcoming her reluctance. During his period of the treatment he used to visit the celebrated Schermann [a Viennese graphologist]. And the latter, on the basis of specimens of the *demi-mondaine's* handwriting, repeatedly told him by way of interpretation that she was at her last gasp, was at the point of suicide and would quite certainly kill herself. This, however, she did not do, but shook off her human weakness, and recalled the principles of her profession and her duties to her official friend. I saw clearly that the miracle-man had merely revealed to my patient his own intimate wish.

After disposing of this spurious figure, my patient set about seriously the task of freeing himself from his real bond. I detected from his dreams a plan that he was forming by means of which he would be able to escape from his relation with his early love without causing her too much mortification or material damage. She had a daughter, who was very fond of the young friend of the family and ostensibly knew nothing of the secret part he played. He now proposed to marry this girl. Soon afterwards the scheme became conscious, and the man took the first steps towards putting it into effect. I supported his intentions, since it offered what was a possible way out of his difficult situation even though an irregular one. But presently there came a dream which showed hostility to the girl; and now once more he consulted Schermann, who reported that the girl was childish and neurotic and should not be married. This time the great observer of human nature was right. The girl, who was by now regarded as the man's *fiancée*, behaved in a more and more contradictory manner, and it was decided that she should be analyzed. As a result of the analysis the scheme for the marriage was abandoned. The girl had a complete unconscious knowledge of the relations between her mother and her *fiancé*, and was only attached to him on account of her Oedipus complex.

At about this time our analysis broke off. The patient was free and capable of going his own way in the future. He chose as his wife a respectable girl outside his family circle – a girl on whom Schermann has passed a favorable judgment. Let us hope that this time he will be right once more.[10]

My notes imply my new intense interest in this case, since for the first time in my reports of interviews with Helene I started out with this story.[11] I regret that my notes do not record any of her comments on what I read, and therefore there is no easy way of differentiating between Helene's reaction to this first narrative from her response to Freud's second account which occurs in a chapter on "Dreams and Occultism" in *New Introductory Lectures on Psychoanalysis*. To repeat: Helene had appeared not to have noticed the first, posthumously published paper of Freud's which clearly identified the uncle. She had herself once written a 1926 paper on telepathy[12], professionally important in psychoanalysis because she had come up with the original idea that countertransference feelings in an analyst can be a constructive source of helping a patient, and one of Freud's five citations of her work was on the subject of telepathy. (The other four had to do with female sexuality.)

When Freud again mentioned the case of that uncle, in the course of his *New Introductory Lectures on Psychoanalysis*, he excluded the brief analysis involving the niece. This report would thus not have been recognized by Helene. I again read a long passage aloud to her:

> A young man in a position of consequence was involved in a *liaison* with a *demi-mondaine* which was characterized by a curious compulsion. He was obliged from time to time to provoke her with derisive and insulting remarks till she was driven to complete desperation. When he had brought her to that point, he was relieved, became reconciled with her and made her a present. But now he wanted to be free of her: the compulsion seemed to him uncanny.

He noticed that this *liaison* was damaging his reputation; he wanted to have a wife of his own and to raise a family. But since he could not get free from this demi-mondaine by his own strength, he called analysis to his help. After one of these abusive scenes, when the analysis had already started, he got her to write something on a piece of paper, so as to show it to a graphologist. The report that he received from him was that the writing was that of someone in extreme despair, who would certainly commit suicide in the next few days. This did not, it is true, occur and the lady remained alive; but the analysis succeeded in loosening his bonds. He left the lady and turned to a young girl who he expected would be able to make him a good wife. Soon afterwards a dream appeared which could only hint at a dawning doubt of the girl's worthiness. He obtained a specimen of her writing too, took it to the same authority, and was given a verdict on her writing which confirmed his apprehensions. He therefore abandoned the idea of making her his wife.

In order to form an opinion of the graphologist's reports, especially the first one, we must know something of our subject's secret history. In his early youth he had (in accordance with his passionate nature) fallen in love to the pitch of frenzy with a married woman who was still young but nevertheless older than he was. When she rejected him, he made an attempt at suicide which, there can be no doubt, was seriously intended. It was only by a hair's breadth that he escaped death and he was only restored after along period of nursing. But his wild action made a deep impression on the woman he loved; she granted him her favors, he became her lover and thence-forward remained secretly attached to her and served her with a truly chivalrous devotion. More than twenty years later, when they had both grown older – but the woman, naturally, more than he – the need was awakened in him to detach himself from her, to make himself free, to lead a life of his own, to set up a house and raise a family. And along with this feeling of satiety there arose in him his long-suppressed craving for vengeance on his mistress. As he had once tried to kill himself because she had spurned him, so he wished now to have the satisfaction of her seeking death because he left her. But his love was still too strong for it to be possible for this wish to become conscious in him; nor was he in a position to do her enough harm to drive her into death. In this frame of mind he took on the *demi-mondaine* as a sort of whipping-boy, to satisfy his thirst for revenge *in corpore vili*; and he allowed himself to practice upon her all the torments which he might expect would bring about with her the result he wished to produce in his mistress. The fact that the vengeance applied to the latter was betrayed by his making her into a confidante and adviser in his *liaison* instead of concealing his defection from her. The wretched woman, who had long fallen from giving to receiving favors, probably suffered more from his confidences than the *demi-mondaine* did from his brutalities. The compulsion of which he complained in regard to this substitutive figure, and which drove him to analysis, had of course been transferred on to her from his old mistress; it was from her that he wanted to free himself but could not. I am not an authority on handwriting and have no high opinion of the art of divining character from it; still less do I believe in the possibility of foretelling the writer's future in this way. You can see, however, whatever one may think of the value of graphology, that there is no mistaking the fact that the expert, when he promised that the writer of the specimen presented to him would commit suicide in the next few days, had once again only brought to light a powerful secret wish of the person who was questioning him. Something of the same kind happened afterwards in the case of the second report. What was there concerned, however, was not an unconscious wish; it was the questioner's dawning doubt and apprehension that found a clear expression from the graphologist's mouth. Incidentally, my patient succeeded, with the help of analysis, in finding an object for his love outside the magic circle in which he had been spellbound.[13]

> I think Helene was as fascinated by what I read as I was. She started off by insisting that Freud's patient had not been "such a young man" – he already had a "pot belly." The illicit affair had gone on for years, when the woman was already married; she was the wife of an older brother of his, "yes, that was the decisive part." The patient had wanted the sister-in-law to divorce his brother, and marry him. When Freud sent the girl to Helene, he had indicated that his own patient was "very important" to him. Helene could not help enviously observing to me that if he had sent the girl to Ruth Mack Brunswick, he would have said in writing that Dr. Brunswick had "analyzed her with her usual clarity, etc., etc." But there was no mention of Helene in either of the texts I read aloud. She held that it was because she was not, like Ruth, a "lady of the court" in Freud's world. Why, she wondered, was she not invited when he read that first paper to a small group. (According to Strachey, those who were present at the Harz mountains at the end of September 1921 included Freud's "closest followers", which meant Karl Abraham, Max Eitingon, Sandor Ferenczi, Otto Rank, Hanns Sachs, and Ernest Jones. These were his political leaders, the members of the so-called secret Committee in Freud's movement.) Although I believe I failed adequately to explain to Helene the exact nature of Freud's audience, she maintained that she had "played an important part in the case."
>
> Helene said she had not been told about the *demi-mondaine*, nor of the

vicious circle that drove Freud's patient away and then back to his original mistress. A son of that family – either of the man who was analyzed or of his brother – now lived in Boston. Helene had never discussed the situation with him, nor was she sure whether he knew about it. Freud's suppression of the uncle-niece relation, which was so important to the case, was "doubtless for reasons of discretion." Vienna was so small, "like Cambridge" now. (Helene was exaggerating, but it is clear what she meant.) Freud would have to have had the patient's permission before proceeding to publish the account. For a discussion of telepathy the story was complete enough in *New Introductory Lectures on Psychoanalysis* (as well as in "Psychoanalysis and Telepathy"). But as a case history what we had at hand, she said, was "very inadequate." That graphologist was "very famous"; when Helene speculated that he was now a professor of graphology "somewhere in America", I ascribed it to some residual anti-American fantasy of hers. In general, Helene thought there was a great deal to learn from handwriting, except for that of "wealthy girls" who go to private schools and are all taught to "write alike."

Helene insisted she believed that what is "preconscious" can be remembered, but what is unconscious is "always a reconstruction." In "three of four sessions" with the girl Freud had sent to Helene, she thought "the secret was out." (I did not think to ask whether, or for how long, Helene continued to see her patient afterwards.) The young woman had a "preconscious" knowledge of the *liaison* between her uncle and her mother, and possessed the fantasy that she was the child of this illegitimate union. The "oedipal fantasy" itself was "preconscious."

To summarize Helene's renewed account to me: when Freud had sent the girl to Helene he had said, "There is a secret, which I will not tell you – come when you find out." (I assumed, based on how she retold the story to me, that Freud had had a kind of twinkle to his manner or voice.) When Helene came back to him, she said, "I have found out the secret, but there is a secret which even you do not know." (I am not sure that the word "playful" would accurately describe the nature of their complicated relationship, but it might be a beginning.) The "secret" she had uncovered was that the girl had fantasized herself as the child of her uncle and her mother. Helene repeated that the man still bore physical marks of his earlier suicide attempt. I thought that it was Helene's analysis of the niece that had decisively prevented the marriage to the uncle. Helene maintained that the girl was not as "good looking" as she might have appeared. She was Jewish (I am not trying to prettify Helene's Polish prejudices), and around eighteen or nineteen years old. So she might well have entertained the fantasy of having been the product of the *liaison* between her mother and uncle, a liaison that I would consider incestuous. Helene reconstructed that the niece had witnessed, not intercourse, but "a passionate embrace" between her mother and uncle.

Helene's work on telepathy had been concerned with the roots of empathy. She agreed with me that Freud always approached telepathy as a problem of thought-transference; he was narrowing the scope of the issue to the communication of ideas without words or conscious intent. Lou Andreas-Salomé had once written about having had a "long conversation (in confidence" with Freud "on those rare instances of thought-transference which certainly torment him."[14] In 1921 Freud had gone so far in a letter to an American psychologist, Hereward Carrington, to maintain:

> I am not one of those who dismiss *a priori* the study of so-called occult psychic phenomena as unscientific, discreditable or even as dangerous. If I were at the beginning rather than at the end of a scientific career, as I am today, I might possibly choose just this field of research, in spite of all the difficulties.[15]

As Freud was to insist in his 1921 paper, both psychoanalysis and telepathy have "experienced the same contemptuous and arrogant treatment by official science."[16] Even today there has been little scholarly inquiry into Freud's fascination as well as distaste for the subject of the occult, though the concept of the uncanny has received much attention from literary critics. Freud reported, it will be remembered, that the patient of his had felt his whole compulsion with that *demi-mondaine* to be "uncanny."

I wondered in talking with Helene Deutsch on June 4th, 1966 whether it had been proper for Freud to write his account of that case of the uncle so early after the conclusion of the treatment. Also, I questioned whether it was not too soon for Freud to be sure of having had a successful therapeutic outcome with his patient. But Helene thought it was not too fast for Freud to come to his conclusion, and that he "knew" what he was writing. (Around the same time she was expressing uncertainties to me about what all this investigatory digging would ultimately do to Freud's historical standing.) When Freud was writing about the girl's oedipal feelings, he was taking for granted both the attraction as well as the repulsion that would be involved in such a set of emotions. Freud wrote up his conclusions about that patient when he did because he needed them then; they fit into his thinking on telepathy at that time. I think it was characteristic of all Freud's case-history writing that he never presented his patients "in the round," or as one might know them as people. What he wrote was always rather directed at a specific (usually theoretical) purpose, in this instance, the problem of thought-transference.

A couple of weeks after Helene and I had discussed intensively the case of that uncle and niece, we came back to it once more.[17] She recalled a meeting with Freud after she had been seeing the girl analytically. He "pulled over a chair for her" and said, "Oh, so, what did you find!" I asked whether he was pleased at her solution to the mystery. Helene said that he had been "very fascinated". After she had told him the extra "secret," not only that the girl knew of the liaison but that she had built a special variety of family romance around her uncle, Freud had said that the marriage was "off." So, I asked, did he take these cases very seriously? "Immensely!" She said that he had "so much honesty" that he was aware that for him "what mattered was what he discovered." He was "not so interested in the effects of therapy." But "for patients he knew that what mattered was the therapeutic results." And "he needed such results for his practice."

In 1975 I gave a preliminary account in my *Freud and His Followers*[18] of how he presented that uncle and niece for the sake of his interest in telepathy. It seemed to me then that Freud characteristically described his case material in a fragmentary manner, for the sake of elucidating some special problems he might be working on. I thought it was therefore difficult to reconstruct from a given case history what might have happened clinically. The marriage choice being contemplated in the example of the uncle and the niece today seems bizarre. (In "Psychoanalysis and Telepathy" Freud had described the brother's wife only as "a married lady in his own circle.") Once Freud's patient decided to marry the young daughter of his former mistress, however, Freud, who could be remarkably emancipated from middle-class values, "supported his intentions, since it offered what was a possible way out of his difficult situation even though an irregular one."

I thought it striking that when the girl had resisted the advances of her uncle, Freud had recommended that she undergo an analysis. (In his written account, Freud chose to put this in a passive-sounding construction: "it was decided that she should be analyzed.") Freud had needed Helene Deutsch's help in order to explain the fiancée's hesitancy to become involved with Freud's patient sexually. (As Freud put what he had learned from Helene in "Psychoanalysis and Telepathy": "The girl had a complete unconscious knowledge of the relations between her mother and her *fiancé*, and was only attached to him on account of her Oedipus complex.") Once Freud was enlightened of the girl's inner world, he dropped the idea of the match.

I pointed out in *Freud and His Followers* that when Freud was writing up this case, he had tried to suppress, no doubt out of discretion, the familial connection between the partners in the proposed union. But, as I added, at the very end of his account of the case there seemed to be a classic return of the repressed. According to Freud, his patient eventually chose as his wife "a respectable girl outside his family circle. . . ." Until this point in the narrative Freud had not hinted that any of the patient's other loves had been within the "family circle." In his account in *New Introductory Lectures*, Freud also concluded that his patient had "succeeded, with the help of analysis, in finding an object for his love outside the magic circle in which he had been spellbound." In actuality, two separate analyses had been of "help." Although Freud's account remained only a vignette, I argued that a disclosure of its full particulars underlined how active a therapist he could be. But Freud's suppression of the details of the family relationships made it virtually impossible to comprehend what was really going on.

Almost twenty years later, in 1993, I heard from Ernst Falzeder, an expert in reading Freud's handwriting, that the original manuscript of Freud's "Psychoanalysis and Telepathy" contained a fuller clinical account than that which had been published in 1941; Falzeder sent me only a key paragraph:

> After overcoming this person used as a pretext, my patient went earnestly about the business of freeing himself from his real chain. From dreams I guessed a plan which had developed in him, how he could dissolve the relationship with the sister-in-law, without offending her severely or doing her material damage. She had a daughter aged 18, who was very tender toward the young uncle, and supposedly knew nothing about his secret role. He wanted to marry this niece, and thus to turn the beloved one back into the mother. Soon after, the plan became conscious, and the man took the first steps to bring it about. I supported this intent, which corresponded to an irregular but nevertheless possible way out of a difficult situation. But soon after there came a dream, which turned hostile toward the girl, and now he consulted Schermann again, who gave the expert opinion that the girl was childish, neurotic, and ought not to be married. The great knower of human beings was right this time – the behavior of the girl, who was already taken to be the uncle's *fiancée*, became ever more contradictory, and it was decided to entrust her to Dr. Deutsch for analysis. The result of the analysis was the putting aside of this plan of marriage. The girl had complete unconscious knowledge of the connections between her mother and her uncle, and adhered to the latter only because of her Oedipus complex.[19]

I was, of course, astonished at this confirmation of how reliable an informant Helene Deutsch had once been, although what I had written about Freud's "suppression" of material in the published text could no longer stand up. I do not believe (although I could be wrong, and it might be necessary to consult all my accumulated notes) that I ever again discussed this case in the course of the many hours I spent with her in the late 1970s interviewing her for the biography that she authorized me to write. But I am sure she would have been delighted to find out that Freud had in fact acknowledged her role in the story. And I of course was pleased that there was now documentary proof of the otherwise possibly unlikely story Helene and I had worked on in the mid-1960s, and for which I had cited her as a source in *Freud and His Followers*. I do not know why Freud's 1941 editors thought it necessary to suppress the fact of the patient's old love being his sister-in-law, or Helene Deutsch's role in the story. I assume, however, that nobody would have had the authority to censor and distort Freud's manuscript without Anna Freud's express permission.

This detective-like inquiry is winding down, but two key details have recently come to light, which amplify what I had already known. In the recently published Vol. III of the Freud-Ferenczi *Correspondence*, the editorial apparatus mentions Freud's having finished on August 18, 1921 a draft of "Psychoanalysis and Telepathy" while on holiday at Seefeld (where Helene Deutsch also went with her husband and son). The editors observe, for the first time in print, that "the text was published posthumously in an abbreviated version."[20]

Later in that same volume Ferenczi, talking about the problem of thought transference in a *Rundbrief* (on February 19, 1925) sent to all the other members of the Committee, commented about Freud's 1921 work: "Too bad that the Harz secret essay cannot be published. Perhaps a somewhat abbreviated communication can be published, or the permission of those concerned can be obtained." The editors go on to explain in a note to Ferenczi's letter:

> A reaction to Freud's *Rundbrief* of the middle of February: "The strongest literary impression of this month came to me from a report about telepathy experiments with Professor Murray... I confess that the impression of these reports was so strong that I am prepared to give up my opposition to the existence of thought transference...I would even be prepared to lend support to the cause of telepathy through psychoanalysis. Eitingon took along the manuscript of the secret essay from which I derived such analytic confirmation of the telepathic hypothesis at our meeting in the Harz. I would decide today to send this essay into the world and would not shy away from the spectacle that it would unerringly produce. But the barrier of medical discretion looms as an insurmountable hindrance...It is precisely the sensation of this publication that makes it obligatory to hold it back; distortions are impermissible, ameliorations won't help. Should fate have the two recipients of the unfulfilled prophecies die before me, then the hindrance would be removed."[21]

Jones had already used this *Rundbrief* in an altered form; once again the editors of the Freud-Ferenczi correspondence report that "an abridged version of the essay was published posthumously."[22]

In *Freud and His Followers* I had observed that the suppression of details about the family relationship (in the two texts I had read) made it virtually impossible to comprehend what was going on in what Freud later called "the secret essay" in writing to his intimate group of disciples. There were even more secrets to the tale than he had put into writing, since he had been so sparse in describing Helene's Deutsch's exact role. But Freud had presented this material to his loyal Committee, and its members certainly took in what he had had to say. Jones in particular, for example, was unhappy about the whole topic of telepathy, which he thought was impolitic for psychoanalysis and likely to bring it into disrepute. (Concerning "Psychoanalysis and Telepathy," Jones explained that Freud had "half-suggested reading it again before the next Congress, the Berlin one of 1922, but Eitingon and I dissuaded him."[23]

In 1915, Freud enunciated a principle that he himself did not always succeed in following: "Before I continue the account," he wrote parenthetically of another case:

> I must confess that I have altered the *milieu* of the case in order to preserve the incognito of the people concerned, but that I have altered nothing else. I consider it a wrong practice, however excellent the motive may be, to alter any detail of the presentation of a case. One can never tell what aspect of a case may be picked out by a reader of independent judgment, and one runs the risk of leading him astray.[24]

And in 1924 Freud added a footnote to one of his earliest case histories, in which he had disguised his material: "Katherina was not the niece but the daughter.... The girl fell ill, therefore, as a result of sexual attempts on the part of her own father. Distortions like the one which I introduced in the present instance should be altogether avoided in reporting a case history."[25]

I have presented this material now since it seems possible to understand it all more thoroughly than ever before. I stumbled upon this story serendipitously. And yet, as the years have unfolded, my interest in the whole "secret essay" has been amply rewarded. (I once wrote a little paper about the last half-paragraph of "Psychoanalysis and Telepathy."[26]) Of course, oral history has its limitations. I think that the unconscious and conscious failures to ask enough adequate questions, lest this undermine the interviewing itself, are at least as great a drawback as are the inevitable inadequacies and biases of any participants in such an undertaking. But I believe that my awkward stumbling usefully supplements what appears in the documentary accounts. The written text, even – or especially – when it is in print and heavily annotated, has its own ways of being misleading, and the musical undertones can go unheard. Mix-ups like those associated with this story illustrate the complexities connected with the idealistic search for historical truth. By bringing together the available evidence that has come to my attention in connection with Freud's "secret essay", I hope that not only the history of psychoanalysis but also the enterprise of oral history itself will be enhanced.

NOTES

1 Interview #10, p. 6, May 22, 1965 (Paul Roazen Collection, Boston University).
2 *The Diary of Sigmund Freud, 1929-39: A Record of the Final Decade*, translated, annotated, with an Introduction by Michael Molnar (New York, Charles Scribner's, 1992), p. 122.
3 Paul Roazen, *Helene Deutsch: A Psychoanalyst's Life* (New York, Doubleday/Anchor, 1985; 2nd edition, with new Introduction, New Brunswick, N.J., Transaction Publishers, 1992), p. 245.
4 Bernfeld wrote: "In 1922 I discussed with Freud my intention of establishing myself in Vienna as a practicing analyst. I had been told that our Berlin group encouraged psychoanalysts, especially beginners, to have a didactic analysis before starting their practice, and I asked Freud whether he thought this preparation was desirable for me. His answer was: 'Nonsense. Go right ahead. You certainly will have difficulties. When you get into trouble, we will see what we can do about it.' Only a week later, he sent me my first didactic case...." Siegfried Bernfeld, "On Psychoanalytic Training," *The Psychoanalytic Quarterly*, Vol. 31, No. 4 (1962), p. 463.
5 Interview # 33, April 2, 1966, pp. 1a & 2.
6 Interview #34, April 9, 1966, pp. 1 & 1a.
7 Helene Deutsch, *The Psychology of Women: A Psychoanalytic Interpretation*, Vol. 1 (New York, Grune & Stratton, 1944), p. 346.
8 Helene Deutsch, *Neuroses and Character Types: Clinical Psychoanalytic Studies* (New York, International Universities Press, 1965), p. 352.
9 For Freud's analytic treatments of Ruth and Mark Brunswick, as well as David Brunswick, see Paul Roazen, *Freud and His Followers* (New York, Knopf, 1975; reprinted, N.Y., Da Capo, 1992), Part IX, Chs. 1-2, and Paul Roazen, *How Freud Worked: First-Hand Accounts of Patients* (Northvale, N.J., Aronson, 1995), Chs. 2 & 3.
10 "Psychoanalysis and Telepathy," *Standard Edition*, Vol. 18, pp. 191-93.
11 Interview #38, June 4, 1966, pp. 1-5b.
12 Helene Deutsch, "Occult Processes Occurring During Psychoanalysis," in *The Therapeutic Process, The Self, and Female Psychology: Collected Psychoanalytic Papers*, ed. with an Introduction by Paul Roazen (New Brunswick, N.J., Transaction Publishers, 1992), pp. 223-38.
13 "New Introductory Lectures," *Standard Edition*, Vol. 22, pp. 45-47.
14 Lou Andreas-Salomé, *The Freud Journal*, translated by Stanley Leavy (New York, Basic Books, 1964), p. 169.
15 *Letters of Sigmund Freud*, ed. Ernst L. Freud, translated by Tania and James Stern (London, The Hogarth Press, 1961), p. 339.
16 "Psychoanalysis and Telepathy," *op. cit.*, p. 178.
17 Interview # 40, June 18, 1966, p. 3.
18 Roazen, *Freud and His Followers, op. cit.*, pp. 157-59.
19 I am indebted to Tom Taylor for his translation. See also Ernst Falzeder, "Preface," *The Complete Correspondence of Sigmund Freud and Karl Abraham 1907-1925*, ed. Ernst Falzeder, translated by Caroline Schwarzacher (London, Karnac, 2002), p. xvi.
20 *The Correspondence of Sigmund Freud and Sandor Ferenczi*, Vol. 3, 1920-1933, *op. cit.*, p. 67.
21 *Ibid.*, pp. 205-06.
22 Ernest Jones, *The Life and Work of Sigmund Freud*, Vol. III (New York, Basic Books, 1957), p. 392; *The Correspondence of Sigmund Freud and Sandor Ferenczi*, Vol. 3, 1920-1933, *op. cit.*, pp. 205-06.

23 Jones, *The Life and Work of Sigmund Freud*, Vol. III, *op. cit.*, p. 392.
24 "A Case of Paranoia Running Counter to the Psychoanalytic Theory of the Disease," *Standard Edition*, Vol. 14, p. 263.
25 "Studies on Hysteria," *Standard Edition*, Vol. 2, p. 134.
26 Paul Roazen, *The Historiography of Psychoanalysis* (New Brunswick, N.J., Transaction Publishers, 2001), pp. 346-49.

13

WINNERS AND LOSERS IN THE HISTORIOGRAPHY OF PSYCHOANALYSIS

Darwinism might lead one to think that in intellectual history too, as in nature, one can count on something like the survival of the fittest. But the history of ideas turns out to be more wayward than biology. To take only one example, from the history of socialism: Marx's great rival within the First International was the Russian anarchist thinker Mikhail Bakunin (1814-76). Turgenev wrote a short novel, *Rudin*, about a character modeled on Bakunin. But if on Ph.D. examinations today one asks graduate students in political science, even those with a special interest in the history of socialism, about Bakunin, there is likely to be a blank stare in response.

Yet as Isaiah Berlin first pointed out, on a series of key issues between them Bakunin was right and Marx wrong.[1] On the question of where revolution was likely to break out for instance, Marx had predicted it would come at the point of highest industrialization; therefore Marx looked hopefully to Germany, England, and America. Bakunin, however, thought that revolution was likeliest when the controls of feudal society had been disrupted, but before the new constraints of capitalism had been imposed; the boiling point of class conflict would come therefore after the industrial revolution had begun to break up the old regime, but before the proletariat had been organized. So, unlike Marx, Bakunin looked to countries like Spain and Russia, and recommended that socialists should make revolution when and as they could.

To take another issue between Marx and Bakunin, the Russian feared Marx's own post-1848 bureaucracy. Bakunin was afraid of any form of government run by "scientists", and thought Marx was too addicted to a theory that could lead to dissecting human beings cruelly. From Bakunin's perspective Marx's proposals meant one more set of dangerous elites, and party leadership could be as bad as any earlier class rule. Marxism was for Bakunin too like old religion that made for an inequality consisting of God and his slaves. Bakunin was instead proposing to promote a different kind of freedom.

Furthermore, unlike Marx, Bakunin thought that nationalism was not a temporary phenomenon. To Bakunin the nation was a genuine force that was unlikely to evaporate in the future. While Marx (and early classical liberals too) held that the nation was a mistake, Bakunin felt nationalism represented energy that needed to be harnessed, and that individual nations must be set to competing with one another. Bakunin was himself a pan-Slav, not an internationalist; and Bakunin held that the existence of nations was a harder nut to crack than Marx thought.

To continue even further the contrast between Bakunin and Marx: to Bakunin the enemy was the state, and he accused Marx of pretense when it came to power. In the 1860's the First International was becoming, Bakunin held, an alternative state form of authoritarianism. Marx was, according to Bakunin, allowing a political hierarchy to grow, and such new vested interests were a fresh menace to liberty. For Bakunin contact with respectability, and not just power itself, was the source of corruption. Bakunin wanted to tame the party within a national framework. But it should be clear that Marx's proposal that the dictatorship of the proletariat would evaporate following a socialist revolution was to Bakunin a snare and a delusion. In short, Bakunin feared that Marx was advocating a fresh form of tyranny.

Now Lenin would make his own special use of Bakunin's anarchist ideas, as well as those socialist theses of Marx himself. And yet it is Marx who triumphed, and Bakunin who got defeated not only within the First International, but within subsequent intellectual history too. It is not simple to account for what happened, but Marx had his system of thought, and a coherent point of view does make it possible to attract disciples. And yet in hindsight, when one examines the differences between Bakunin and Marx, it can be striking that on so many points Bakunin was prophetic about exactly where Marx went wrong. Still, it will probably always be the case that Marx gets remembered, whereas Bakunin seems destined to remain a sidelight in the history of socialist thought.

Many examples of the waywardness of reputations could be collected. The ideas of Giambattista Vico were little known in the eighteenth century, only to become famous long after his death. In our own time the writings of Italo Svevo, for instance, seem to continue to still be enhancing his standing. Think of the list of writers who won Nobel Prizes in literature, as opposed to those notable ones never so honored, to remind us how capricious such recognition can be.

Now within the history of psychotherapy, we also do not find that those who appear to have won are necessarily superior, either in their originality or in their hold on the truth, to those who seem to have lost. If psychotherapy were like an established science, where knowledge becomes cumulative, this would not be the case. But the history of psychotherapy is to today's psychotherapy nothing like the history of dentistry is to dentistry now. And natural sciences like chemistry and physics are entirely different. For inevitably there is within psychotherapy the problem of how society, and ethics too, affect how we have thought. Psychotherapists have rarely been taught that their field is unique, as much an art as a science; and I think that there are more analogies between psychotherapy and social philosophy than have ever been acknowledged.

Instead of thinking of the past in terms of anything like progress, I believe that history can be like a giant seesaw, a teeter-totter in which it is impossible to raise one reputation without simultaneously lowering another. It took me years to learn that the act of trying to rescue any figure from oblivion may unintentionally lead to the charge of attempting to detract from the standing of others. Yet the scales of historical justice may be harder to tilt than one might imagine.

To take an example from popular political history, in America right now the second President of the United States, John Adams, has only recently been the subject of an immensely successful biography[2], one whose notoriety can probably be linked to the recent fall-off in the standing of the third President, Thomas Jefferson. (Jefferson's views about blacks, and the likelihood that he fathered children by a house-slave, have helped to precipitate the recent decline in his stature.) For the first time there has now been a movement afoot to build a national memorial to Adams. He and Jefferson were once allied as revolutionary friends, then became rivals and opponents, although they were reconciled in their last years. But it has taken two hundred years in order to begin to redress the striking imbalance between Adams and Jefferson in their respective historical positions that was first initiated by the results of the election of 1800, when Jefferson displaced Adams in the White House.

Modern psychotherapy does not have a history as old as two centuries, yet the sectarianism between rival schools has continued to be every bit as partisan as what one encounters in the bitterest quarrels of political warfare. Those figures who are valued are apt to be the ones that one wants to identify with, and take as models. Nevertheless, ours is a peculiarly ahistorical period of time. As we legitimately search the record for heroes and villains, it is not hard to allow a presentistic orientation about history to mislead us about the relative standing that earlier figures deserve. To take a recent example from the history of the American Supreme Court, a recent devastating study of the great Justice Oliver Wendell Holmes, Jr. has a chapter called "Would You Have Wanted Justice Holmes As A Friend?"[3] I tried to deal with the problems associated with looking at history through the wrong end of a present-day telescope with an essay called "Was Freud A Nice Guy?"[4]

It is of course inevitable that we use today as the starting point for how we approach history. But there should be some check on the easy assumption that we are now inevitably the products of progressive forces, enabling us to be so superior to the past that we can readily hand out a report card grading people. Do we really expect a giant in the history of jurisprudence, like Holmes, to be a friend like one of our neighbors now? And do we imagine that a pioneer in the history of thought like Freud (any more than Marx) would rank as a "nice guy" by today's expectations and standards?

For in the history of psychotherapy we are particularly likely to be misled by the possible role of technique. I suspect that the use of the couch, for example, was, at least in America, one of the key sources of the popularity of psychoanalysis. Freud seemed to hold out the possibility of a neutral approach to clinical situations that was readily teachable to his followers. But I would like to remind us of a comment of Freud's that Marie Bonaparte recorded in her journal from her analysis: "More important than what one does is what one is."[5] Any such principle need not mean that Freud was proposing something like the idea that anything goes; and he was talking to someone he had confidence in, not the kind of beginner for whom he published his famous essays on technique. And yet the notion that the analyst amounts to the most important model that the patient has needs to be worked into our ideas about what kind of science psychotherapy can ever expect to be. To me at least, the comment of Freud's that Marie Bonaparte noted down means that the artistic, and moral, sides of psychotherapy ought never to be overlooked. And I share Peter Lomas's recently expressed conviction that every clinical encounter inevitably is also simultaneously an ethical one.[6]

As one looks back over the past one hundred years, the issues that were front and center at the turn of the twentieth century are likely to appear still lively to our contemporaries. For the biological psychiatry started by Emil Kraepelin (1856-1926) emphasized the importance of diagnosis, classification, and heredity in ways that are now once again, in the era of DSM-III and IV, so important. The success of new psychopharmacological drugs like Prozac has once again awakened an interest in Kraepelin's formalistic orientation that once seemed securely dated. Although German psychiatry had been in disrepute partly thanks to how the Nazis relied on it, in America the old debates between Kraepelin and his detractors have once again surfaced as timely. Psychoanalysis in particular has recently been criticized by the movement of thought known as neo-Kraepelinism. Yet it seems to me hard not to think of much of today's psychopharmacology as part of the kind of pragmatic orientation toward technology that once helped account for the American receptivity to Freud. And I suspect that William James's indictments of brain mythologizing, as well as his tolerance for the relevance of religious beliefs, are as immediately relevant now as they were a hundred years ago.

In any discussion of winners and losers in psychotherapy it obviously is necessary to make plain which geographical area one is talking about. As an American I am obviously most aware of what has happened in my own country, even if it can be hard to generalize about so big an entity. But I have traveled around more than a bit, and have at least some idea of what has been the case elsewhere. So that in the Far East, for example, where psychodynamic psychology has been relatively rare, it is still possible to describe the initial impacts that Freud (1856-1939) and Jung (1875-1961) have had. The direction in which a country like China, as well as the rest of the underdeveloped world, chooses to go may turn out to be decisive in determining what the long-term story of these ideas may be. If the Confucian family system should decline, for instance, problems in intimate human relations that hitherto seemed unthinkable there are going to seem strikingly alive. Western ideas of selfhood and individualism may become increasingly relevant in China; and in that context I think a psychodynamic orientation can be expected to flourish. (In contrast to what is still the case on the mainland, in Hong Kong for example clinical psychology is now being taught.)

For now, however, this past century has had as its most notably influential psychologist the Viennese Freud. This success could turn out someday to have been a passing fluke, but for now I consider him the greatest psychological writer of that era. It is a well-known irony that the America Freud despised was for a long time his most enthusiastic supporter. He might not now be disappointed as psychoanalysis has become an increasingly rare procedure there; he was convinced that the initial American reception of psychoanalysis was shallow and too pragmatic. Literary people and philosophers do by and large continue to treat Freud as a central figure in the history of ideas. But American departments of psychiatry, which forty years ago were generally headed by psychoanalysts, are by now almost all in non-analytic hands. The once high-flying American analysts held out too long against the possible reliance on medication; and in following Freud's advice to keep analytic training institutes separate and apart from other educational institutions, analysis grew isolated from proposals about newer currents of treatment.

I do not know what has been happening in the Netherlands recently, but psychoanalytic practice was once important enough as a cultural phenomenon there for book-length studies of the Dutch history of psychoanalysis to be undertaken; that would be true for Germany as well as Russia, where there has been a notable revival of psychoanalytic interest in the post-Soviet period. Argentina has been such an unusual source of interest in Freud that there is now one book in English covering the tale.[7] Italy has been a country open to a variety of ideological influences from abroad, and Freud's standing there is now finally considerable. In Israel, on the other hand, despite the role that Jews have played in the general history of modern psychotherapy, there has been a striking lack of enthusiasm for Freud.

In writing Freud's 1914 polemic "On the History of the Psychoanalytic Movement,"[8] he set the central contours of the world's understanding of his work. He had been bent then on distinguishing his ideas from those of Alfred Adler (1870-1937) and Jung, and in general Freud succeeded partly by virtue of his willingness to engage in such a dispute. Adler, who never systematically answered Freud, is relatively ignored nowadays. However undistinguished as a writer Adler may have been, it is worth remembering the fact that the American Supreme Court in its historic 1954 decision outlawing segregated schools relied on psychological research that can be traced back to Adler.[9] The Nazi period meant that Adler's following in his "individual psychology" was decimated; relatively more successful in Vienna than Freud, the Adlerians had had relatively less incentive to go abroad. Even today little literature about Adler has been published.[10] Group therapy, early childhood education, and the position of women have all been enhanced by Adler's impact.

Jung, who I think was Freud's most profound early critic, proved to be far more successful as a leader than Adler. Not only did Jung come to found a world wide movement in behalf of his "analytic psychology," but the literature about Jung's work has begun to become abundant. (Jung did belatedly, in a 1925 seminar, try to answer Freud.[11]) Although many of the books on Jung are essentially trots, designed to introduce newcomers to the relatively arcane world of Jungian psychology, first-class biographical work on Jung has now been undertaken.[12] Although Jung's texts have been allowed to appear in print with nothing like the scholarly apparatus that James Strachey brought to his *Standard Edition* of Freud's psychological works, the world of Jung studies has started to look historiographically serious. Ernest Jones's (1879-1958) three volume biography of Freud in the 1950s, written endorsing and amplifying Freud's own bias against "renegades" like Jung and Adler, proved immensely influential in shaping the general public's acceptance of Freud's outlook on such early quarrels.[13] For years the intelligentsia was surprisingly credulous about Jones's view of things, even though it essentially just enlarged on Freud's own point of view. So the mythology about the history of psychoanalysis was largely established by the legends Freud promoted about his early "backsliding" supporters like Adler and Jung. (There is still almost as little literature about Wilhelm Stekel as about Otto Gross.[14])

Jung remains largely a taboo subject within orthodox psychoanalysis. Yet he made a notable batch of telling points against Freud, and their pre-World War I differences have still not been adequately untangled. Jung was intent on challenging Freud's excessive rationalism, as well as the implicit authoritarianism of the classical psychoanalytic set-up. Jung insisted that the past might be revived defensively, so that the factor of infantilism became for Jung a defense against current reality. Jung thought that symptoms could be looked on as positive achievements, and so on. A full account of Jung's contributions would be a lengthy one. The story of the growth of the Jungian movement has only begun to be told.[15] And Jung's links to European intellectual history need to be further developed.[16]

Other early analysts have enjoyed relatively short-run successes, which may or may not continue in the future. The impact of modern feminism meant a striking revival of the work of Karen Horney (1885-1952), although she was once shunned by "mainstream" psychoanalysis. (The commonly invoked image of a mainstream illustrates by itself the latent authoritarianism of this field.) Horney is now regularly cited and quoted throughout the world of orthodox psychoanalysis that is associated with the International Psychoanalytic Association (IPA). Books about Horney, all sympathetic to her, have continued to come out,[17] and the Institute she founded continues. My own efforts to revive a complicated figure like Helene Deutsch (1884-1982), once a favorite of Freud's but who does not fit neatly into a linear view of the emancipation of women, have to be written off as a failure[18]; even her two-volume *The Psychology of Women* has long been out of print. (In Paris, however, her clinical papers are coming out from a major publishing house in a two-volume trade edition.[19]) Lou Andreas-Salomé (1861-1937) is another strikingly original woman who does not readily fit into today's North American feminist categories; not even a full collection of her psychoanalytic writings exists.

Wilhelm Reich (1897-1957), like Horney another so-called troublemaker, enjoyed for a time a special notoriety; he was one of the earliest to try and bring Marxism and psychoanalysis into some relationship with one another, and his books have not only stayed in print but his *The Mass Psychology of Fascism*[20] has even appeared in pirated editions. (Yet as we have already noted, two recent biographies of Freud, written from different ideological outlooks, both completely ignored the troublesome name of Reich.[21]) Although Freud had no personal or intellectual relationship with Horney, Freud was upset enough about Reich to compose his *Civilization and Its Discontents* against him. Still, Reich not only pioneered in developing "character" analysis, but also notably contributed to the growth of psychoanalytic technique. The literature about him continues to expand, and his books have proved highly popular, even though his last phase marked by his interest in "orgone" energy, which ended in his death in a federal penitentiary, did tarnish, as might have been expected, his earlier contributions.

The one outstanding success story in the historiography of psychoanalysis in recent years has been the remarkable comeback staged by Sandor Ferenczi (1873-1933). Thanks to Jones's slanderous way of dismissing Ferenczi's differences with Freud as due to the fruition of a long-simmering psychosis in Ferenczi, not long ago he was regularly bypassed as a figure in this field. (Unfortunately Freud seems to have started the tradition of pathologizing opponents with diagnostic categories.) Thanks however to the publication of the three-volume edition of the correspondence between Freud and Ferenczi, as well as to the appearance of Ferenczi's *Clinical Diary*, Ferenczi has staged a notable revival.[22] The Hungarian school of psychoanalysis, even when scattered abroad, has hung together enough to have succeeded in re-establishing Ferenczi's genuine stature. His emphasis on the significance of trauma in personality development has also helped ensure that his ideas seem relevant now, and the whole interpersonal approach has been infused with the warmth of his therapeutic optimism. International Ferenczi gatherings are a sign of the vitality of this major alternative to the clinical approach recommended by Freud.

Otto Rank (1884-1939), another analyst Jones tried to tarnish with the accusation of mental instability, has not fared nearly as well as Ferenczi. Books by Rank, as well as an early diary, still remain untranslated into English today. Rank developed an idiosyncratic vocabulary, but although works by him continue to come out, he failed to establish anything like a separate school of his own. He deserves credit for highlighting the role of emotions in therapy as opposed to the value of a rationalistic reconstruction of the childhood past, as well as his interesting work on the psychology of art. Best-sellers like Ernest Becker's *The Denial of Death*[23] may have helped keep Rank's name going, and for awhile there even was a *Journal of the Otto Rank Association*, but by and large Rank's ideas have been either unacknowledged or simply used by other more popular psychologists, such as Rollo May or Carl Rogers for instance.

In France Jacques Lacan (1901-81), driven out of the IPA by Anna Freud and Marie Bonaparte in 1963, not only single-handedly managed to get psychoanalysis into the center of that nation's intellectual life, but shaped the way Freud's ideas were received there. In reading books coming out of France it is sometimes hard to follow what is meant by citations to Freud since those references are apt to be so colored by the novel concepts that originate in the Lacanian movement. (The fact that there are about twenty translations into French of Freud's little 1925 paper "Negation" testifies by itself to Lacan's powerful impact.) Francophilic circles abroad have been similarly influenced by Lacan's teachings. Although Freud's works were relatively slow to be received in France, and there is still no standard edition of his writings in French, it is now well established that there is such a phenomena as a French Freud.[24] (The current world wide impact of Lacan has to make earlier valiant efforts to revive the ideas of Pierre Janet look mainly like a hot-house endeavor.[25]) Disenchantment with Marxism has undoubtedly allowed psychoanalysis, at least within the Left, to become so central in France.

In England the ideas of Melanie Klein (1886-1960) are uniquely central. Klein's work, starting in child analysis, has also had its impact abroad, in Argentina for example, but the British Freud means that the Kleinian *weltanschauung* has succeeded in being taken-for-granted there. This triumph of Klein came only after a bruising battle among British analysts at the end of World War II[26]; Anna Freud (1895-1982), who essentially withdrew to concentrate on building up her own training facilities in Hampstead, was to prove a notable loser in psychoanalytic warfare. For some reason, lack of political skill or an altruistic surrender on her part toward her father, she was unable to combat the Kleinian apostles who knew how to gain power. They were inspired by a millennial-seeming passion, reflected in Klein's early belief that all children need analysis; psychosis too was considered a matter of environmental failure. The most unlikely-seeming ideas appear to flourish as Bolshevism did, at least for a time, seem to succeed historically. Perhaps the existence of Anna Freud's many allies in the States misled her about the necessity of being more decisively active in Britain. Kleinianism did have its eventual beneficial effects in shaping British psychotherapy, and today she has to be counted among the more surprising of Freud's heirs. Every success in this field, however, appears to me to be a sign of the need for more critical thinking.

I think we have to be on our toes about any apparently triumphant school of thought, just as we need to be sure that good ideas among "losers" have not been needlessly forgotten. I am implying the liberal conviction that all power needs to be questioned. And so the recommendation that seems to me most apt is that we pursue a counter-cyclical approach, which means skepticism about the present and special generosity about the easily forgotten past.

Britain had other notable analytic figures, and — besides Klein — the work of Donald W. Winnicott (1896-1971) has probably been the most broadly influential. More books of his appeared following his death than he personally saw into print. His idiosyncratic originality meant that there was nothing remotely comparable to Kleinian dogmatism for potential followers to hang onto. And he did little to organize any such movement in his own behalf. Since Winnicott failed to anoint any apostles it is all the more impressive how his ideas have succeeded in spreading. Winnicott therefore seems to me to be the exception that proves the rule, when it comes to the attraction of comprehensive systems like those of Marx as opposed to the individual insights of someone like Bakunin.

Ronald D. Laing (1927-89) probably sold more books than any other member of the British Psychoanalytic Society, and for a time he seemed to have created an anti-psychiatry cause that might endure. But his own personal falling-apart, doubtless connected with his earlier out-of-control alcoholism, was different and less dramatic than Reich's prosecution by the U. S. Food and Drug Administration, but still comparable in serving to discredit his prior writings.[27] As a result others have had to confront a fresh challenge posed by the recent developments within biological psychiatry.

The American contribution has been distinctively different, following more Anna Freud's emphasis on the importance of putting any pathology within the general context of normality. For a time the ego psychological ideas of Heinz Hartmann (1894-1970) seemed to be a dominant force, but that work, largely tidying up Freud's concepts, now seems sterile and without much contemporary influence.[28] On the other hand, the pioneering ideas of Harry Stack Sullivan (1892-1949), an untutored American original, continue to have clinical relevance. Sullivan was ambitious not only about treating psychosis, but he sought to extend his hopefulness to the spheres of race relations, poverty, and world politics. (In Italy today at least as many, if not more, of Sullivan's books are studied as in America.) The critiques of psychiatry of Thomas Szasz have lost some of their force as the biological nature of the great mental illnesses seem more established than ever. But Szasz did notably highlight how psychiatry can make use of social conformism, a point the recently fashionable Michel Foucault subsequently made. Adolf Meyer (1866-1950), who led the single most influential school during his lengthy Chairmanship of the Department of Psychiatry at Johns Hopkins, is remembered now mainly by specialists in the history of psychiatry. Meyer was, despite his tortured prose with neologisms that failed to catch on, a great teacher with a broad-minded outlook, and he pioneering for example with his skepticism about the institution of training analyses.

But the most notable and successful independent school of thought in American psychoanalysis is undoubtedly that of Heinz Kohut (1913-81). He did consciously set out to found a movement called "self-psychology", and was even important enough as an original thinker to have earned Anna Freud's disapproval; when she stigmatized him as "anti-psychoanalytic" that was meant to be decisive in marking him as a "deviation", but instead his work has continued to attract ardent followers – eager to pinpoint the legitimacy of his Freudian lineage. Although Kohut's writings are at least as difficult to follow as either Sullivan's or Meyer's, self-psychology served to fill a felt need among American analysts to get away from the instinctual reductionism associated with traditional Freudian teachings.[29]

Oddly enough Kohut's "heresy" originated in Chicago, at the Institute that Franz Alexander (1891-1964) had initially founded; Kohut had enough problems of his own without taking on Alexander's controversial mantle. Although Alexander was once well known as a publicist, historian, as well as an analytic pioneer, by now his name has substantially disappeared. Like his Hungarian friend Sandor Rado (1890-1972), who created the Institute at Columbia's medical school in defiance of the powers-that-be at the New York Psychoanalytic Society, Rado is now a forgotten figure.[30] Although Alexander's work on the "corrective emotional experience", as well as experiments in scheduling appointments, prefigured many later innovations in psychotherapy, and Rado too stuck his neck-out about what was missing therapeutically in classical psychoanalysis, they both exist only on the margins of people's awareness. The interest of Abram Kardiner (1891-1978) in anthropology and society has also pretty well evaporated as an influence, even though he notably led the way in criticizing libido theory and in extending psychoanalytic influence to the area of race relations.

Three of the most publicly well-known analysts, Bruno Bettelheim (1903-90), Erich Fromm and Erik H. Erikson, have also suffered relative declines, even though their many books continue to be read. Bettelheim's reputation, while still secure in France, entered in the United States on the steepest possible collapse following the public scandal associated with the use of physical restraints at his orthogenic school at the University of Chicago that became public at the time of his suicide. The storm that his death set off was led by former patients at a time when Bettelheim could no longer answer critics; but his once popular writings had never hinted at the use of even spanking, much less the environment of terror that seems to have been associated with his clinic. No doubt some of the critiques of Bettelheim have been unbalanced if not unfair[31], still it would be reasonable to put at least a question mark around much that Bettelheim reported.

Although Fromm (1900-1980) was once so important in putting the social environment into the center of psychoanalytic thinking, and his books may have out-sold even those by Laing, starting in the 1960s Fromm's aspirations as a political prophet turned many off his work. His former Marxist allies at the Frankfurt school of critical sociology were almost fanatically intolerant when it came to the undoubted merits of Fromm's work. Neo-Freudianism as a movement proved unsuccessful[32], even if many of Fromm's ideas may have been silently incorporated within modern social science. Fromm's influence, such as it now is, has been carried on by the analysts he trained in Mexico and New York City, as well as by his literary executor in Germany.[33] Although there is an international Fromm group with its headquarters in Germany, it is largely a German organization, with some key Italian supporters. At Fromm's 100th birthday the IPA German analysts did not seem to want to acknowledge Fromm's significant part in the history of the discipline. Even though he wrote little on technique, so much else on that subject has now been discredited that one would not think that the failure to add any distinctive mistakes of his own would prove damaging to his reputation.

Erik H. Erikson (1902-94) played his cards differently from Fromm. Rather, the example of how Fromm had been excluded from the IPA[34] helped ensure that Erikson would pursue an organizationally safer path. Erikson had many ideas about society and individual development that were similar to Fromm, and also Kardiner, but Erikson stuck to his own individual course that had started with his beginnings as an artist. Although trained as a child analyst by Anna Freud, Erikson grew critical of many key features to orthodox analysis; Erikson typically muffled the independent direction that he chose to go in, and even as he wrote loyally about Freud's own biography, he never dared explicitly to found his own separate school. For many years before his death he had been afflicted by

Alzheimer's, and his greatest influence probably came in the 1960s. By the mid-1970s there was already a noticeable fall-off in how well his books did.[35] Like Bettelheim and also Fromm, Erikson had felt drawn away from strictly clinical concerns; Erikson turned to the field he called "psycho-history", as well as the broadest kinds of social and ethical questions. It remains to be seen whether someone as privately gentle as Erikson can ever hope to match the influence of those as ideologically intransigent, for example, as Klein or Lacan.

Fanaticism has paid all too well in the history of psychoanalysis. Even a figure like Otto Fenichel, who wrote an obsessional textbook but inspires those on the Left who want to think of themselves as loyal to the "mainstream" of psychoanalysis, has aroused a surprising amount of recent interest. Frieda Fromm-Reichmann's work on the psychotherapy of the psychoses meant that she deserved, I think, a recent biography.[36] But one on Clara Thompson, a leader in interpersonal psychoanalysis and a notable student of Ferenczi's, has never been undertaken, even though she wrote one of the most fair-minded early histories of psychoanalysis[37]; rather like Helene Deutsch, Thompson has had the bad luck to run into feminist sectarianism, which has complained in her case of her having failed to follow up adequately on Ferenczi's interests in trauma and incest.[38]

To generalize: whatever intellectual historians might be inclined to think ranks in importance, by and large it has been the conformists behind today's IPA bureaucracy whose work is most likely to get cited in the professional literature. While in principle originality pays off in terms of the history of ideas, I regret to say that in the short-run the costs of ostracism seem a heavy penalty to have to pay. Being a company man or woman pays off to a remarkable degree. Psychoanalysis became a church in which in each locality the presence of local transferences means that home grown pundits, who look parochial from the broadest perspective, are likely to get surprisingly acknowledged and taught.

"Pluralism" has been much talked about, but so far has amounted to verbal adherence. Jung's work, for example, is still too controversial to get discussed among analysts; yet he proposed so many challenging ideas that it is hard to see how they can continue to be ignored without damage to the whole subject of the history of depth psychology. (He proposed, for instance, that transference is a sign of lack of rapport between patient and analyst, an idea that I think deserves far more attention.) It is not only that implicit sectarianism continues to persist; while the wars among the Freudians have gone on for almost a hundred years now, the biologically oriented psychiatrists have been allowed to continue relatively unchallenged with their diagnostic shell-games.

The ideal of toleration in psychoanalysis still remains an undeveloped entity. That is to say, no support has been given to the notion that given how many mistaken roads have been taken in the past, respect deserves to be paid to any original ideas that get proposed. Any metaphor like that of a "deviation" means that old-time religiosity has not been overcome. One would have thought that reflecting back on all the controversies in this field it would be more apparent to people today that they might be wrong. Skepticism about being right should promote toleration for the legitimate points of views of others. The faith that through broadening interchanges one might learn something precious would facilitate a kind of openness that could help ensure the survival of this whole way of thinking.

Threats to free thought come from many different sources. In Toronto recently an expert on anti-depression medication was offered a professorial psychiatric appointment. But when he gave a lecture that included a discussion of the possible suicidal reactions to taking Prozac in a subgroup of depressive patients, the academic invitation was withdrawn, and a legal suit ensued.[39] Drug companies have acquired that much power over medical appointments that they can sabotage thinking that might look like it was not good for their business, and billions of dollars can be at stake.

Recent successful television programs like *The Sopranos* or *Six Feet Under* should be enough to demonstrate, at least for America, the extent of the success of the Freudian revolution in the history of human thought. We still need to investigate the implications this has had in a variety of areas, such as the kinds of powerful drugs that get given, and on what grounds this is being done, especially to small children. The current extent of the reliance on pharmacology may be misleading about the degree to which the underlying thinking remains indebted to earlier psychological theorizing. Caretaking will likely remain an essential component of all psychotherapy, regardless of the school of thought that may be currently triumphant. Also, in what ways human privacy has gained or lost remains, I believe, an open question that demands investigation. And the whole subject of confidentiality is one which ethical inquiry should be equipped to try to handle.

In terms of Freud's contemporaries he was himself a great heretic, and there is little doubt that he attracted to his movement people with similarly subversive inclinations. His approach respected failures in life, and paid attention to the problems of outsiders. Those who have felt they were forced to break with Freud, or with the "mainsteam" following his death, would seem to have been in keeping with his own most daring spirit. But any moralistic denunciations of predecessors can often be unaware of the full circumstances surrounding earlier thinking. So it remains to be seen just what the transformation in ideas that his work initiated will add up to. Will analysts, for example, be able successfully to challenge the current vogue for psychopharmacological remedies, or behavioristic ones? One wonders whether as profound a philosopher of psychiatry as Karl Jaspers (1883-1969) will ever be adequately credited for his own early trenchant critique of Freud. The more attention gets paid to the inevitable limitations of the founder of psychoanalysis, the more epochal his achievement can become. Of course this new twenty-first century has scarcely begun to unfold. The great American baseball manager Leo Durocher is said to have once maintained that "nice guys come in last," and perhaps the next generation will be in a better position to decide whether that principle applies also to the history of psychoanalysis.

NOTES

1. Isaiah Berlin, "Herzen and Bakunin on Liberty", in *Russian Thinkers*, ed. Henry Hardy (London, The Hogarth Press, 1978), pp. 82-113. See also Isaiah Berlin, *Karl Marx: His Life and Environment* (Oxford, Oxford University Press, 1942).
2. David McCullough, *John Adams* (New York, Simon and Schuster, 2001).
3. Albert W. Alschuler, *Law Without Values: The Life, Work, and Legacy of Justice Holmes* (Chicago, University of Chicago Press, 2000), pp. pp. 31-40.
4. Paul Roazen, "Was Freud a Nice Guy?", in *The Historiography of Psychoanalysis*, op. cit., pp. 23-36.
5. See Celia Bertin, *Marie Bonaparte: A Life* (New York, Harcourt Brace Jovanovich, 1982), p. 176.
6. See, for example, Peter Lomas, *Doing Good? Psychotherapy Out of Its Depth* (Oxford, Oxford University Press, 1999).
7. Mariano Ben Plotkin, *Freud in the Pampas: The Emergence and Development of a Psychoanalytic Culture in Argentina* (Stanford, Stanford University Press, 2001).
8. *Standard Edition*, Vol. 14, pp. 7-66.
9. Paul Roazen, *Freud and His Followers* (New York, Knopf, 1975; reprinted, New York, Da Capo Press, 1992), p. 211.
10. But see Bernhard Handlbauer, *The Freud-Adler Controversy* (Rockport, Mass., Oneworld Publications, 1998), translated by Laurie Cohen, and Edward Hoffman, *The Drive for Self: Alfred Adler and the Founding of Individual Psychology* (Reading, Mass., Addison-Wesley, 1994).
11. C. G. Jung, *Analytical Psychology: Notes on the Seminar Given in 1925*, ed. William McGuire (Princeton, Princeton University Press, 1989).
12. See the forthcoming books on Jung by Deirdre Bair and Sonu Shamdasani.
13. Ernest Jones, *Sigmund Freud*, 3 volumes (New York, Basic Books, 1953-57).
14. See Roazen, *Freud and His Followers*, op. cit., pp. 211-22; Martin Green, *Otto Gross, Freudian Psychoanalyst 1877-1920: Literature and Ideas* (Lewiston, Edwin Mellen Press, 1999).
15. See Thomas B. Kirsch, *The Jungians: A Comparative and Historical Perspective* (London, Routledge, 2000) and William McGuire, *Bollingen: An Adventure in Collecting the Past*, revised edition (Princeton, N.J., Princeton University Press, 1989).
16. Petteri Pietikainen, *C. J. Jung and the Psychology of Symbolic Forms* (Helsinki, Academia Scientiarum Fennica, 1999).
17. See most recently Bernard Paris, *Karen Horney: A Psychoanalyst's Search for Self-Understanding* (New Haven, Yale University Press, 1994).

18 Paul Roazen, "Women and History," *Psychologist/Psychoanalyst*, Spring 2000, pp. 29-33. (Also in Paul Roazen, *Cultural Foundations of Political Psychology* [New Brunswick, N.J., Transaction Publishers, 2003]), pp. 264-74.
19 Helene Deutsch, *Les Introuvables: Cas Cliniques et Autoanalyse* (Paris, Seuil, 2000).
20 Wilhelm Reich, *The Mass Psychology of Fascism*, op. cit.
21 Peter Gay, *Freud: A Life For Our Time* (New York, Norton, 1988) and Louis Breger, *Freud: Darkness in the Midst of Vision* (New York, Wiley, 2000).
22 *The Clinical Diary of Sandor Ferenczi*, ed. Judith Dupont, translated by Michael Balint and Nicola Zarday Jackson (Cambridge, Harvard University Press, 1988), and *The Correspondence of Sigmund Freud and Sandor Ferenczi*, ed. Eva Brabant, Ernst Falzeder, and Patrizia Giampieri-Deutsch, translated by Peter T. Hoffer, 3 volumes (Cambridge, Harvard University Press, 1993-2000).
23 Ernest Becker, *The Denial of Death* (New York, Basic Books, 1973).
24 See, for example, Sherry Turkel, *Psychoanalytic Politics: Freud's French Revolution* (New York, Basic Books, 1978), and Elisabeth Roudinesco, *Jacques Lacan & Co.: A History of Psychoanalysis in France, 1925-85*, translated by Jeffrey Mehlman (Chicago, University of Chicago Press, 1990).
25 Henri Ellenberger, *The Discovery of the Unconscious: The History and Evolution of Dynamic Psychiatry* (New York, Basic Books, 1970), pp. 331-417.
26 Paul Roazen, *Oedipus in Britain: Edward Glover and the Struggle Over Klein* (New York, Other Press, 2000).
27 See Adrian C. Laing, *R. D. Laing: A Biography* (London, Peter Owen, 1994), and also Daniel Burston, *The Wing of Madness: The Life and Work of R. D. Laing* (Cambridge, Harvard University Press, 1996).
28 *The Hartmann Era*, ed. Martin S. Bergmann (New York, Other Press, 2000).
29 Charles B. Strozier, *Heinz Kohut: The Making of a Psychoanalyst* (New York, Farrar Straus & Giroux, 2001).
30 Paul Roazen and Bluma Swerdloff, *Heresy: Sandor Rado and the Psychoanalytic Movement* (Northvale, N.J., Aronson, 1995). See also Paul Roazen, *The Trauma of Freud: Controversies in Psychoanalysis* (New Brunswick, N.J., Transaction Publishers, 2002). Ch. 13.
31 Compare, for example, Richard Pollak's unremitting indictment, *The Creation of Dr. B.: A Biography of Bruno Bettelheim* (New York, Simon & Schuster, 1997), with Nina Sutton's sympathetic but not uncritical portrayal in *Bettelheim: A Life and Legacy* (New York, Basic Books, 1996).
32 Neil McLaughlin, "Why Do Schools of Thought Fail? Neo-Freudianism as a Case Study in the Sociology of Knowledge", *Journal of the History of the Behavioral Sciences*, Vol. 34, No. 2 (Spring 1998), pp. 113-34; Neil McLaughlin, "How to Become a Forgotten Intellectual: Intellectual Movements and the Rise and Fall of Erich Fromm," *Sociological Forum*, Vol. 13, No. 2 (1998), pp. 215-46.
33 Rainer Funk, *Erich Fromm: His Life and Ideas*, translated by Ian Portman and Manuela Kunkel (New York, Continuum, 2000).
34 Paul Roazen, "The Exclusion of Erich Fromm from the IPA," *Contemporary Psychoanalysis*, Vol. 37, No. 1 (2001), pp. 5-42. (Also in Roazen, *Cultural Foundations of Political Psychology, op. cit.*, pp. 1-34.)
35 Lawrence J. Friedman, *Identity's Architect: A Biography of Erik H. Erikson*, op. cit., Kit Welchman, *Erik Eikson: His Life, Work, and Significance* (Buckingham, Open University Press, 2000), and Carol Hren Hoare, *Erikson on Development in Adulthood: New Insights from the Unpublished Papers* (New York, Oxford Univ. Press, 2002).

36 Gail A. Hornstein, *To Redeem One Person Is to Redeem the World: The Life of Freida Fromm-Reichmann* (New York, Basic Books, 2000).
37 Clara Thompson, *Psychoanalysis: Evolution and Development*, with the collaboration of Patrick Mullahy, new Introduction by Paul Roazen (New York, Grove Press, 1950, New Brunswick, N.J., Transaction Publishers, 2002).
38 Sue A. Shapiro, "Clara Thompson: Ferenczi's Messenger with Half a Message," in *The Legacy of Sandor Ferenczi*, ed. Lewis Aron and Adrienne Harris (New York, Hillsdale, N.J., The Analytic Press, 1993), pp. 159-173.
39 David Healy, *The Anti-Depressant Era* (Cambridge, Harvard University Press, 1997); David Healy, "Conflicting Interests in Toronto: Anatomy of a Controversy at the Interface of Academia and Industry," *Perspectives in Biology and Medicine*, Vol. 45, No. 2 (Spring 2002), pp. 250-63.

14

THE VITALITY OF NEUROSIS

An unusual degree of polarization has afflicted the subject of Freud and his creation of psychoanalysis, so that informed opinion continues to seem to remain as partisan as it been over the past hundred-odd years. On the one hand there are those practitioners who lead the trade unions of analysts, for whom it has been tempting to mythify Freud so that he appears to become what today's practitioners might like a man born in 1856 to have been. Controversial subjects are passed over as bad for business, and a shortsighted need to make Freud into a man of our own time takes precedence. And others are too eager to protect him from what might be regarded as "slander," even though one might have supposed that Freud was well-enough established in intellectual history to need no such defensiveness. The historical Freud is to me far more interesting, and challenging for us now, than partisan idealizations of him. Yet it is also true that a further rugged band of critics seems to share the same essentially anachronistic approach to Freud, so that he gets narrowly weighed by contemporary standards of what a great man might have been like. All Freud's intended critiques of Western civilization's ethics are apt to get lost in the hubbub that continues to surround his work. Between his allies and his enemies it is too easy for the greatest Freud to slip into oblivion. For political philosophers, I am going to contend, the place to start with Freud is not his own explicit attempts at political theorizing but rather the more elusive implications of his work for our understanding of the human condition – what I want to incorporate under the notion of the vitality of neurosis.

The meetings called "Contested Legacies: A Conference on the German-Speaking Intellectual and Cultural Emigration to the United States and United Kingdom, 1933-45" at Bard College in August 2002, for which this chapter was written, could include Freud by the skin of his teeth, since he emigrated to England only a bit over a year before his death in 1939. The most significant emigration in Freud's life was probably when his family moved from Moravia to Vienna in 1859, although the exact circumstances of that exile remain largely unexplored by scholars. Like so many other old Viennese, Freud was not actually born in the city his life has helped to immortalize. To exclude Freud from "Contested Legacies," while including relatively secondary figures like Erich Fromm and Erik H. Erikson, would have been odd indeed. For as Arnold Zweig wrote to Freud during early 1938 (in one of those early and tendentiously edited collections of Freud's letters that will have to be redone someday), "Your achievement will in any case be sufficient to guarantee the immortality of Viennese cultural life in the 19th and 20th centuries."[1]

Why Freud should matter to political theorists? (As Erikson once pointed out, it is hard for anyone of us to escape our earliest professional discipline, and political philosophy is for me what artistry was for him.) Isaiah Berlin, Hannah Arendt, and Leo Strauss may have been intensely rivalrous with one another, yet it would be impossible to evaluate which one of the three deserves the laurel for having the most contempt for Freud.

To start off with the issue of rivalry, and how different these thinkers might appear to be: Berlin wrote a reader's report for a British publisher saying that Arendt's *The Human Condition* was unworthy of publication, and he singled her out following her death in a *Times Literary Supplement* survey of over-rated thinkers; she had fully reciprocated Berlin's feelings, and evidently thought he had conspired to promote the pro-Zionist opposition to her Eichmann book. Both Berlin and Arendt shared a similar negative outlook on sociologists, even if he was committed enough as a liberal never to have been so imprudent as to have put into print anything along the lines of her notorious essay on the crisis at Little Rock. Meanwhile continentals like Arendt and Strauss seemed too quick to see each other as fascists, although I should leave it to others more intimately acquainted with their work to elucidate what they in fact thought about each other. Strauss's conviction that Berlin was a "relativist" seems to me far too facile an assessment.

Berlin had actually wrangled a meeting with Freud in London, but was so little impressed by Freud's presence that he never bothered to write up the encounter. Although Berlin scattered various references to Freud throughout his writings, I do wonder how much of Freud Berlin ever actually read; I know that once on a trip to the States in the 1960s, Berlin bought a copy of the old large Modern Library edition of Freud, but that seemed to me then a sign of Berlin's presence in America only reminding him of the inevitability of Freud's stature. (When I was enrolled at a great Oxford college in 1959-60 the library had not one single book by Freud.) Berlin saw Freud, I believe, as an enemy of freedom perhaps at least as dangerous as Marx, and it would be possible to interpret Berlin's "Two

Concepts of Liberty" inaugural lecture in the light of Berlin's antagonism toward Freudian notions of positive liberty. Therapists regularly proceed on the premise of the legitimacy of Rousseau's doctrine of forcing people to be free, even if there remains too little attention in psychoanalytic literature to the Kantian problem of using people in a way that could be construed as manipulative.

In Arendt's case we know that she had at least four volumes by Freud in her library that is now housed at Bard College, but it seems to me striking which books she chose to exclude – the greatest Freud, *The Interpretation of Dreams* or the case histories, do not get represented there, as she chose to collect works readily accessible to a political theorist. It is not just in her Eichmann book, where she sounds triumphant that psychiatrists could be comical soul experts in certifying Eichmann's normality, but a revealing passage comes up in a 1950 letter from Arendt's husband (Heinrich Blücher) to her about a friend in psychological need:

> Kurt is showing signs of true psychosis. (Having a dentist look inside your mouth is indecent.) I am trying to get him to see Fromm, but he manifests that true resistance about which psychoanalysts otherwise only talk; any day now he'll start thinking of us as insane. I don't want this kind of talent to end up in an insane asylum. Unfortunately Goldstein was all thumbs, and only scared him even more. Furthermore, the poor man keeps quoting our own arguments against psychoanalysis. We should never talk to others the way we talk to each other – and in this case we have helped wreak havoc.[2]

Among Freud's favorite lines was the maxim from Goethe's Mephistopheles in *Faust*: "After all, the best of what you know may not be told to boys." Blücher was warning her that their anti-psychoanalytic prejudices were having unfortunate practical consequences for their friend in need of therapeutic help.

In Leo Strauss's case, I remember a graduate seminar of his on Nietzsche at the University of Chicago, in the winter of 1958-59, in which he paused in discussing the concept of sublimation in *Beyond Good and Evil* in order to distinguish what Nietzsche had in mind from anything that Freud might have intended. Even though I was then only at the beginning stages of learning about Freud's importance for political theory, it was obvious that Strauss did not share any such conviction. Strauss's Chicago Department of Political Science antagonist, David Easton, did on the other hand encourage me in pursuing Freud's significance. (Easton allowed a few of us to be given a graduate seminar on Weber, Mannheim, & Freud.) Someday an intellectual biography of Strauss, or the multi-volume edition of Berlin's letters that will be appearing, may explicate their respective antagonisms toward Freud.

But while the immense reputations of Berlin, Arendt, and Strauss are a late twentieth century success story that extends beyond political science, they each shared a bitterness about psychoanalysis, so that Freud himself remains a failure within political theory. (A look at Karl Popper and others too would extend the general anti-Freudian professional tale.) At the same time, practicing political psychologists are as hostile to theoretical matters as the crudest behavioralist could be.[3]

One might suppose that the issue of what is natural would be central to a political philosopher's concerns. Also, it should be impossible to begin to understand what might be rational without also entertaining an inquiry into other sides of reason, such as the non-rational or irrational. Further, traditional concepts like authority, anxiety, individualism, conformity, punishment, and freedom also are part of what psychoanalysis centrally purports to deal with. Notions of the self, and the whole question of personhood, have become pivotal in political theory without its becoming commonplace to consider what bearing on it Freud might have had. And family life – here Freud was most explicitly challenging preceding values – may be the one key area that helps to decide whether psychoanalysis has a secure future, as countries like India and China move closer to western models of how children and parents deal with one another. (Traditional Confucian values may be a good deal closer to ancient Greek ideas than to what we in the individualistic West trace to the heritage of the 18th century European Enlightenment.)

If I had to select one book to epitomize the civilization Freud represented, it would be Stefan Zweig's *The World of Yesterday*[4] that best recaptures a whole lost era. In the course of my own interviews with some seventy people who had known Freud personally, I concluded that Stefan Zweig did the best job of describing what those people were like. Old world culture would now seem to have almost vanished from Europe. For example, at a recent conference in Vienna I was preceded by a speaker whose standing-room only talk was officially summarized as: "collect the positive aspects of your life and save them for the dark times. Your own experiences are expensive. Others' experiences are valuable." (Most of the audience for this Norman Vincent Peale-like presentation had left before I began to speak.) Only a couple of years earlier, while traveling in Germany for some lectures, I got curiously defended by one analyst on the grounds that I was reminding the clinicians of their European past. I felt it was a topsy-turvy situation that an American should be on the continent for the sake of reminding analysts of a continental heritage that was so unfamiliar to me.

I do not think that these personal anecdotes are idiosyncratic and without general implications; for social bases help account for creativity — including its absence – and by and large North America has lacked the fundamental conflicts that have afflicted so much of the rest of the world.[5] Tragedy is an inescapable aspect of human experience that even someone as friendly toward psychoanalysis as Herbert Marcuse chose to ignore in his utopian reading of what he regarded as a "hidden trend" in Freud's heritage. I would not want to share in romanticizing old world culture, or ignore its barbarities and hypocrisies. My European analytic friends are as capable of extravagantly engaging in what Freud stigmatized as "wild analysis," in interpreting a recent event like 9/11, as Freud himself was in approaching someone like Woodrow Wilson almost three quarters of a century ago; Freud was appalled by Wilsonian democratic pretensions.[6]

As grandiose as Freud could be in approaching questions of social philosophy, the *Totem and Taboo* side of his work that Arendt would seem to have paid attention to, it is the more clinical aspect of his contribution, as I tried to suggest at the outset, that I have believed to be central to what he bequeathed to history. And this is why I have chosen to write about the vitality of neurosis, since it is a subject so at odds with today's understanding of psychoanalysis. Current editions of DSM (Diagnostic and Statistical Manual Of Mental Disorders) III and IV, widely used by clinicians not just for insurance purposes but for the sake of diagnoses, have replaced neurosis by the notion of "disorder." With the vanishing of the term neurosis also went Freud's civilized respect for outsiders; psychoanalysis stood, I think, for an unusual amount of regard for failure and disability.

Ours is I think a peculiarly materialistic era, one that was heralded by Aldous Huxley in his 1932 *Brave New World*. A half a century ago people like myself first read that novel alongside Orwell's *1984*, but Orwell's vision of totalitarian regimes probably was seriously misleading; the concept of totalitarianism was built on a mere twelve years of German history combined with twenty years of Stalin's Soviet rule, and supposedly that totalitarian concept was critical in explaining the modern era. We now know not only how fragile and transitory the successes of Hitler and Stalin were, but early critics of the notion of totalitarianism, those who saw its limits and parochialism, were once brushed aside. I am thinking for example of how rough a time someone like George Kennan had from Kremlinologists, who for years saw his approach as too much that of a kind of religious mystic.[7] Boris Pasternak's *Doctor Zhivago* came as such a notable shock in reminding the world of the miraculous endurance of the spirit of the greatest Russian culture even in the face of Stalinist tyranny.

While Orwell has had a vast social and political influence, Huxley has gone relatively unheralded. Yet it was his novelistic conception of "soma," a drug by the way without any of the side effects associated with today's popular anti-depressants, that anticipated what is now known as cosmetic psychopharmacology. Huxley has a "Controller", in a line of reasoning "not to be published," engage in thinking that is more relevant now than ever:

> once you began admitting explanations in terms of purpose – well, you didn't know what the result might be. It was the sort of idea

that might easily decondition the more unsettled minds among the higher castes – make them lose their faith in happiness as the Sovereign Good and take to believing, instead, that the goal was somewhere beyond, somewhere outside the present human sphere; that the purpose of life was not the maintenance of well-being, but some intensification and refining of consciousness, some enlargement of knowledge.[8]

Huxley's Controller admits that such reasoning was "quite possibly true," but considered it not "admissible"; and he feared the creation of "less than human monsters." Huxley's world, like that of Orwell, did not have "any use for old things here." Huxley accurately foresaw that "you can't have tragedies without social instability." One way of describing the future Huxley was painting was for him to write: "Christianity without tears – that's what *soma* is." And Huxley's "Savage" protests: "Nothing costs enough here."[9] Appropriately enough Huxley's *Brave New World* reminded readers of William James's great assault on materialism, *Varieties of Religious Experience*.

In the face of the form of barbarism Huxley was describing, and which has become I think all too prevalent, Freud had meant by the concept of neurosis a universal human quality. For him the achievement of an Oedipus complex was a sign of culture and civilization. Of course at the same time Freud was critical of the constraints of society, and labored to alleviate the consequences of oedipal feelings. But for him the absence of an Oedipus complex was either a tip-off to psychosis or an indication that patients were riff-raff, good-for-nothings that an analyst should have nothing to do with. The concept of worthiness in Freud implied the anti-Christian idea that some human beings might be unworthy.

As with the questionable influence of all great literature, Shakespeare for example, in misleading us about what we can expect of limited human capacities, one can wonder whether fallible human beings in reality can be expected to live on the plane of great drama. And many of the analytic followers of Freud did in fact try to humanize his heritage, and widen the scope of psychoanalysis beyond the narrow confines Freud had in mind.[10] Clinicians found it necessary to broaden the kinds of people Freud chose to work with, and to embrace more of humanity than Freud thought was accessible to psychotherapeutic influence. But whereas the analytic tradition started from neurosis and worked outward, sometimes imposing the neurotic model too ambitiously, the current tendency has gone in the opposite direction, so that diagnoses and medication designed for psychotics are now being administered to what Freudians once considered garden-variety neuroses, and sometimes even young children.

Freud took for granted the capacity of human beings to internalize conflicts, and therefore people inclined, for example, to drink their problems away were in his view not entitled to psychoanalytic attentions. (Jungians have long been more adept at dealing with alcoholism than those brought up in the more strictly Freudian tradition.) But both Freud and Jung worked from a starting point that assumed the legitimacy of suffering. When Huxley's Controller speaks of the faith in happiness as the "Sovereign Good," or the "maintenance of well-being," one can almost hear in the background the protests of Dostoevsky's underground man against the British utilitarian approach. Nietzsche shared in the disdain for groundling-like happiness. Freud even maintained that an analyst ought not to rush into alleviating suffering too quickly, and that pain is a critical incentive to the insight that makes genuine change lasting. Short-term anxiety can have its purposes, and Jung for instance emphasized how symptoms can have a constructive purpose.

Neurosis was not in Freud's view like some sort of toothache, to be removed by a version of psychological dentistry. No one can, or at least should be, "cured" of the human condition; whatever Freud might sometimes have implied, I think in the end he held that none of us can be purified of conflicts. I was delighted to be able to use as the epigraph for a recent book of mine[11] some lines from *Measure for Measure*:

> They say best men are moulded out of faults,
> And, for the most, become much more the better
> For being a little bad. . . .

And I once had relied on how Nietzsche's friend Lou Andreas-Salomé had understood the interconnections between her psychoanalyst lover Victor Tausk's weaknesses and achievements: "from the very beginning I realized it was this very struggle in Tausk that most deeply moved me – the struggle of the human creature. Brother-animal. You." She remarked too of Freud: "Confronted by a human being who impresses us as great, should we not be moved rather than chilled by the knowledge that he might have attained his greatness only through his frailties?"[12]

Whatever Freud might sometimes have suggested, I think he sought at his best to teach people how to live with distress, and the multiple ways of dealing with pain. He had notorious disdain for American culture, with its legal Prohibition of alcohol and its barbaric-seeming approach to mental life. Pragmatism ought not to mean that the goals of life be so simplified that savagery be substituted for refinement. The way we now often invoke the notion of zero tolerance would fulfill his worst expectations about the New World's naivete. He could not have approved of either our all or nothing approach to divorce, nor the expectations about marriage that lead to such primitive resolutions of enduring human dilemmas. It took someone inspired largely by the Jungian tradition, Anthony Storr, to write a book about solitude originally called *The School of Genius*[13], starting from the fact that so many great philosophers were predominantly solitary. Storr believed that

> The burden of value with which we are at present loading interpersonal relationships is too heavy for those fragile craft to carry. Our expectation that satisfying intimate relationships should, ideally, provide happiness and that, if they do not, there must be something wrong with those relationships, seems to be exaggerated. . .If we did not look to marriage as the principal source of happiness, fewer marriages would end in tears.[14]

Freud did, as his early critics were able to point out, take society too much for granted. In their different ways Fromm and Erikson performed an important service in insisting on the social dimension of human experience, something Freud had tried to banish from what he considered the proper subject of what he chose to consider suitable for "science." At the same time that Freud tried to universalize his insights, and therefore over-emphasized the significance of the Oedipus complex. Consequently, each of the so-called dissidents in his movement thought it necessary to repudiate this concept.

Although it was important to relativize Freud's achievement, and put it in cultural context, he also can be credited with having aimed at the statelessness of thought, the cross-cultural universe symbolized by Erasmus. It is the exile's fate to be torn away from rootedness, and Freud was in a sense making a virtue of necessity. He and Jung, for example, were in different ways competing for the right to consider themselves emancipated from their narrow origins. Freud was struggling to get away from the confines of his own religious background, and he dearly wanted to conquer in the Christian world Jung represented. Freud's relationship to Judaism is complicated; his reliance on Augustinian-like introspectiveness can be seen as a form of defiance of Freud's own religious background. Meanwhile Jung was seeking out the collective unconscious, and when he talked about India and China for example, he was trying to get beyond the confines of therapeutics to something underlying neurosis. Both Freud and Jung were caught up in a struggle between parochialism as opposed to cosmopolitanism, and it requires emancipated intellectual historians to try to understand the different conflicts they were trying to deal with.

All of this is beyond the ken of most North American psychiatric residents today. They are apt to think that the profession they have entered into is some version of dentistry. The side of Freud who denounced the ethic of "love thy neighbor as thyself" is simply incomprehensible to today's clinicians.[15] Therapists who feel comfortable seeing clients while wearing white coats are unlikely to be receptive to the idea that every clinical encounter is simultaneously an ethical one. As a matter of fact, American medical schools are having great trouble attracting residents, and psychiatry in particular is populated by young foreigners; seeing patients for a matter of minutes before writing a prescription is not an enticing inducement for American medical school graduates. Yet without such residency programs psychiatric departments risk the loss of their accreditation.[16]

It is particularly striking that residents drawn from all over the world are being enticed into using a system of thought which denies the significance of the variety of societies they in fact come from. Our whole era now preoccupied with diagnostic thinking presumes that the Almighty was so limited as to have created a universe of only a few hundred types of people. A diagnosis is in itself, I believe, a kind of insult to humanity, and at odds with the kind of catholic range of a great artist like Charles Dickens. Any Dickens novel contains food for expanding the narrow range of most contemporary psychiatric thinking. We need clinicians who are willing to question what a bad marriage might be like, and that which can constitute a legitimate disappointment in love. A recent fashion for finding clients who are "bi-polar" reflects as much about the state of today's medication as it does changes in diagnostic fashion. Once the term "borderline" was similarly abused, and even neurosis was once taken to be a wastebasket term. That Freud really intended a new moral ethic to arise out of psychoanalysis has simply been obliterated. At the same time childhood itself has been medicalized, so that medication is being prescribed to preschoolers in a way that nobody can adequately predict the future human consequences.

If one asks of American psychologists who were the most eminent figures in the twentieth century, a survey reports that the hands-down winners will be B. F. Skinner and Jean Piaget. (I used to teach Skinner's *Walden Two*, and I found his psychological system had important anti-political implications.) Freud does come in at least third in that survey; Erikson ranks 12th, William James 14th, Jung 23rd, Adler 67th, and Anna Freud 99th. Fromm does not make it to the first hundred. The most cited in the journal literature turns out to be Freud, and he is also the most mentioned in introductory textbooks.[17] But one has to suspect that there is a special American twist to the way Freud is being understood. He rightly objected to the instrumental approach to his work, which helped to fuel the contempt he felt for the state of our civilization.

A complicated issue about humaneness is not easy to confront. I once published an essay asking "Was Freud A Nice Guy?"[18] Surely by many contemporary standards Freud deserves to appear frightening. And still I believe that he can be used humanely, even if he personally cannot rank among the lovers of mankind. I hope it does not appear too paradoxical if I also maintain that Erikson and Fromm can be relied upon for humaneness even if they were partisans of humanity. Marcuse may have been foolish in pronouncing his beliefs in the primal horde and in the death instinct, but he had the right impulse in citing Adorno to the effect that in psychoanalysis it is only the exaggerations that are true.

Surely Freud stands for the proposition that not everything is political, even if his own politics were less than exemplary. At the end of his life he was supporting an unfortunate political regime in Austria, and he wrote rather more enthusiastically about Mussolini than one might have liked.[19] He not only did business with Hitler's regime in Germany for longer than any of us had once realized[20], but a loyal student of his like August Aichhorn traveled to Berlin from Vienna to teach at the Göring Institute.[21] The whole tradition of depth psychology that Freud started has been notably weak on its political side, but then those of us who have not known the most painful choices of old world culture are in no position to be excessively judgmental. Freud's psychoanalysis was asking the ancient question of how we should live, even if none of the answers anybody has come up with should ever appear entirely satisfactory. It is part of the vitality of the concept of neurosis that it should lead us to the struggle of further ethical quests.

An essential spirit to Freud's psychoanalysis seems to me missing today. A key cosmopolitanism appears to have been lost. Skepticism and irony, everything that links Freud to Nietzsche, appear out of place in clinical thinking now. For me Freud should be an aspect of great world literature, and the stoicism associated with ancient philosophizing has to be at odds with those eager to invoke medication now. Idealism has its own special dangers; Satan comes disguised by good intentions, evil has multiple masks, and just as psychosurgery or electric shock were once recommended for those not yet at the end of their clinical ropes, now lithium can be a dangerous technology. Nobody should want to be a Luddite about any of the most recent advances in psychopharmacology; nor is callousness about short-term suffering in order. But the utopianism behind "soma" has its own dangers, entirely aside from the continuing pressures of trade unionism among therapists.

Lord Acton's warning about the corrupting possibilities of power cannot be repeated too often. Authoritarianism can be implicit in every therapeutic proposal. The drug companies, whose business now is a question of billions of dollars annually, can hardly be expected to help in protecting the ideals of autonomy and individualism. General practitioners may prescribe drugs to patients they hopefully know well, but the best psychiatrists are those most cautious in dispensing clinical wisdom. The popular new insurance-driven categories seem to me hardly superior to the earlier Freudian notion of neurosis. "Progress" in human affairs seems to me, as to Freud, one of the most dangerous of our illusions. Sectarianism, whether psychotherapeutic or chemical, has had an unfortunate hold on too much of the life of the mind, and the ideals of charity and toleration have scarcely had much of a foothold in clinical thinking. Humaneness should mean that there be limits to clinical ambitiousness. To conclude: in opposition to Berlin, Arendt, and Strauss, I think that psychology and political theory need one another as much as ever.

NOTES

1. *Letters of Sigmund Freud and Arnold Zweig*, ed. Ernst L. Freud, translated by Prof. & Mrs. W. D. Robson-Scott (London, The Hogarth Press, 1970), p. 155.
2. *Within Four Walls: The Correspondence between Hannah Arendt and Heinrich Blücher 1936-1968*, ed. and with an Introduction by Lotte Kohler, translated by Peter Constantine (New York, Harcourt, 2000), p. 139.
3. Paul Roazen, *Cultural Foundations of Political Psychology* (New Brunswick, N.J., Transaction Publishers, 2003), Preface.
4. Stefan Zweig, *The World of Yesterday* (London, Cassell, 1943).
5. Louis Hartz, *The Liberal Tradition in America: An Interpretation of American Political Thought Since the Revolution* (New York, Harcourt Brace & Co., 1955).
6. Paul Roazen, *Freud: Political and Social Thought*, 3rd edition with new Introduction (New Brunswick, N.J., Transaction Publishers, 1999), "Epilogue: Woodrow Wilson".
7. See, for example, "Discussion," in *Totalitarianism*, ed. Carl J. Friedrich (New York, Grosset & Dunlap, 1954), pp. 31-36; see also David Riesman's 1952 essay, "The Limits of Totalitarian Power," in *Abundance for What? And Other Essays* (N.Y., Doubleday & Co., 1964), pp. 80-92.
8. Aldous Huxley, *Brave New World* (London, Flamingo, 1994), pp. 160-61.
9. *Ibid.*, pp. 161, 194, 199, 200, 217, 218.
10. See, for instance, Paul Roazen, editor, Helene Deutsch, *The Therapeutic Process, the Self, and Female Psychology* (New Brunswick, N.J., Transaction Publishers, 1992).
11. Paul Roazen, *Oedipus in Britain: Edward Glover and the Struggle Over Klein* (New York, Other Press, 2000).
12. Paul Roazen, *Brother Animal: The Story of Freud and Tausk*, second edition with New Introduction (New Brunswick, Transaction Publishers, 1990).
13. Anthony Storr, *The School of Genius* (London, Andre Deutsch. 1988).
14. *Ibid.*, p. xiii.
15. Sigmund Freud, "Civilization and Its Discontents," *Standard Edition*, Vol. 21, pp. 109-110. See Paul Roazen, *Political Theory and the Psychology of the Unconscious* (London, Open Gate Press, 2000), pp. 28-48.
16. J. Allan Hobson and Jonathan A. Leonard, *Out of Its Mind: Psychiatry In Crisis, A Call for Reform* (Cambridge, Mass., Perseus Publishing, 2001).
17. Steven J. Haggbloom, "The 100 Most Eminent Psychologists of the 20th Century," *Review of General Psychology*, Vol. 6, No. 2 (2002), pp. 139-152. I am grateful to William McKinley Runyan for bringing this survey to my attention.
18. Paul Roazen, "Was Freud a Nice Guy?", in *The Historiography of Psychoanalysis* (New Brunswick, New Jersey, Transaction Publishers, 2001), pp. 23-36.
19. Paul Roazen, "Ethics and Privacy," in *The Trauma of Freud: Controversies in Psychoanalysis* (New Brunswick, N.J., Transaction Books, 2002), pp. 111-127.
20. Roazen, *Cultural Foundations of Political Psychology*, op. cit., Ch. 1.
21. See Geoffrey Cocks, *Psychotherapy in the Third Reich: The Göring Institute*, 2nd edition (New Brunswick, N.J., Transaction Publishers, 1997), p. 417.

A PERSONAL EPILOGUE: SECRET SPACES

Memory is notoriously tricky, and I think formal autobiography only justified by the most talented, but I would like to venture on trying to recreate what has always seemed to me a paradise from my early childhood – a little beach which was part of the small town at the beginning of Cape Cod where we used to go summers during World War II. This topic seems to me a suitable one since I cannot remember ever discussing it before, and I have never checked about my version of things with any surviving relatives; so it remains a personal realm even as I am writing about it now.

Since I was born in 1936, I am thinking of the years when I was, let us say, four to six or seven years old. I have looked at some photo albums, and there are shots of me at this beach in those years. (The photos were almost certainly taken by our long-standing housekeeper.) What strikes me now as most memorable about that time is just how unprepossessing the beach can look from adult eyes. I happened to go back there a few years ago, and I can testify to how lacking in glamour it looks like now. Yet it is very much today as it was then: a smallish stretch of sand adjoining a good-sized body of water ultimately connected to Buzzards Bay. There was no surf, just the changing of tides; on exceptionally windy days there might be white caps, but so tranquil that there was never any need for a life guard.

I can still vividly remember exhilaratingly setting off alone, barefoot, in the early morning with my pail and shovel heading for a wonderful day at the beach. I would most likely have known whether it was going to be high-tide or low-tide, or in which direction in-between the water was moving. Probably it was a weekday. On the day in question I remember no issue of cars as a source of danger; but then our house was close to the beach, and the traffic so minimal, that even on Saturdays and Sundays traffic could not have been any problem. The street I have in mind lacked a sidewalk, but there were some side-walks in our section of town. The cottages were all set close together but at the start of the day everything was quiet.

The beach itself was wholly transformed as the hours passed, and on weekends people came who would never be there in the normal course of events; on holidays it could be said to have been crowded. (The absence of a parking lot meant that it was restricted to the local people who got there almost entirely by foot.) Such changes in the quantity of people would be the case at most beaches. But this one sticks in my mind because of how absolutely fascinating it was at the time, even though it is likely to look run-of-the-mill through adult eyes. First of all it was possible to go and come from it all on one's own; I am presuming it was a nice day, and therefore I could expect my older brother and younger sister to come along at some time during the morning. One of my cousins, who lived nearby, was also a reliable playmate, and we had a fun live-in grandmother. But I could get incredibly absorbed with building and digging in the sand; castles with moats were designed to withstand the elements coming from the sea. Even a crumbling structure could be reinforced to endure for at least awhile the ravages of water. If the tide were coming in, then my objective would be to start off by making constructions that were far enough back so that they would withstand the on-coming water for a good bit. The low tide (at which the beach was technically at its most expanded) seemed to last awhile, and would not be the time of greatest excitement. The day's work would be interrupted at least once daily by the arrival of an ice-cream truck, and small change on-hand would enable one to join in the line-up. A simple popsicle, a "push-up," or the more expensive ice-cream sandwiches, tasted perfect in hot weather. Those were the days before modern refrigerators in the country, and small ice-trucks came regularly to the house.

Talk at the beach was more significant to me than the swimming; but the water was warmer when the tide was not at its highest. At the lowest tide the sand was unattractively squishy on the feet, and one seemed almost to sink in. There were a couple of large rocks towards the shore by which one could estimate just at what stage the tide was at. Special excursions were possible, such as walking a bit along the edges of the bay; the shells of dead horseshoe-crabs seemed reminders of incredibly dangerous possibilities which had been miraculously rendered safe. The agony of stepping on a upright tail of such a live creature seemed too dreadful to contemplate except as an imaginary horror. There would be occasional dinghies sitting in the sand; getting in and out of them was an adventure in itself. Late in the war we had the use of a small war-surplus inflatable raft, but I don't remember our ever paddling very far. Sometimes we had the inner tubing of tires for swimming, but that pail and shovel were the main essentials of my beach life. I am unable to remember anything ever more fascinating than watching minnows move around. I must have had a towel with me too, but that was not an instrument for the work I undertook in the sand.

The excitement came from the small beach itself, all the daily changes that took place in it, and the shifting sets of people who arrived. An almost endless variety of things seemed to be going on. For special occasions like birthdays we children would get taken by car to Silver Beach near Falmouth, and although that always seemed an unusual treat, our own little beach never lost its special allure. In hindsight, it was such a dull place that older children would have been bored by it, and so small children and their caretakers mainly frequented it. I honestly can't recall going home for lunch, and as a matter of fact the memory that stands out most in my mind is the unadulterated pleasure of going there on my own; maybe that was a special event because it was unusual. I presume that mainly I went with my brother and sister, but that I could do it on my own had to add to the allure of the place.

Although the sand and the water were both perfectly clean, objectively it was one of the worst beaches I ever saw later; when I think of the world-class beaches on Martha's Vineyard, for example, that I later took my own children to it scarcely seems possible that I was ever once so content with the space once given to me. But I don't think that as a parent I ever adequately succeeded in looking back on beaches with the eyes of a small child. Spectacular expanses of sand or broad vistas were not what attracted me as youngster; waves are of course only for older children. I suppose, now that I have spent so much of my time writing, that I have continued to live in my imagination; but the reality of that beach, and how it could ever have so entranced me, brings back how much I lived largely on my own resources. The stability and predictability of the outside world then made possible my happiness; but how busy I kept, and how entirely content I was, is some kind of testimony to the different perspective a child brings to things. The relative autonomy of my existence at that beach lends a special glow to my whole childhood. The fact that a world war was going on only entered our lives in the form of special costumes that were worn for dancing occasions. The main part of town had places which were part of the world of soldiers, but that only bore on our lives in the most distant way.

Rainy days did happen, but then there would be movie-houses which would open up for the occasion. One could walk (a long way) to a couple of them too, but in the rain that would not have been likely. A whole separate set of memories would be associated with the break in our normal schedule that was involved in going to movies in bad weather. But I am writing now to commemorate how absolutely magical and joyous was the social entity associated with that one small beach. At the time it seemed completely fulfilling, and one of the highlights of a city-kid's whole year. However claustrophobic and secure the extended family life of which I was a small part, that beach, so unprepossessing to my grown-up eyes, provided an escape hatch to the outside world. Now matter how crowded a life we led, with schools, lessons, hobbies, and religious routines, for me I think the beach itself remained a reality as well as a symbol of how the external world could be beckoning. The simplicity of summer-time manners has always appealed to me; and that beach became an everyday reality for at least two months every year. If I put my mind to it, I could think of other special areas of autonomy in my childhood, but I do not think any of the others can match how gloriously beautiful that one beach seemed.

INDEX

Abraham, Hedwig, 137
Abraham, Hilda, 133
Abraham, Karl, 21, 32, 34, 62, 73, 130, 133–137, 181
Ackroyd, Peter, 37
Acton, Lord, 18, 215
Adams, John, 192
Adler, Alfred, 19, 20, 37, 53, 75, 106, 136, 143, 144, 146, 155, 195, 214
Adorno, Theodor, 214
Aichhorn, August, 215
Alexander, Franz, 35, 128, 199
Andreas-Salomé, Lou, 20, 42, 43, 59, 60, 61, 62, 64, 66, 67, 68, 69, 73, 102, 125, 133, 183, 196, 212
Aquinas, St. Thomas, 21
Arendt, Hannah, 121, 207, 208, 209, 210, 215
Augustine, St., 21, 213

Bakunin, Mikhail, 190, 191, 198
Barker, Lewellys F., 159, 160, 162, 163
Baruch, Elaine Hoffman, 108, 109, 110
Barrymore, John, 95
Baudelaire, Charles-Pierre, 98
Becker, Ernest, 197
Bercuson, David, 166, 167, 168, 169
Berlin, Sir Isaiah, 19, 190, 207, 208, 209, 215
Bernays, Martha (Freud's fiancée and later wife), 82, 125, 134
Bernays, Minna (a sister-in-law of Freud's), 110, 111, 112
Bernfeld, Siegfried, 56, 106, 129, 134, 175
Bettelheim, Bruno, 34, 200, 201
Billings, Richard N., 110
Binion, Rudolf, 102, 103
Binswanger, Ludwig, 21

Blücher, Heinrich, 208
Blum, Harold, 107, 108
Blumgart, Herman, 177
Boehm, Felix, 37
Bonaparte, Marie, 37, 63, 130, 193, 197
Borovoy, Alan, 169
Bouchard, Lucien, 172, 173
Bourassa, Robert, 168, 170
Boyer, Patrick, 171, 172
Braun, Ludwig, 129
Brentano, Franz, 122
Breuer, Josef, 105, 108
Brill, A. A., 53
Brownell, Will, 110
Brunswick, Mark, 177
Brunswick, Ruth Mack, 81, 130, 177, 181
Bullitt, William C., 110, 128
Burke, Edmund, 153
Burlingham, Dorothy, 61
Burnham, John C., 94

Caplan, Paula, 113, 114
Carrington, Hereward, 183
Chessick, Richard, 120, 121
Clark, Joe, 171
Clark, Kenneth, 144
Conrad, Joseph, 32
Cooper, Barry, 166, 167, 168, 169

Davies, Robertson, 166
Davis, David Brion, 18
Deutsch, Felix, 21, 109, 129, 130
Deutsch, Helene, 21, 32, 34, 62, 66, 67, 68, 72, 73, 74, 81, 104, 105, 108, 109, 110, 122, 123, 130, 155, 156, 174–187, 196, 201
Dickens, Charles, 37, 81–92, 152, 214
Diderot, Denis, 56

221

Donaldson, Scott, 116, 117
Dostoevsky, Fyodor, 82, 152, 212
Dupont, Judith, 125
Durocher, Leo, 203

Easton, David, 208
Eichmann, Adolf, 207, 208
Eisenhower, Dwight, 152
Eissler, Kurt R., 22, 36, 43, 58–78, 102, 104, 105, 106, 107, 108, 109, 128
Eitingon, Max, 133, 181, 186, 187
Ellenberger, Henri, 23
Emerson, Ralph Waldo, 95
Erasmus, Desiderius, 213
Erikson, Erik H., 29, 33, 35, 38, 81, 82, 90, 110, 150, 151, 154, 200, 201, 207, 213, 214

Falzeder, Ernst, 134, 136, 185
Fanon, Frantz, 144
Federn, Ernst, 73, 104
Federn, Paul, 69, 70, 74, 104
Fellini, Federico, 18
Fenichel, Otto, 23, 201
Ferenczi, Sandor, 21, 30, 49, 53, 63, 65, 73, 81, 82, 90, 92, 125–133, 134, 181, 186, 196, 201
Flaubert, Gustav, 32
Flexner, Simon, 162
Fliess, Wilhelm, 125
Fluss, Emil, 135
Forster, John, 87, 88, 89, 91
Foucault, Michel, 199
France, Anatole, 14
Fraser, Sylvia, 119, 120
Freud, Anna (Freud's youngest child), 9, 22, 27, 34, 35, 36, 37, 38, 41–50, 57, 60, 61, 62, 63, 64, 70, 76, 78, 83, 104, 108, 111, 112, 113, 175, 186, 197, 198, 200, 214
Freud, Ernst (Freud's youngest son), 111
Fromm, Erich, 55, 103, 117, 145, 146, 147, 154, 200, 201, 207, 208, 213, 214
Fromm-Reichmann, Frieda, 201

Galbraith, John Kenneth, 175
Gandhi, Mahatma, 151
Gay, Peter, 21, 38, 63, 110, 111, 112, 120, 121
Gide, Andre, 126
Gifford, Sanford, 123

Glover, Edward, 30, 34, 36, 38, 49, 54, 81
Goethe, J. W., 78, 208
Goldwater, Barry, 172
Gomperz, Theodor, 122
Göring, Matthias, 149
Gosse, Edmund, 107
Graf, Max, 136
Greene, Graham, 27, 175
Gross, Otto, 75, 195
Grosskurth, Phyllis, 115, 116
Grote, George, 122
Grotjahn, Martin, 104

Hall, G. Stanley, 68
Hamilton, Alexander, 17, 153
Hammett, Dashiell, 117
Hartmann, Dora, 33
Hartmann, Heinz, 33, 199
Hawthorne, Nathaniel, 16, 17
Haynal, Andre, 134, 135
Hegel, G. W. F., 119
Heidegger, Martin, 121
Hellman, Lillian, 117
Hirst, Albert, 70
Hitler, Adolf, 17, 37, 121, 122, 149, 149, 158, 172, 173, 210, 215
Hobbes, Thomas, 14, 21
Holmes, Oliver Wendell, Jr., 192
Hoover, J. Edgar, 116, 117
Horney, Karen, 21, 147, 155, 156, 196
Hughes, Charles Evans, 160
Hughes, Ted, 118, 119
Huxley, Aldous, 210, 211, 212

Ibsen, Henrik, 66

James, Caryn, 118, 119
James, Henry, 16, 17
James, William, 54, 95, 147, 193, 211, 214
Janet, Pierre, 160, 197
Jaspers, Karl, 202
Jay, John, 17, 153
Jefferson, Thomas, 169, 192
Jekels, Ludwig, 61, 74, 106
Jelliffe, Smith Ely, 94, 95, 99, 100
Johnson, Lyndon, 172
Jones, Ernest, 28, 36, 45, 65, 70, 76, 81, 82, 106, 122, 126, 128, 133, 134, 135, 136, 164, 181, 186, 187, 195, 196, 197
Joyce, James, 90

INDEX

Jung, Franz, 53
Jung, Carl G., 9, 20, 21, 35, 36, 37, 41, 47, 49, 51, 52, 53, 59, 60, 67, 68, 81, 94, 98, 99, 100, 106, 111, 125, 131, 133, 134, 135, 136, 147, 148, 150, 154, 163, 194, 195, 201, 212, 213, 214

Kafka, Franz, 63
Kant, Immanuel, 208
Kardiner, Abram, 199, 200
Katan, Anny, 43
Kazin, Alfred, 116
Keegstra, James, 169
Kennan, George, 210
Kernberg, Otto, 56
Keynes, Lord, 24, 25, 174
Khan, Masud, 34
King, William Lyon Mackenzie, 158–166, 171, 173
Klein, Melanie, 27, 30, 34, 35, 54, 197, 198, 201
Kluckhohn, Clyde, 118
Knopf, Alfred, 102
Knopf, Olga, 72
Kohut, Heinz, 33, 35, 199
Kraepelin, Emile, 193
Kreuger, Ivar, 174, 175, 176, 177
Kris, Ernst, 34, 82
Kris, Marianne, 34
Kronold, Edward, 109
Kubie, Lawrence S., 11

Lacan, Jacques, 22, 49, 54, 197, 201
Laing, Ronald D., 35, 198, 200
Landsberg, Michelle, 114, 115
Lasswell, Harold, 21, 48, 160, 164
Laurier, Sir Wilfrid, 165, 171
Laurvik, Elma, 24, 127
Lenin, 143, 191
Levesque, Rene, 167
Lewis, Anthony, 103
Lewis, Aubrey, 103
Lewis, Sinclair, 171
Likierman, Meira, 112
Lippmann, Walter, 110, 116, 117, 151, 152
Lipton, Samuel, 103
Locke, John, 21
Loewi, Hilde, 74
Lomas, Peter, 35, 36, 102, 193
Luther, Martin, 151

MacArthur, Douglas, 17
MacDonald, Jeffrey, 119
Machiavelli, Nicolo, 14
MacLeish, Archibald, 116
Madison, James, 17, 153
Major, Rene, 56
Malcolm, Janet, 72, 78, 107, 113, 118, 119
Mannheim, Karl, 208
Marcuse, Herbert, 102, 116, 146, 154, 209, 214
Marx, Karl, 59, 147, 153, 190, 191, 193, 198, 207
Masson, Jeffrey M., 78, 107, 113, 114, 118, 119
May, Rollo, 196
McGinnis, Joe, 118, 119
McGuire, William, 94, 135
Melville, Herman, 9, 82
Menninger, Karl, 19
Meyer, Adolf, 159, 162, 163, 165, 199
Mill, John Stuart, 122, 153, 167
Millet, Kate, 114
Milton, John, 25
Monahan, Patrick J., 170
Morgan, Christiana, 117, 118
Mosbacher, Eric, 133
Müller-Braunschweig, Carl, 37
Mulroney, Brian, 166, 170
Murray, Henry A., 68, 117, 118
Mussolini, Benito, 17, 151, 166, 215

Napoleon, 48
Nietzsche, Friedrich, 42, 49, 63, 97, 155, 208, 212, 215
Nixon, Richard, 159
Nunberg, Herman, 52

O'Neill, Eugene, 94–100
Olden, Christine, 109, 123
Orwell, George, 210, 211

Pasternak, Boris, 210
Payne, Sylvia, 35, 37
Peale, Norman Vincent, 209
Perot, Ross, 171
Peterson, David, 170
Pfister, Oscar, 125, 133, 134
Phillips, Adam, 112
Piaget, Jean, 214
Plath, Sylvia, 118
Plato, 122
Popper, Sir Karl, 209

Puner, Helen Walker, 29, 76, 77, 78

Rado, Sandor, 134, 137, 199
Rakoff, Vivan, 172, 173
Rank, Beata ("Tola"), 128
Rank, Otto, 33, 41, 49, 52, 53, 81, 127, 128, 129, 130, 133, 134, 181, 197
Reich, Wilhelm, 22, 35, 41, 53, 116, 121, 144, 145, 148, 155, 156, 196
Reik, Theodor, 68
Rilke, Rainer, 63
Robbins, Natalie, 116
Robertson, Heather, 163, 164
Robinson, Forrest G., 117, 118
Robson, John, 122
Rockefeller, John D., Jr., 159, 160, 162
Rogers, Carl, 197
Roosevelt, Franklin, 173
Rosen, Lea, 73
Rosenfeld, Eva, 37
Rousseau, Jean-Jacques, 14, 95, 141, 208
Roustang, François, 64
Rycroft, Charles, 27–38, 55, 67

Sachs, Hanns, 181
Salle, David, 59
Sandler, Joseph, 71
Sarasin, Philipp, 97
Sartre, Jean-Paul, 31
Schermann, Rafael, 178, 179, 185
Schmideberg, Melitta, 35
Schorske, Carl, 122
Schur, Max, 129
Scott, Ian, 170
Semrad, Elvin, 9, 11
Shakespeare, William, 32, 98, 170, 211, 212
Silberstein, Eduard, 82, 108
Silver, Ann-Louise, 94, 100
Skinner, B. F., 214
Smith, Al, 171
Sokolnicka, Eugenia, 126, 127
Solzhenitsyn, Alexander, 24
Spinoza, Benedict de, 74
Spitz, Rene, 51
Stalin, Joseph, 158, 173, 210
Steel, Ronald, 110
Steinach, E., 130
Stekel, Wilhelm, 53, 195

Stern, J. P., 116
Stevenson, Adlai, 83
Storfer, Adolf, 134
Storr, Anthony, 36, 212
Strachey, James, 112, 181, 195
Strachey, Lytton, 25
Strauss, Leo, 207, 208, 209, 215
Sullivan, Harry Stack, 21, 147, 199
Svevo, Italo, 191
Szasz, Thomas, 101, 102, 199

Tausk, Marius, 63, 72
Tausk, Victor, 20, 36, 42, 43, 49, 52, 58, 59, 61, 62, 63, 64, 65, 66, 67, 68, 69, 71, 73, 74, 81, 102, 103, 104, 105, 106, 108, 110, 120, 121, 212
Taylor, Harriet, 122
Thackeray, William, 83
Thomas, D. M., 58
Thompson, Clara, 201
Thwaite, Ann, 107
Tito, Marshal, 172
Tolstoy, Leo, 32
Trevor-Roper, Hugh, 59
Trotsky, Leon, 144
Trudeau, Pierre Elliott, 168, 169, 170
Truman, Harry S., 83
Turgenev, Ivan, 190
Tyson, Alan, 35

Veblen, Thorstein, 158
Vico, Giambattista, 191
Victoria, Queen, 25

Wagner-Jauregg, Julius, 22, 34
Wallas, Graham, 151
Weber, Max, 24, 208
Weiss, Edoardo, 69, 70, 106
Wilson, Woodrow, 110, 159, 160, 210
Winnicott, Donald W., 28, 32, 35, 198
Winnik, Dr., 73
Wittels, Franz, 70, 72, 75
Wolff, Antonia, 60

Yeats, William Butler, 91, 92
Young-Bruehl, Elisabeth, 112

Zundel, Ernst, 169
Zweig, Arnold, 106, 125, 133, 207
Zweig, Stefan, 209